MODERN IDEOLOGIES

MODERN IDEOLOGIES

MAX MARK
Wayne State University

St. Martin's Press
New York

Library of Congress Catalog Card Number: 72-95748

Manufactured in the United States of America.
For information write: St. Martin's Press, Inc., 175 Fifth Avenue, New York, N.Y. 10010

AFFILIATED PUBLISHERS: Macmillan Limited, London—also at Bombay, Calcutta, Madras, and Melbourne.

CONTENTS

INTRODUCTION

Man is in an ambiguous position: he is both part of nature and estranged from it, both part of society and estranged from it. Man's consciousness tells him that the laws of nature (to which he is subject) are responsible not only for his existence but also, in the end, for his destruction. His consciousness creates a sense of individuality and a desire for personal happiness, but at the same time it makes him aware that it is only through the group that he can fulfill himself. His awareness of being a distinct self creates the desire to be free, but at the same time he must admit that in the interests of an ordered social life he must submit to some authority. The process of socialization, which has worked on him since birth, creates an attachment to the particular group into which he was born, but his awareness of other groups in the world makes him question the rationality of dividing humanity into distinct groupings. In order to deal with these seeming paradoxes, man needs a more or less organized body of thought for his orientation.

The vital problem that has always faced mankind is finding purpose for existence, and on this subject nature is mute. In fact, by showing complete indifference to the existence of individual man, and even of mankind itself, nature rather suggests that life is meaningless. But as a matter of elementary impulse, man wants to go on living. Under these circumstances, he has to create a world of his own making that will accommodate his need for meaning and purpose. It is, however, in many ways an artificial, threadbare world. Discomfort or disappointment eventually bring most individuals to the existentialist question: What is the purpose of it all? But as long as a person is mentally healthy, he will dismiss such a question as "morbid." He rules out the questioning of purpose because of his internalization of a social taboo. Though every society as a matter of course has notions about human purpose, these notions must be reinforced by a taboo because the problem of human existence is essentially insoluble.

The knowledge that there are other people like oneself and that these people have as much claim to happiness as oneself creates the idea of justice. Thus the basis of justice is regard for our fellow men because they are *like* ourselves. (It is interesting to note that depriving other people of equal rights is always based on the notion that they are not like ourselves.) In the biblical command "Love your neighbor as yourself," the connotation is that your neighbor is *like* yourself. The command is thus not only prescriptive but explicative: "Love your neighbor as yourself because he is like yourself." The ideas of purpose and justice are so intimately connected that they are usually part of every belief complex. Man apparently cannot conceive of a world that is meaningful and at the same time unjust.

In prehistoric times, mankind lived in small groupings such as tribes in which people accepted each other as fellow men because they had face-to-face contacts. As time went by these groupings grew larger, through either peaceful or forcible mergers. Occasionally a group made itself the carrier of a wider civilization or a religious mission, with the result that those who accepted this civilization or religion became fellow men. Thus, once groupings became too large to be based on face-to-face relationships, it was an *idea* that defined the orbit of human fellowship. And it was the idea of nationalism that established the nation as the modern orbit of human fellowship.

Part of group living, and a precondition for it, is a pattern of social relationships, involving the relationships between parents and children, the relationships between leaders and followers, and the assignments of rights and duties. Essential to any ordered relationship is authority, or the acknowledged right of some to set policies for all. And again, it is an idea that provides the basis for authority.

An amazing facet of the human story is man's ability to formulate ideas that have given purpose to his life, established the orbit of human fellowship, regulated social life, and sanctioned authority. For a very long time these ideas were embedded in folkways and myths that were handed down from generation to generation with little change; hallowed by religion, they found expression in various rituals. But at some point folkways were elevated to the level of consciousness—and more often than not by men who began to question tradition. Such questioning usually remained within the religious framework and led to innovation via changes in religious beliefs. But the questioning of tradition gradually assumed a secular character, paralleling the gradual yielding to secular interpretation of areas hitherto controlled by religion. The only area that religion has continued to dominate is that articulating the purpose of life, but, as we will see, even this area has not been preserved from secular rivals.

Once the questioning of tradition becomes a matter of secular concern, social philosophy is born. From this point on the issues of human fellowship, the patterns of social relationship, and the legitimacy and ends of government will be dealt with in reference to human experience. Through the ages social philosophy was either contemplative or action oriented. But prior to the nineteenth century, action-oriented social philosophies exerted only an indirect influence through their impact on elites. For the masses, established religion continued to provide direction and emotional satisfaction. With the progressive secularization and democratization of social life, social philosophy became less remote; it entered the arena of social struggle out of which ideology was born.

The turning point in this chain was the French Revolution. Though the term *ideology* has had a checkered career, today we understand it to refer to emotionally charged beliefs about the substance of the "good life," the most desirable orbit of human fellowship, the ideal form of social organization, or the conditions for the legitimacy of government—or all of these together. In the latter case we speak of an ideological *system,* such as Marxism.

Every ideology contains, either explicitly or implicitly, two elements: a particular value and the assertion that social or psychological reality calls for the implementation of this and no other value. For example, the ideology of nationalism holds that all people who have a language and culture in common ought to have a political home of their own that will be independent of foreign dictates. This "ought," in turn, is based on the proposition that only such an arrangement can lead to the happiness and development of the individual.

It therefore follows that an attack upon an ideology must concentrate on its interpretation of social and psychological reality, but the elements of reality are so complex and contradictory that objective proof of what is and what is not becomes rather difficult. While it is possible to prove that racism has no basis in scientific fact, it is not possible to prove that society requires free enterprise rather than socialism for its best development. Even if proof for free enterprise could be adduced, the argument could still be made that human nature is not a closed book, that man can be educated into being a more cooperative being than he is today. Thus, argument about reality must not only deal with what *is* but with what *is possible.* Arguments about ideology are themselves ideological, however much they try to appear in scientific garb. And one of the major problems of the social sciences is that they always contain an ideological element.

Although ideologies rise in response to particular situations and needs, it would be an oversimplification to say that there is a linear development between a situation and an ideology; a situation may allow for a whole spectrum of ideologies. However, a situation sets definite limits on the revelance of an ideology. The attempt to export liberal democracy to backward countries, for example, proved to be frustrating and ineffective.

The age of ideology, which began with the French Revolution, has reached its apogee in our times. The role of ideology in the present era reflects the fact that ours is an age of revolution. This revolution, which transcends national boundaries, questions the traditional organization of societies and has pitted different interpretations of the good life against each other. It has often centered on societies that thus far had been overshadowed by the West, societies whose problems are radically different from those experienced by Western man. On the international scene, it has led to a worldwide competition for men's minds in terms of different conceptions of the good society.

PART ONE

THE FUNDAMENTAL IDEOLOGIES

CHAPTER ONE

MAN, THE MEASURE

THE RISE OF THE MODERN WORLD

The modern world is characterized by the placement of man at the center of the universe. With the change in emphasis from what is beyond to what is here, from the religious to the secular, man denied the earlier belief that this world is only the antechamber of a world to come. The new belief stressed the importance of life on this earth and man's capacity for enjoying it. It was the Renaissance that ushered in the new age and created a new model of man: man as the master of his fate.

The change from the medieval to the modern world not only involved the abandonment of earlier beliefs, it also brought an abandonment of old loyalties and the destroying of many traditional institutions. This process was accompanied not only by great physical suffering but also by great mental anguish. Men are basically conservative, and the imposition of new loyalties was experienced as a violation of the very essence of their being. Consequently, new institutions are too often seen as evil. When, with the Renaissance, the modern state arose, the idea of a world composed of artificial units, each claiming to be sovereign and equal, appeared to the traditional mind as a repulsive anarchy or, even worse, a violation of a divine order that could be conceived only in hierarchical terms.

Furthermore, though the new is always the child of the old, in many cases the new, in the role of a usurper, took over through the use of raw power. The veil of legitimacy that had grown around power was torn aside and power as the basis of social life stood in its full nakedness. With the old moorings gone and confusion reigning, man looked in the mirror and saw a rather unattractive figure. Henceforth the challenging question became the role and meaning of power. This is a theme that will recur over and over throughout modern history.

The new discoveries in science and technology played an important role in man's conception of himself as master. As man discovered the laws of nature, his belief in reason grew immeasurably. And the shift from faith to reason released man from his submission to a hierarchical order and led to his assertion of himself as an individual. From this point on the relationship between the individual and society became a source of unending debate.

Finally, with the new emphasis on what is here rather than what is beyond, the question of the good life in this world received a preeminent place. Increasingly, the good life became identified with the materially abundant life. But since the quest for the abundant life took place under conditions of scarcity, the question of the allocation of resources arose. Who should get what, and why, began to dominate politics, and ultimately became the issue around which ideological struggles revolved. A central concern in these struggles was the place and justification of private property in the means of production.

Though the Renaissance represented a break in tradition, the old was not completely destroyed. In fact, during the centuries following the Renaissance there was an almost continuous struggle between the older Christian tradition and the newer secular ideas. Gradually, however, the old was incorporated into the new—much like old wine into new bottles. In some cases, however, even the wine was new.

A good illustration of such an extreme development is the emergence of the modern state. In the medieval period the common man had two loyalties: a strong spiritual one to the Pope in Rome and a weak secular one to his immediate feudal superior. If the Pope excommunicated a feudal noble, the allegiance of his subjects lapsed. The Protestant Reformation broke the power of Rome—even in the Catholic countries it was substantially weakened—and secular authority became dominant. But tradition still required that authority have religious sanction. Hence a king became king by the grace of God, though this grace more often than not followed success on the battlefield. Later, when the dynastic state was succeeded by the national state, religious sanction disappeared. Thus the modern state is a thoroughly secular institution.

Less drastic than the above development were the cases where religion maintained itself as a force but became permeated by secular values, as in Calvinism. Calvinism accepted the values of the emerging business community but gave them a religious rationalization. Thus success in business was identified with divine grace and failure with divine rejection.

The Role of Power

In the medieval period secular power was not only subordinated to religious power, it was also greatly decentralized. Each feudal lord ruled in his own bailiwick, and the king or prince was a mere figurehead. The rise of commerce brought a new class into being, the middle class or bourgeoisie, which found itself greatly limited by the fragmentation of secular power. How could one conduct business if one was always in danger of running afoul of petty feudal lords? The bourgeoisie needed a centralized authority that would make commerce over wide areas secure.

Another element also contributed to the obsolescence of the feudal distribution of power. To be meaningful, a territorial unit had to be a unit of protection. During the medieval period, when an enemy assaulted a fortified castle with bows and arrows and swords, a feudal lord could protect his people. But when gunpowder was invented, the single bailiwick ceased to be a dependable unit of protection.

Thus, the aspirations of the incipient bourgeoisie and the military obsolescence of the bailiwick provided new opportunities for ambitious kings and princes to become more than mere figureheads, and a great scramble for power set in. When the dust settled, the feudal nobility had been destroyed and supplanted by a court aristocracy. The king had become a king in fact.

Theories of Power

In the struggles that led to the emergence of the centralized monarchy, moral scruples played little part. Evil means did not necessarily lead to evil ends. With the disintegration of medieval values on a wide scale, brute force appeared to be the only ordering principle that could alleviate the chaos.

How respectable it would be in the centuries to follow for a person to be a Frenchman, how happy he would be, in looking at the continued particularism of Germany and Italy, that in his country there had been people on the top who were ruthless enough to forge a great nation. In addition, how pleasant it would be for him to be able to feel morally superior in the face of the struggle of these others, who had to repeat what history in his own case had already covered with its merciful veil.[1]

Niccolò Machiavelli (1469–1527) became the ideologue of the modern state. Deeply disturbed by the continued fragmentation of Italy in the face of the rise of strong national monarchies in France, Spain, and England, he looked for the prince who would do for Italy what those other monarchs had done for their countries. Here is his prescription:

You should know, then, that there are two ways of fighting: one by legal means, the other by force. The first way is proper to man, and the second to beasts, but since the first is often not effective, recourse must be made to the second. Thus a prince has to learn well how to make use both of the beast and the man. . . . Since a prince is forced to avail himself deliberately of the beast, he should choose the fox and the lion. For the lion cannot defend himself against snares, nor can the fox against wolves. Therefore one must be a fox in recognizing snares and a lion in terrifying wolves. Those who rely simply on the lion do not know their own interests. Thus a prudent ruler cannot keep his word, nor should he do so, when such a scruple will turn against him and when the reasons that caused him to make the promise have been removed. If all men were good, this precept would not be fitting, but since they are bad and would not keep their word with you, you do not have to keep yours with them. . . .[2]

Under conditions of anarchy, Machiavelli thought it better to use power cruelly than not to use it at all.

Cesare Borgia was considered cruel. Yet his cruelty had reconciled the Romagna, and had united it and restored it to peace and loyalty. If this be carefully considered, then he will be seen to have been more merciful than the Florentines who, in order to avoid the reputation for cruelty, allowed Pistoia to be destroyed. Therefore a prince, in order to keep his subjects united and loyal, should not be concerned about a bad reputation for cruelty. For with but a very few examples he will be more merciful than those who through an excess of mercy allow disorders to break out from which killings and robberies may result. For such civic disorders are wont to harm a whole people, while executions ordered by the prince harm only the individual. . . .[3]

A similar emphasis on order over justice was assigned by Thomas Hobbes (1588–1679), who had witnessed the ravages of civil war. Concerned with the justification of an absolute monarchy, he depicted man's "state of nature" in the gloomiest colors. As he saw it, life in the state of nature is brutish and short, and man needs government in order to make civilized life possible. The government Hobbes had in mind was absolutist—that is, a government to which people have given absolute power and given it irrevocably. According to Hobbes, only such a government can substitute a single will for the many divergent wills that inevitably, sooner or later, must lead to chaos. Once men have become firmly socialized in a new loyalty, and hence the basis of their society has become securely established, their concern can shift to the question of justice.

This was the subject taken up by John Locke (1632–1704). According to him, government must be based on the consent of the governed. But the purpose of the government is not order as such; its purpose is to secure certain inalienable rights. If government does not fulfill this role, or becomes oppressive, citizens have a right to revolt.

Whensoever, therefore, the legislative shall . . . either by ambition, fear, folly, or corruption, endeavour to grasp themselves, or put into the hands of any other, an absolute power over the lives, liberties, and estates of the people, by this breach of trust they forfeit the power the people had put into their hands for quite contrary ends, and it devolves to the people, who have a right to resume their original liberty. . . . What I have said here concerning the legislative in general holds true also concerning the supreme executor. . . .[4]

Within the modern nation-states power became civilized and restrained, but in the relationship between states, power—in all its rawness—continued to be the ultimate arbiter. Each state, by claiming sovereignty, became instrumental in creating international anarchy, which made for an almost continuous chain of wars, interrupted only by brief interludes of uneasy peace.

THE MANY FACES OF REASON

The Age of Reason

The Age of Reason began with men doubting the body of inherited wisdom, and thus reason began its reign as *critical* reason. The philosopher who made doubt the permanent companion of reason was René Descartes (1569–1650). The source of the new prestige of reason was the discovery of the laws of nature; as this prestige grew, reason was held to be a guide for all human efforts, on the assumption that the same reason that had established the laws of nature also governed human behavior. It was recognized that man had emotions, but they were considered subordinate to his reason, and in general man was considered to be endowed with a rather neat and well-ordered character.

The parallelism between nature and society was best expressed in the work of Baruch Spinoza (1632–77). According to him, the actions of men were as predetermined as the motions of the heavenly bodies. Man should therefore be investigated in the same way as one studies mathematics. "I will write about human beings as though I were concerned with lines and planes and solids. . . . I have labored carefully not to mock, lament, or execrate, but to understand human action." [5]

According to this interpretation society was static. The assumption was that once man, by using his fully developed reason, had established the reasonable society, no changes in social institutions would be necessary. There was no assumption of historical change, in the sense that what was considered a reasonable society in one era might be considered unreasonable in the next.

Abstract reason assigns universal and unchanging characteristics to society. It does not connote qualitative change in society but implies only more of the same. Abstract reason provided the intellectual justification for both the age of absolutism and the French Revolution. The French Revolution, which attacked the old regime for its violation of reason, assumed that the new institutions it was fashioning corresponded to the "laws" of reason, and hence had the hallmark of permanency.

Ethics of the Age of Reason

The Age of Reason, having postulated that not only nature but also human behavior were subject to laws, found itself confronted by the issue of moral behavior—that is, how to reconcile objective laws with personal choice, Immanuel Kant (1724–1804), who addressed himself to this question, argued that a moral law is inborn in man. This law is experienced by man as duty, as a compulsion created by reason. Kant's expression for this duty was the categorical imperative: "Act in such a way that the maxim of your will could form the basis for general legislation."

Kant considered an act ethical if it is undertaken with no other consideration than that of duty. He explicitly rejected a hedonistic interpretation of ethics. His position was that man was not created for the purpose of being happy. He stressed the point that the more man makes happiness his object, the less contentment he will experience.

Laissez Faire as a Rationale

As the bourgeoisie became the dominant class and business began to dominate man's thinking, economic activity became the center of man's concern. Thus reason's point of reference came to be the operation of the economy; the "laws" governing the economy replaced the "laws" of nature. It was assumed that in the pursuit of gain people would bring their wares to the marketplace, which would determine who would be successful and who not. Since only those who offered the best wares at the cheapest price would be successful, and since buying the best wares at the cheapest price was in the best interest of society, a harmony of interests was assumed between the individual and society. The fact that some people would fall by the wayside was considered parallel to the occurrence of calamities in nature. Historical evolution was not involved in the assumptions about this type of economy, which we refer to as *laissez faire* ("let people do as they please").

Laissez faire's first critics were a group of writers who are referred to as utopian socialists. They denied the "naturalness" of laissez faire and argued that society should organize the national economy from the standpoint of social justice. Reason and justice were now combined; to be unjust was to be irrational. But the utopian socialists were *utopian* because of their belief in abstract reason—or more specifically, because their schemes were not based on historical or social analysis. They assumed that if people were persuaded of the reasonableness of their propositions, they would accept them regardless of how their own interests would be affected.

Dialectical Reason

Opposed to the notion of abstract reason and its assumption of a static social order was the dialectical reason developed by G. W. F. Hegel (1770–1831) and later taken over by Karl Marx (1818–83) within a different context. Hegel believed that what is rational changes with the times. But historical relativism is not identical with historical fortuitousness. Hegel maintained that history follows a logical pattern.

Much as the human mind evolves a consistent logical system as a result of clashing ideas, so human society evolves in a historical process as a result of conflicting forces. This is the essence of Hegel's dialectic.

Applied to social development, dialectical reason has revolutionary implications in that it suggests that no social order is permanent. But Hegel did not apply his dialectic ad infinitum. He accepted the nation-state as the highest form of organization beyond which history could not move. (In this respect Hegel was a conservative, and, as we will see later, it was as such that he made his impact on German political thought.) Hegel's limitation on the extent of change was extraneous to the principle itself. Likewise, since the historical process describes a mere method of change, it is not tied to any particular driving force in history. For Hegel, the driving force was a metaphysical idea, for Marx it was matter.

Custodians of Reason

The age of rationalism coincided with the beginning of the age of absolutism. Reason was thought to be the exclusive preserve of the rulers, and the intellectuals of the day gave themselves the role of advisers on reason. The truly rational man was the philosopher. The common man could become rational only through the enlightenment of the philosopher and, in a practical sense, through the acts of his king or prince.

The increasing democratization of social life brought a shift in the identity of the carriers of reason. Gradually, the common man came into his own. The belief in the reasoning ability of the common man was most forcefully propounded by utilitarians such as Jeremy Bentham. Nevertheless, the reasoning ability of the common man did not go unchallenged, and the question arose: Can the common man understand revolution? As a rule, revolutions are made by minorities, though they may have the support, in varying degree, of the rest of the people. Those who undertake a revolution must, therefore, claim superior insight into the demands of the hour or the age.

The custodians of reason at the time of the French Revolution were the Jacobins, whose self-imposed duty was to make citizens virtuous and to eliminate those who were beyond redemption. There is no doubt that the Jacobins believed their terrorist dictatorship was a necessary means for reaching a harmonious society in which compulsion would be superfluous.

Similarly, the Bolsheviks in Russia took it upon themselves to create a new society by coercion, their goal being the creation of a new man who would be free from all the afflictions of the old Adam. The aim of the revolution of 1917 was to establish a society of complete freedom and equality. The activities of the revolutionaries were not to be interpreted as arbitrary or capricious; they merely reflected the movement of reason in history. If people were to understand their own best interests, they would enthusiastically support what history had prescribed for them.

MAN'S PSYCHOLOGICAL BASES

Rational Man

The typical man of reason may have been a philosopher who tried to live a life of order and serenity, or he may have been a man who calculated profit and loss in fulfillment of his duty to progress. But whatever he may have been, he did not subject himself to psychological analysis or scrutiny. It was only much later that he was confronted by the awareness of his emotions and impulses. Did reason determine his goals, or were his goals determined by his emotions?

David Hume (1711–76) took the position that reason is effective only in determining means, and that goals are established by man's passions. "Reason is and ought only to be the slave of the passions and can never pretend to any other office than to serve and obey them." Hume also denied that values can have objective justification; he considered them a matter of individual propensities. This position ushered in the era of moral relativism, which would later find powerful support in anthropology and sociology.

What, then, is the goal in life? Kant had said it is the fulfillment of one's duty as a rational being; Jeremy Bentham (1748–1832), the founder of the utilitarian school, said it is happiness. In the first chapter of *An Introduction to the Principles of Morals and Legislation,* Bentham stated:

Nature has placed mankind under the governance of two sovereign masters, pain and pleasure. *It is for them alone to point out what we ought to do, as well as to determine what we shall do. On the one hand the standard of right and wrong, on the other the chain of causes and effects, are fastened to their throne. They govern us in all we do, in all we say, in all we think: every effort we can make to throw off our subjection will serve but to demonstrate and confirm it. In words a man may pretend to abjure their empire; but in reality he will remain subject to it all the while.* The principle of utility *recognizes this subjection, and assumes it for the foundation of that system, the object of which is to rear the fabric of felicity by the hands of reason and law. Systems which attempt to question it deal in sounds instead of sense, in caprice instead of reason, in darkness instead of light.*[6]

Bentham assumed that everyone will pursue maximum pleasure for himself. At the same time, society's goal must be the greatest happiness for the greatest number.

When egoism—which is what the pursuance of pleasure really means—became the frame of reference for one's action, the whole idea of ethics was dealt a severe blow. If everything we do is done for the pleasure of doing it, every altruistic act is in essence egoistical, for it is done for the sake of self-gratification. Under these circumstances, we can no longer have an ethics of motivation, only one of consequence. Hence if a man is drowning, both the person who does nothing to save him and the rescuer who jumps in after him act out of egoism—the first because he is afraid he may come to grief, the second because he wants to be, in his own eyes or in the eyes of others, a hero. However, while both acts are egoistical, the second is more ethical than the first because its consequences are more beneficial for somebody else.

Turning away from the psychology of pleasure and pain, thinkers in the latter part of the nineteenth century and most of the twentieth century started to look at man on a deeper psychological level. After the subconscious and the irrational were discovered, a number of new and politically relevant themes about human behavior were developed.

1. Emotion-based myths, rather than rational philosophy, keep people going and hold societies together. The external manifestations of these myths change, giving the impression of development and novelty, but their core is always the same, catering to the unchanging basic needs of human nature.

2. Men are basically confused and aimless; hence what they need above all is leaders.

3. The obvious actions of men are seldom significant; their hidden motives are usually much more important.

4. Man's mastery over nature does not necessarily lead to beneficial applications; he may use science for making war, and even for committing suicide.

In a way, all these themes represent an attack on the model of man as a rational being and the gradual substitution of a new idea of man: man as an irrational being.

Irrational Man

The discovery of man's irrational side, and particularly the discovery of the unconscious, led to two different reactions and two different applications. Freud emphasized the usefulness of man's reason in psychoanalysis, for controlling his irrational side. The other reaction was the glorification of irrationality, which was put to both a literary and a political use.

In the literary sphere, irrationalism and romanticism were two sides of the same coin—of the tendency to oppose other methods of understanding to intelligence. Intuition, empathy, and introspection were now assumed to be superior forms of insight. The feelings of a genius were thought to reveal more understanding of the world than the dictates of common sense. The mysterious forces of the unconscious were credited with being the source of creativity. Reason was superficial, whereas man's emotions had depth. Reason was said to lead to conventionality, whereas the irrational was the mainspring of originality.

As long as these ideas were confined to the literary realm or to pure philosophical speculation, they were socially harmless. But when they were transferred to the political realm serious problems arose. One thinker who glorified irrationalism in both the artistic and political spheres was Friedrich Nietzsche (1844–1900). An admirer of the creative artist, he translated his admiration into the political realm, where his "transvaluation of values" led to attacks on the "philistinism" of democracy and the "slave morality" of Christianity.

The irrational interpretation of social life amounted to a denial of purpose in man's striving; but Nietzsche maintained that man fulfills himself in the mere act of striving and that history is shaped by the activities of great men who had "followed their destinies." The age of democratization suggested the idea of the hero-people. In Germany, for example, the Folk—that mysterious protocommunity out of whose womb the German nation was born—was made the carrier of all virtue, admitting no constraints on the fulfillment of its destiny. Shorn of all bombast, heroism in politics amounts to a quest for power solely for the sake of power.

The rise of political irrationalism in continental Europe toward the end of the nineteenth century (Victorian England was spared this development) reflected a continent in social, national, and international crisis. All three elements tended to interact. In France, the battle between the forces of the republic and those of the monarchy (which the French Revolution had not settled) created tensions and fissures. The lost war against Prussia only exacerbated the conflict because the defenders of the *ancien régime* ascribed the defeat to the decay that allegedly inhered in the republican way of life. In Germany, the conflict between liberal nationalism and its romantic counterpart became a battle between rationalism and irrationalism, from which irrationalism emerged triumphant. All over Europe, the claims of the newly emerging proletariat led to frightened reactions by the threatened bourgeoisie. At the same time, many intellectuals who despised both the bourgeoisie and the working class made themselves the carriers of a romantic elitism. Furthermore, international tension, armaments races, and the impact of overseas competition on the home fronts in Europe created pessimism about man's ability to master his fate.

In contrast to these developments, the United States at the turn of the century could regard itself with great confidence. The tremendous industrial developments subsequent to the Civil War, the social mobility of the people, and the feeling of moral superiority over Europe enhanced this positive self-image. At the same time, the confident belief in democracy and individual opportunity created conditions that were not conducive to the acceptance of irrationalism. It was only with the Great Depression, the Second World War, and the great social dislocations of more recent times that a new mood has taken hold in the United States and the earlier optimism about automatic progress has given way to a mood of skepticism.

THE INDIVIDUAL AND THE COMMUNITY

The medieval conception of society was organic and hierarchical. The individual did not count as an individual but only as part of a larger whole; his place in life was by and large determined by the group into which he was born. The Renaissance led to an emancipation of the individual, but this emancipation applied only to the upper classes; the mass of people continued to be individually anonymous within the hierarchical order. It was only with the rise of the bourgeoisie that the individual came into his own.

In contrast with the organic interpretation of society of the earlier age, society was now viewed as the sum of its individuals. This view, in turn, led to the assumption that public interest was not distinct from private interests; or to put it differently, the public interest was supposed to be the result of the interplay of private interests. This was the position held by John Locke. As mentioned earlier, Locke believed that the purpose for the establishment of organized society was the protection of certain inalienable rights. A government had no functions in its own right, except, perhaps, to guarantee security against foreign attack and to maintain domestic tranquility. On the assumption that society is nothing but the sum of the individuals who compose it, a society was viewed as having life only in the present. Tradition, or responsibility for continuing the work of earlier generations, was not considered a proper social issue.

The conservative answer to Locke was given by Edmund Burke (1729–97). His position was that society is *not* the sum of its individuals. Society, Burke held, precedes the individual, for without society man is not man. Society, in turn, is held together by a body of conventions and customs that have been hallowed over a long period of time. It does not represent merely the living but encompasses everything that bygone generations have bequeathed; and the present generation owes it to those who came before to safeguard their patrimony.

Prescription is the most solid of all titles, not only to property, but, which is to secure that property, to government. . . . It is a presumption in favor of any settled scheme of government against any untried project, that a nation has long existed and flourished under it. It is a better presumption even of the choice *of a nation,—far better than any sudden and temporary arrangement by actual election. . . . The individual is foolish; the multitude, for the moment, is foolish, when they act without deliberation; but the species is wise, and, when time is given to it, as a species, it almost always acts right.*[7]

Another answer to Locke—with possibly revolutionary implications—was given by Jean-Jacques Rousseau (1712–78). While

Burke looked to the customs and conventions of the past, Rousseau's frame of reference was the movement toward the realization of man's better self, which implied an orientation to the future. Rousseau saw this better self expressed in something he called the *general will.* Rousseau was a democrat who believed in the equality of men, but not in the sense that each individual should be permitted to determine his own destiny; his equality was the equality of the parts in an organic whole. The whole had a will of its own, the general will, that should have precedence over individual wills. Thus Rousseau made a distinction between the will of the majority and the general will. The will of the majority is the summation of individual interests; the general will represents the common good in whose creation all must participate because it is a precondition for the private good.

Each of us puts his person and all his power in common under the supreme direction of the general will, and, in our corporate capacity, we receive each member as an indivisible part of the whole. . . .

. . . the general will is always right and tends to the public advantage; but it does not follow that the deliberations of the people are always equally correct. . . .

There is often a great deal of difference between the will of all and the general will; the latter considers only the common interest, while the former takes private interest into account, and is no more than a sum of particular wills. . . .[8]

Rousseau's distinction between the sum of private interests and the public interest is particularly important in a highly complex society. In our society, for example, the private interest is usually identical with interest in making a profit. But many things that should be done cannot be done through appeals to the profit motive. For example, solutions to some of our urban problems, such as the building of parks, playgrounds, and low-cost housing, cannot be achieved on the basis of the profit motive. Indeed, city planning is impossible if the overall consideration is not to interfere with the desires of private builders. Thus the will of all and the general will often come into conflict. But there are great difficulties in institutionalizing the general will. Who is to represent the general will? Surprising as it may seem, the United States has an institution that represents the general will, for in declaring a law unconstitutional, the Supreme Court in effect says that a particular statute is not in the best interests of the United States or does not represent the noblest traditions of the United

States. One should not be deceived by the reference the Supreme Court makes to the Constitution in declaring a law unconstitutional, for, after all, the Constitution means what the Supreme Court says it means. However, the role of the Supreme Court is limited in the sense that few laws are contested and even fewer are declared unconstitutional. There is a further limitation in that the members of the court are appointed by the President and confirmed by the Senate. And because both the President and the Senate are elected, they must be responsive to public opinion. Finally, the Supreme Court itself must be sensitive to the trends operating in society.

If all these restrictions did not exist, the notion of the general will in our society would lend itself to the legitimation of an elitist regime. Moreover, Rousseau's position that the individual has no rights that run counter to the general will can become a justification for totalitarian rule.

The Many and the Few

As we mentioned earlier, the expansion of individual freedom during the Renaissance applied only to the elite. The masses remained in their traditional state of dependence and were not considered important by society. It was only with the rise of the bourgeoisie that democracy became a principle of political organization. However, democracy was highly restrictive in the beginning. In Great Britain, for instance, before the Reform Act of 1832, the electorate consisted of 500,000 people, or approximately 5 percent of the population aged twenty years or over. The Reform Act of 1832 increased the electorate to 720,000, or approximately 7.1 percent of the population of voting age. At the beginning of the twentieth century, the electorate represented 30 percent of the voting age population. Only in 1928 was universal suffrage instituted.

Thus it becomes clear that democracy was first understood not as rule by all the people but rule by the people of property. The argument that was generally made for excluding the majority was that only people who had a stake in the state should have a right to participate in the decision-making process, and property was the all-important determinant.

At the inception of the American republic, the decision-making process was similarly restricted. For example, only about forty people signed the draft of the Constitution in September 1787, and, according to Article VII, approval by the elected delegates of nine state conventions was sufficient to ratify it. The people who voted for the delegates were a rather small group inasmuch as only adult males who qualified on the basis of property and other restrictive tests had the right to vote. Thus out of a population of 3,900,000, only 500,000 had the right to vote; only 160,000 made use of it; and perhaps only 100,000 favored the Constitution. The Founding Fathers were very suspicious of the majority. However, the spirit of the new nation, its freedom from an aristocratic past, the accessibility to the ownership of property, and the impact of the frontier became major forces for egalitarianism.

The fact that democracy did not apply in all aspects of society should be pointed out here (though we will deal with this aspect in a more detailed manner in the next chapter). When democracy arose in the Western world, social activities had been divided rather arbitrarily into two distinct spheres: one political and the other economic. Democracy was supposed to operate only in the political sphere; the economic sphere was managed by the owners of unequally distributed wealth. It was only toward the end of the nineteenth century, and particularly in the twentieth century, that the division between these two spheres began to break down. The modern democratic state accepts the responsibility for the economic welfare of its people, and economic decisions are increasingly brought within the purview of the political process.

It should also be pointed out that the meaning of democracy is not the same in all eras and in all societies. There is a common starting point for all interpretations of democracy—namely, that the many are more important than the few. But what constitutes the many? The relationship of their interests to those of the individual, the scope of concern with the many, the priority of concerns, and the techniques used to give expression to them have varied over time and among societies. At the same time all modern Western democracies accept the proposition that the individual has rights (as against society) that have to be protected. The type of democracy in which the individual has such rights is called *liberal* or *constitutional* democracy and stands in contrast to the Rousseauean type of democracy, which is referred to as *totalitarian* democracy and underlies the revolutionary regimes of the left.

Within liberal democracy, different degrees of emphasis may be placed on the individual or society. Where the focus is on the individual's freedom from government interference, we have *libertarian* democracy. Where the interests of the majority are stressed, *majoritarian* democracy is involved. (Philosophically, the difference can be traced to that between Locke and the utilitarians.) Further, the scope of democratic government may encompass only what has traditionally been considered the political realm, in which case we speak of political democracy, or it may also involve the economic sphere, which makes it an *economic* or *social* democracy.

Mass Society

The standards of traditional democracy have characteristically been shaped by an educated elite, although there has been broad popular participation in the decision-making process. However, many writers now see a decline in this particular role of the elite and a consequent debasement of standards.[9] According to these writers, popular opinion creates our present standards of taste and behavior. And these writers maintain that public opinion reflects the anomie and rootlessness of modern society.

While modern transportation and communication have brought people closer together, and, through the division of labor, the elements of society have become more interdependent, people have become more estranged than ever. The individual is anonymous, no longer rooted in the primary association of the family. Greater geographical mobility does not permit the establishment of meaningful ties with people. And greater social mobility creates status anxiety and discontent. Under these circumstances, the individual no longer has a self but consists of a number of different roles that ever-shifting situations impose on him. Man is no longer an individual; he is a creation of mass society. He can find security only by trying to be whatever everybody else is and by participating in all the fads and fashions that happen to come along; thus he becomes a conformist. In those societies that have an authoritarian tradition, mass society gives rise to a need for the leader who, by calling on the masses for devotion and sacrifice, seems to supply a sense of purpose. The modern mass movements of fascism are reflections of mass society.

There is a certain truth to this theory of mass society, but on close inspection we find important flaws. When we look at the rise of fascism in Germany and Italy, we see that it was not the abstraction of mass society that was responsible for these phenomena but the breakdown of a particular socioeconomic order. Without the mass unemployment of the 1930's, Nazism would not have arisen in Germany; without the disorganization of Italian society following the end of the First World War, fascism would not have arisen in that country. After all, if there is such a thing as mass society, given the acceleration of technological development and its consequences, German society would have to be more of a mass society today than it was in the 1930's and it would follow that the politics of West Germany would be even more authoritarian today than during the earlier period. Nothing, however, is further from the truth. There is general agreement that so long as no severe economic crisis erupts in Germany, its parliamentary system will remain democratically sound.

Looking at our own society, we see that the alleged conformism and the flourishing of fads and fashions are not primarily the result of the aspirations and needs of the masses; rather, they reflect the interests of the elites. In order to maintain their position, these elites are constantly engaged in creating new wants. The concept of mass society provides a convenient scapegoat for the unpleasant results of this undertaking. Perhaps it is therefore correct to say that the elites have the masses they deserve.

WHAT IS MAN?

This is obviously a purely rhetorical question, for what the brief survey undertaken in this chapter has shown is the complexity of man. There is no such thing as "human nature." Man, instead, is self-defined. In turn, how man defines himself depends on his challenges and opportunities. If one observation can be made, it is that man finds himself in constant movement between a number of poles: between chaos and order, between the rational and the irrational, between the individualistic and the communal—to name just a few.

NOTES

1. Max Mark, *Beyond Sovereignty* (Washington, D.C.: Public Affairs Press, 1965), p. 10.
2. Niccolò Machiavelli, *The Prince,* tr. Robert J. Cunningham (unpublished), Chapter 18.
3. *Ibid.,* Chapter 17.
4. John Locke, *Of Civil Government* (New York: Dutton, 1924), p. 229.

5. Quoted in Will Durant, *The Story of Philosophy: The Lives and Opinions of the Greater Philosophers* (Garden City, N.Y.: Garden City Publishing, 1926), p. 196.

6. Jeremy Bentham, *An Introduction to the Principles of Morals and Legislation* (London: The Clarendon Press, 1907), pp. 1–2.

7. Edmund Burke, *Writings and Speeches,* Vol. VII (London: Bickers & Son, 1865), pp. 94–95.

8. Jean-Jacques Rousseau, *The Social Contract,* tr. G. D. H. Cole (New York: Dutton, 1913), pp. 15, 25.

9. One of the first to deal with mass society was the Spanish philosopher José Ortega y Gasset (1883–1955), who wrote: "The multitude has suddenly become visible, installing itself in the preferential positions in society. Before, if it existed, it passed unnoticed, occupying the background of the social stage; now it has advanced to the footlights and is the principal character. There are no longer protagonists; there is only the chorus" (*The Revolt of the Masses* [New York: Norton, 1932], p. 13).

CHAPTER TWO
LIBERALISM

Liberalism postulates the idea that freedom is central to the realization of the human personality. The idea of freedom won a hold on popular imagination in the seventeenth century and from then on was one of the moving forces in history.

ROOTS OF LIBERALISM

In its historical course, the idea of freedom underwent many changes in meaning. To understand this process, we must realize that freedom is a very ambiguous concept. Freedom takes many forms: freedom of speech, of assembly, of political and economic action, and so on. These freedoms, in turn, can be interpreted in various ways. Is economic freedom the right to use one's economic power however one sees fit, or does it mean freedom from want? Then there is the question of the interrelationship among the various freedoms. Which are prior and which are derivative? Does political freedom depend on economic freedom, or does political freedom lead to economic freedom? There is also the question of where one man's freedom ends and another man's freedom begins. If the decision of one man affects the interests of another, how much freedom should the former have in making his decisions? Finally, there is the general question of freedom versus responsibility. Thus there is a world of complexity behind a term that, in its emotional resonance, seems so simple.

The Beginnings of Liberalism

At first, liberalism did not have to grapple with matters as complex as those we have described; its task was simple—to free man from oppressive authority. There was wide agreement on what was needed and what should be done. In the evolution of liberalism, freedom of speech holds a central place. After the Reformation had established freedom of conscience, freedom of speech was placed on the agenda of human aspirations. Since the realization of freedom of expression requires tolerance more than anything else, tolerance became the hallmark of liberalism.

One of the earliest defenses of the freedom of expression was made by John Milton (1608–74) in his *Areopagitica.* For an understanding of Milton and his successors in the defense of the freedom of expression, it should be pointed out that liberalism does not operate on the assumption that one idea is as good as the next; it assumes, rather, that freedom of speech will lead to that free competition of ideas from which truth will emerge. As Milton declared:

And though all the winds of doctrine were let loose to play upon the earth, so Truth be in the field, we do injuriously by licensing and prohibiting to misdoubt her strength. Let her and Falsehood grapple; who ever knew Truth put to the worse, in a free and open encounter. . . .

. . . For who knows not that Truth is strong, next to the Almighty; she needs no policies, no stratagems, nor licensings to make her victorious; those are the shifts and the defences that error uses against her power. . . .[1]

Two hundred years later John Stuart Mill (1806–73), in *On Liberty,* made what has become the classical defense of the freedom of expression. What makes Mill particularly interesting for us today is that he addressed himself not to government but to society. No longer concerned with oppression by government but with the oppression of dissenters by a majority, Mill understood that in order to have a liberal government there must be a liberal society—one that is tolerant of dissenting minorities and unconventional individuals.

LAISSEZ-FAIRE LIBERALISM

As the bourgeoisie fought its way into power, it appropriated liberalism as its ideology and gave it a narrow class interpretation. It selected from the many ideas of freedom the ones that would most cogently support its claims. Its central notions were the natural right to private property and the economic freedom that is based on it. The bourgeoisie took the position that complete economic freedom for its members would lead to an ever-increasing expansion of wealth for society. On the basis of the argument that the production of wealth is the most important social function, the bourgeoisie claimed political predominance. In so doing the bourgeoisie challenged the dynastic state, which was based on royal absolutism in politics and mercantilism in economics.

Royal absolutism means that the king or ruling prince is above the people and the laws, which apply solely to the subjects. (*Absolute* comes from the Latin *absolutus,* meaning absolved or free; that is, free from the ordinary laws.) Mercantilism involves state control of the economy in the interests of the state—in actuality, in the interests of the court. The economy was geared to making the ruler wealthy so that he had the resources for his wars. And since wealth was defined as the amount of gold possessed, the question was one of acquiring gold. This was achieved by mining gold and by having a surplus of exports over imports, the surplus being made up by gold. Under mercantilism, the establishment of a business required government approval, and since the government wanted to encourage exports, it favored export industries. Such encouragement often took the form of monopolistic grants to particularly important enterprises. The need for monopolies resulted from the fact that, in an age of scarcity of capital, novel ventures and high risks were not economically attractive.

As the bourgeoisie became stronger and more assertive, it challenged royal absolutism in the name of democracy, and mercantilism in the name of laissez faire. Democracy at that time was viewed essentially as government by the bourgeoisie. The doctrine of laissez faire maintained that if the economy were freed from government shackles, the energies of individual entrepreneurs would be optimally productive.

Laissez faire assumed that there should be a sharp separation between the government and the economy and that government should be restricted to the maintenance of external security and domestic tranquility and to the enforcement of contracts. A state that was characterized by such a government was ironically referred to by its opponents as a "night-watchman state." The economy operated in an autonomous sphere and obeyed its own laws, which were viewed as the embodiment of rationality. In a sense, government was considered to be an evil that was made necessary only because of the irrational element in human affairs, while the economy was assumed to express all that is rational in man. It would, of course, follow from this that "that government governs best that governs least."

The heart of the economy was the market, for which people would produce in anticipation of consumer demand and in expectation of a profit. The market was said to be democratic because the consumer was king, but its relationship to income was often overlooked. To take a contemporary example, there is a lower limit in price at which it becomes unprofitable to build homes. For a consumer to have an influence on this market he must have an income sufficiently great to allow him to buy a house whose production is still profitable.

Under laissez faire, the market did not operate only for commodities; it operated also for labor. Wages, accordingly, were considered to be rationally determined by supply and demand. And since wages determined prices, the idea of raising wages "artificially" through unionization was considered to be nonsensical. Higher wages would make for higher prices and thus be self-defeating. The possibility of increased productivity was not taken into consideration in the argument.

An economic order that is based on the private ownership of the means of production is referred to as *capitalism.* Laissez-faire capitalism involved six more elements in addition to the private ownership of the means of production: (1) a multitude of competing producers, (2) the market as regulator of competition, (3) no government interference in the economy, (4) each entrepreneur accepting the profit as well as the risk of his activity, (5) the owner of an enterprise serving also as its manager, and (6) no responsibility by the state for its people's economic welfare.

Freedom Under Laissez Faire

Although freedom of the individual under laissez faire was identified with individual autonomy, this did not apply to the worker unless we view him as that abstract entity who is free to sell or withhold his services regardless of the consequences. Freedom, therefore, was the freedom of the man of property, because only property made a person truly independent. Property, in turn, was conceived as an inalienable right, and Locke, in Chapter 5 of his *Of Civil Government,* provided the rationale for this status of private property. Once a person has "mixed his labor" with the production or development of an item, the product is his, and he can do with it whatever he pleases. Property carried exclusive rights for the owner, but these rights were not accompanied by social obligations.

If we view freedom in its relationship to private property and assume a society based on a multitude of small entrepreneurs, freedom implies a self-contained, independent person. This conception of freedom holds true in a situation where the economy has no great complexity and there is no interdependence of the sort where the decisions of one enterprise have far-reaching ramifications. Obviously, if one is an independent farmer who is able to produce everything he needs or can buy what he needs from a variety of independent producers, such a definition of freedom makes sense. But in a complex and interdependent economy, where the decisions of giant enterprises send ripples across the whole of society, freedom cannot be defined as independence and autonomy.

In regard to government, Lockean freedom means privacy, so that the ideal man is the private man who tends to his own business. If it is necessary to serve the government, this should be viewed only as an interruption of one's private life—as an onerous duty. Hence if duty to the public conflicts too much with one's private interests, return to private life must be viewed with sympathy. Participation in government is best left to substitutes—to lawyers who are trained to look after the interests of their clients. Obviously, this conception of the relationship between government service and private life is in sharp contrast to an aristocratic tradition, where the idea of noblesse oblige applied particularly to government service.

If we are to understand what later happened to the concept of freedom, we must understand the relationship of freedom to purpose. If freedom is understood as the absence of restraint and nothing more, then, for example, unrestrained opportunities for a person to become intoxicated would be an aspect of his freedom. But the men of the laissez-faire era had a much more serious view of life. In their minds, absence of restraint was connected with release of energies for constructive purposes. But, as so often happens in the development of ideas, means and ends became disconnected. The memory of royal absolutism, the spirit of competitiveness, and the desire of the wealthy to use their wealth as they wished led to an emphasis on the absence of restraint, and the question of the uses of freedom was ultimately ignored. Freedom was thus defined as the opportunity to do as one pleases. It was freedom "from."

Equality Under Laissez Faire

Given the fact that the economy was outside the public decision-making process, equality meant having an equal say in those decisions that were defined as political. Under conditions of representative institutions, it meant universal and equal suffrage. And since decision-making was restricted to things narrowly defined as political and did not seem to affect the socioeconomic order, the limitations on suffrage in terms of property qualifications were gradually abolished. But even in the political process, the wealthy were protected by their special position. Political decisions were not merely a matter of "one man, one vote"; obviously, money played a part in financing candidates, in running their campaigns, and in lobbying with those who were elected. Moreover, the position of private wealth in all these matters was particularly strong at a time when labor had no countervailing power because of its lack of organization.

Equality also meant equality before the law, but without reference to the unequal conditions that might exist at the time when a law was being applied. The French writer Anatole France once said that, in its majestic equality, the law forbade rich and poor alike to sleep under the bridges of the Seine.

Finally, equality referred to the legal opportunity to use one's freedom. Since it was assumed that only the government could circumscribe the freedom of an individual, this equality was tantamount to equality in the enjoyment of civil liberties. The entire issue of the circumscription of freedom by private individuals, such as employers, which is at the heart of modern problems of civil rights, was alien to the laissez-faire conception of liberalism.

The Transformation of Liberalism

Laissez-faire liberalism was transformed because of criticisms of the system as well as changes that occurred in laissez-faire capitalism. The criticisms of laissez faire came chiefly from the socialists, who showed that laissez faire was not a "natural" order, that it operated in the interests of the bourgeoisie, and that the workers had been its victims. Socialists attacked the idea of the separation between the political and the economic spheres as artificial, and they initiated the process that would lead to government's assuming some responsibility for the economic welfare of its people.

Let us examine the structural changes that took place in capitalism. First, the multitude of individual entrepreneurs was replaced by a smaller number of corporations. Second, the free market as the regulator of competition was challenged by the rise of monopolies and oligopolies. Third, the free market in labor was abolished through the establishment of unions. Fourth, the state became involved in regulating business and labor, in assuming responsibilities for the functioning of the economy, in becoming an important customer, and in establishing businesses. And fifth, production became so costly that there was a need for advance planning in manufacture; it would have been uneconomical to produce in anticipation of consumer demand; thus the manufacturing of demand became part of the production process itself.

The change from entrepreneurial capitalism to corporate capitalism was the result of an advanced technology that required investments beyond the means of individuals. Thus corporations assumed ever-increasing significance, until they came to dominate the economy. In a corporation, the professional manager guides the destinies of the enterprise instead of the owner-entrepreneur; thus the separation of ownership and management is a characteristic of corporate capitalism.

As ownership became divorced from management, ownership also became divorced from all those opportunities for initiative and self-expression it had provided earlier. The owner of stock, because of his wealth and income, might live quite well, but if he did nothing but collect his dividends, his life would indeed be empty. He might, in a sense, be free, but this freedom would be meaningless because it lacked purpose.

The corporation also had major consequences in regard to the worker. It revealed, first of all, the weakness of unorganized labor. Pressure for organization increased, and organization was facilitated by the concentration of many workers in one place. The emergence of trade unions meant the abolishment of the "free" market in labor. As labor became stronger, it put pressure on the government for various protective measures, such as the determination of maximum hours of work, restriction of female and child labor, and enforcement of safety measures—important breaches of the laissez-faire policy. Ultimately, the people demanded that government protect them against the vagaries of capitalism. Unemployment compensation, social security, minimum wages, pensions, and the like were introduced. With these developments, laissez-faire capitalism became transformed into welfare capitalism.

The rise of monopolies and oligopolies accompanied the development of government as a regulator of business. In the case of such monopolies as utilities, government would have to approve the rates because of the nature of their functions. In some countries attempts were made to prevent the formation of monopolies or, where they had developed, to curb them.

Where private business did not have the means for the necessary investments, governments often stepped in—as in the railroads on the European continent, which to a great extent were built by governments and have been run by them ever since. Occasionally, underdeveloped areas also called for government aid; in the United States, the Tennessee Valley Authority (TVA) is an example. Subsidization of certain branches of an economy, such as agriculture, also has been widespread. Other examples of government intervention are the subsidization of airlines through mail contracts and financial contributions to shipbuilding (which has often been made more palatable by provisions to use the ships built by public subsidy as troop transports in case of war). Finally, over the years governments have become customers of increasing importance through armament contracts and space exploration. Capping all these developments has been government's acceptance of responsibility for the depression-free functioning of the economy. More than that, there is an almost moral commitment on the part of government to foster a steady rate of economic growth.

An organization of the economy in which the means of production are privately owned but the government has assumed a dominant role in the economy is referred to as *state capitalism*. The idea of state capitalism is to preserve the capitalist system—or, in essence, the private ownership of the means of production—by reducing business risks. When a government operates as a customer on a cost-plus basis, there is even an assured profit. In general, the modern capitalist economy tends toward stable markets, with the result that in many areas, such as the automobile industry, there is no major price competition but only competition in the appearance of the products. State capitalism may also go as far as the nationalization of industries, provided such industries have operated at a loss. As compensation, the owners receive bonds they can use for profitable investments.

In regard to nationalization, there is a difference between state capitalism and socialism. Under socialism, even enterprises that have operated at a profit may be nationalized; under state capitalism, nationalization applies only to enterprises that have operated at a loss. It is interesting to note that when the British Labour government came to power in 1945, it nationalized the coal industry, which was a sick industry, *and* the steel industry, which was profitable. When the Conservatives returned to power, they did not think of denationalizing the coal industry, but they attempted to denationalize the steel industry.

An interesting change, to which John Kenneth Galbraith refers in his *New Industrial State,* has occurred in the relationship between consumer and producer. Galbraith maintains that it is no longer true that the consumer determines what is to be produced. As lead times for production increase and investments for new products or new models become larger, it has become increasingly difficult to base production on estimates of future customer inclination. At the same time,

the high production and income which are the fruits of advanced technology and expansive organization remove a very large part of the population from the compulsions and pressures of physical want. In consequence their economic behavior becomes in some measure malleable. No hungry man who is also sober can be persuaded to use his last dollar for anything but food. But a well-fed, well-clad, well-sheltered and otherwise well-tended person can be persuaded as between an electric razor and an electric toothbrush.[2]

Thus the combination of the production requirements under modern technology and the availability of income beyond the necessities of life leads to a situation where demand can be manufactured by the producer.

Finally, in some countries capitalism has moved toward some form of national planning. Under the auspices of the government, producers are asked to cooperate in setting targets for their production and to interrelate these targets among all the industries involved in the stages that lead to the end products. The government helps in providing the necessary data, in making projections of growth rates, and so on. The planning process may even involve the setting of priorities by the government, which are achieved through various credit measures.

As we look back at all these developments, we can see that the laissez-faire elements were either eliminated or eroded one after another. Obviously, there have been differences among capitalist countries in terms of the extent of changes, but the general tendency away from laissez faire has applied to all of them. Depending on the angle from which we view modern capitalism, it is *welfare* capitalism, *corporate* capitalism, *monopoly* capitalism, or *state* capitalism.

The Redefinition of Freedom

Changes in the economy were bound to raise questions about individual freedom and autonomy. It had become clear that people are not free if they are economically insecure. The correlation between freedom and physical security had always been taken for granted. Now a similar correlation had to be accepted in regard to economic security. However, the inclusion of economic security among the responsibilities of society would require an enlargement of the scope of organization both within and outside of government. But how far could society go in this respect before organization came into conflict with freedom?

This question obviously led to a reexamination of the purpose of freedom. As we have seen, under laissez faire freedom was defined as the opportunity to do as one pleases. Now the purpose of freedom had to be rediscovered. As it turned out, what purpose could freedom have other than individual growth and development? Certainly a worker under a union contract had a better opportunity to develop himself than one who worked under conditions of "free" labor. Not every case is as clear-cut as this, but the new definition of freedom did at least provide some general orientation.

Modern economic development created another problem: that of specialization and division of labor. On the one hand, the high degree of specialization and division of labor made possible an efficiency of production which put a great range of complex commodities within the reach of people of moderate means. On the other hand, the very same division of labor would make many people small cogs in a big machine. What would remain of the autonomous individual, the well-rounded man engaged in a variety of productive activities? (This problem is now being examined at the place of its dreariest manifestation, the assembly line. Manufacture of large parts of a product by teams of workers is one of the attempted solutions.)

The Redefinition of Equality

We have noted the limited character of equality. When the economic sphere was brought within the purview of the government, public attention had to be given to the role of economics in the judgment on equality. Inasmuch as rich people do not sleep under bridges, the law prohibiting it was directed against poor people. Similarly, the equal treatment of people in competitive examinations has an element of inequality if, because of sharp economic differences, the opportunities for preparation have been different. The fact that, pending the redress of social injustice, society is compelled to seek competence at the expense of equality is, of course, a different matter.

The concern of government with economics had another consequence for equality. Once economics becomes public business, the economic activities of individuals and corporations cease to be completely private. People now have the same claim for equal treatment vis-à-vis private business as they had vis-à-vis the government. And this becomes the new core of civil rights.

Thus the redefinition of equality paralleled the redefinition of freedom. Just as freedom was defined as the opportunity for individual growth and development, equality became defined as the *equal* opportunity for individual growth and development.

JOHN DEWEY AND THE NEW LIBERALISM

The direction of social change required by the new socioeconomic developments became a central concern of the American philosopher John Dewey (1859–1952), who started from the proposition that the goal of human existence is general growth. To achieve it, the impediments of a faulty social organization would have to be removed, and one of these impediments is an economy that is based on senseless consumption. The following lines in many ways parallel the criticism of the New Left: "Making things is frantically accelerated; and every mechanical device used to swell the senseless bulk. As a result most workers find no replenishment, no renewal and growth of mind, no fulfilment in work." [3]

Dewey maintained that this form of economic order is based on class interests. His critique of the present economic order is therefore a critique of capitalism, and in this sense he is not far removed from the Marxist interpretation. But whereas Marxism considers the class struggle as the means for overcoming the present order, Dewey believed in the method of intelligence. He argued that, although the present socioeconomic order is tied to certain class interests, a great part of its unsatisfactory nature is due to ignorance, and although man has been rational in the exploration and mastery of nature, he has remained backward in his handling of social relationships. It is sheer ignorance that permits man to maintain obsolete institutions that obstruct individual growth. However, once the need for social change becomes accepted, a process of freeing man is set in motion. And there is no reason why he cannot move to ever greater heights. In some ways Dewey's emphasis on intelligence as the solution of social problems reflects an affluent society, where relief of the suffering of the poor does not diminish the position of the rich and where such suffering continues only because of inertia and disinterest.

In conclusion, the chief contribution of liberalism is found in the development of constitutionalism—in the development of those safeguards that protect the individual against the arbitrariness of government. In its general concern with the individual, liberalism has insisted that whatever values society achieves must contribute to the enrichment of the life of the individual. Thus liberalism assumes that the pursuance of individual happiness can be harmonized with the requirements of the common good. As an effective ideology, liberalism requires stable societies where conflicts of interest between groups can be reconciled within procedures accepted by all—where the basic agreement exists that whatever the disagreements, they must be resolved peacefully and without too much disruption of existing institutions.

NOTES

1. John Milton, *Of Education, Areopagitica, The Commonwealth*, ed. Laura E. Lockwood (Boston: Houghton Mifflin, 1911), pp. 130–31.
2. John Kenneth Galbraith, *The New Industrial State* (Boston: Houghton Mifflin, 1967), pp. 4–5.
3. John Dewey, *Human Nature and Conduct: An Introduction to Social Psychology* (New York: Modern Library, 1930), p. 271.

CHAPTER THREE

MARXISM

In the history of ideas, Marxism represents the articulation of the aspirations of the working class as it emerged at the beginning of the nineteenth century in Europe. But to view Marxism only in this light would not do justice to its claims of providing general insights into the workings of history and society that transcend a particular period. Marxism represents an especially powerful blend of general propositions about man and society, a pungent criticism of the society of its time, the advocacy of policies of radical change, and a view of a millennial world. The particular strength of Marxism lies in its assertion that what morally *ought* to be, scientifically *must* be—or, to put it differently, what is desirable is not only feasible but historically inevitable.

For an objective discussion of Marxism, it is first of all necessary to dissociate it in one's mind from modern communism.* It would be regrettable indeed if Marxism were to be yielded to the communists as their special patrimony. Given Marx's outlook on life, he would hardly view the Soviet or Chinese communist regime as the embodi-

* For an understanding of what follows, it is necessary to bear in mind that *communism* and *socialism, communist* and *socialist* have different meanings, depending on the context and on who uses them. Marx and Engels referred to their movement as socialist up to 1847, when they published their famous *Communist Manifesto.* As Engels explained in the preface to the English edition of the Manifesto in 1888, Marx and he decided to use *communist* because by 1847 *socialist* had become a catch-all term for utopian socialists, social reformers, and so forth, while *communist* had an aggressive, working-class flavor. However, when the German Social Democratic Party was founded in 1875, its members reverted to calling themselves socialists.

Today the terms have different meanings. If used by communists, *socialism* refers to that stage of development where people still receive compensation on the basis of the quantity and quality of their work, while *communism* refers to the higher stage, where people receive their income on the basis of their needs, although communists tend to refer to themselves interchangeably as communists or socialists. When the terms are used by noncommunists, *socialism* means social democracy (the system the British Labourites, for instance, advocate), while *communism* refers to a system of total control of social life by a self-appointed elite.

ment of his ideas. Hence what these regimes are doing today should not be "read backward" as the intentions of Marx and Engels. Since communism's most conspicuous features have been violence and the suppression of opposition, Marxism has been erroneously identified with these characteristics, although they are rather peripheral to Marxist theories. Besides, Marx's bark was worse than his bite, as his practical political activity in the workers' movement showed. Identifying Marxism with communism would also have the adverse effect of misinterpreting the many diverse groups all over the world that call themselves Marxist.

Marx the Humanist

Karl Marx (1818–83) in his youth was first attracted to social criticism by his interest in the alienation of man in capitalist society. He was concerned that man was being exploited, made into a means for somebody else's gain, and more or less chained to a machine that dictated the rhythm of his work. In short, the worker had been made into a thing (*reification*). Contrary to the present-day assumption that man's alienation is the result of a complex industrial society, irrespective of whether or not that society is based on private ownership of the means of production, Marx's view was that alienation was primarily a function of private ownership. His position on alienation was elaborated in *Economic and Philosophic Manuscripts* (1844), in which Marx was concerned with man as an individual and man's intellectual and emotional development (see Chapter 13 for further discussion). The belief that Marx held man as nothing more than a class unit is the very opposite of the truth; Marx followed in the footsteps of classical humanists. His concern with economics was based on the belief that economic development is a precondition for individual freedom. And acting on his concern for men, Marx examined the causes of man's plight and plotted the direction in which history was taking him. Marx's philosophy of history is called *dialectical materialism*—and the very term has given rise to the worst kind of misconceptions. Hence, before we begin the discussion of his philosophy of history, let us make certain semantic clarifications.

Materialism

The terms *materialism* and *idealism* are used in two completely different senses: They may refer to ethical motivations or to views on the essence of reality (*ontology*). In an ethical sense, a materialist is a person whose interests are chiefly oriented toward material gains and material comforts, while an idealist is committed to spiritual values and the transcendence of self-interest. Ontologically speaking, *materialism* connotes the position that the essence of reality is matter and that human consciousness is a reflection of the material world. *Idealism,* in contrast, views reality either as the emanation of a metaphysical idea (for example, God, or Hegel's World Spirit), in which case we speak of *objective idealism;* or as being "created" by man's mind, *subjective* (human) *idealism.* In the latter case, the assumption is that what gives shape to the world is human consciousness. In the following discussion, references to idealism mean subjective idealism.

A materialist asserts that social reality has an existence all its own, following objective, determinable laws. An idealist denies the existence of such laws; he insists that human development is open-ended and amenable to a wide latitude of human action. From these differences it follows that while the materialist minimizes the active role of man in shaping the world, the idealist insists on the active relationship between man and the world.

The rise of materialism was closely connected with the rise of physics in the seventeenth and eighteenth centuries, in that the discovery of natural laws (such as those of motion) convinced people of the reality and significance of matter. In the nineteenth century, through the discovery of evolution, biology added to materialism the idea of orderly change. Two achievements are credited to Marx and Engels: the meaningful application of materialism to social life and, in connection with this, the introduction of dialectics into the social process.

What did Marx's application of materialism to social life mean? Marx took the position that the real basis of social life is the way people make their living, and the way of making a living—the *mode of production*—determines the ideas and mores of a particular society. Ideas, mores, beliefs are the so-called superstructure, while the mode of production is the essence of social life and determines the social structure and the political order.

The general result at which I arrived, and which, once won, served as a guiding thread for my studies, can be briefly formulated as follows: in the social production of their life, men enter into definite relations that are indispensable and independent of their will, relations of production which correspond to a definite stage of development of their material productive forces. The sum total of these relations of production constitutes the economic structure of society, the real foundation, on which rises a legal and political superstructure and to which correspond definite forms of social consciousness. The mode of production of material life conditions the social, political and intellectual life process in general. It is not consciousness of men that determines their social being, but, on the contrary, their social being that determines their consciousness.[1]

This passage gives a somewhat exaggerated impression of Marx's commitment to a strict materialism. Marx rather viewed the relationship between consciousness and reality as reciprocal:

The chief defect of all hitherto existing materialism . . . is that the thing, reality, sensuousness, is conceived only in the form of the object *or of* contemplation, *but not as* human sensuous activity, practice, *not subjectively. Hence it happened that the* active *side, in contradistinction to materialism, was developed by idealism. . . .*[2]

Actually, then, Marxism is a mixture of materialism and idealism. It is the idealist element that allows social action and moral choices. A strict materialism, being fully determinist, would make both impossible. Henceforth, the issue in the various ideological conflicts among Marxists would be how much emphasis to put on the materialist or idealist element. A materialist emphasis would involve constantly waiting for the right time to bring about the new social order, while an idealist emphasis would mean forcing the pace of history.

Class and Mode of Production

What characterizes all societies once man emerged from his primitive condition is their division into classes, which is simply a reflection of the specialization of functions. But one characteristic division of classes became predominant in capitalistic societies—the division between those who control the means of production and those who work for and with the "owners." In capitalist society, the capitalist owns the machines and the worker works with them. Thus the type of class division—and the ultimate elimination of classes—is the result of changes in technology.

Every new technology leads to a new mode of production, which in turn leads to new production relationships. But the shift from one to the other is not simple. The beneficiaries of an old order try to maintain production relationships even though they have become fetters on progress. In the beginning, when a new socioeconomic order has arisen, it represents the best possible order (though people may suffer under it). This also applies to the bourgeois capitalist order in its heyday. As Marx and Engels remark in the Communist Manifesto:

The bourgeoisie during its rule of scarce one hundred years has created more massive and more colossal productive forces than have all preceding generations together. Subjection of nature's forces to men, machinery, application of chemistry to industry and agriculture, steam navigation, railways, electric telegraphs, clearing of whole continents for cultivation, canalization of rivers, whole populations conjured out of the ground—what earlier century had even a presentiment that such productive forces slumbered in the lap of social labor? [3]

But there comes a time when what used to be progressive becomes reactionary:

At a certain stage of their development the material forces of production in society come into conflict with existing relations of production or—what is but a legal expression of the same thing—with the property relations within which they had been at work before. From forms of development of the forces of production these relations turn into their fetter. Then comes the period of social revolution. With the change of the economic foundation the entire immense superstructure is more or less rapidly transformed.[4]

The Dialectics of Social Change

How does a social revolution occur and what is its outcome, according to Marx's dialectics? As he explains, every dominant class creates its counterclass: a class of landowners creates a class of slaves or serfs or tenant farmers; a capitalist class produces a proletariat. As long as the relationships of production correspond to the mode of production, class antagonism remains in a suspended state. But as changes in the mode of production occur, antagonisms ("contradictions" in Marxist terms) sharpen and lead to class struggles. Ultimately, a new order is born. The struggle of opposites (*thesis* and *antithesis*) and the emergence of the new (*synthesis*) is called the *dialectics*. The synthesis, however, does not represent a complete break with the past, for elements of the old order are still embedded in the new.

It was the rise of the bourgeoisie to preeminence that created a proletariat, and as long as capitalism remained healthy and competitive, the antagonism between capitalist and worker was subdued. But when, through capital accumulation and advances in technology, large-scale enterprises arose and free enterprise started to decline, capitalism as an economic order became obsolete.

Public ownership of the means of production and economic planning became the most rational forms of economic organization. The bourgeoisie, of course, had to resist this, so that the struggle between capitalists and workers broke into the open. The synthesis of this struggle was socialism. The new feature in socialism was the public ownership of the means of production and the planned economy; the old feature was the continued need to compensate people according to the quantity and quality of their work. But once full socialism had been introduced, classes and class antagonisms were bound to disappear, and though the dialectics would still be at work, it would work within a classless society and lead ultimately to that stage where people would receive compensation in line with their needs.

Revolution and Evolution

Marx saw the change from one order to another as accompanied by strife, and even violence, because no dominant class would voluntarily give up its power; but he made allowance for the peaceful transition to socialism in countries such as Great Britain and the United States:

Some day, the workers must conquer political supremacy, in order to establish the new organisation of labour; they must overthrow the old political system whereby the old institutions are sustained. If they fail to do this, they will suffer the fate of the early Christians, *who neglected to overthrow the old system, and who, for that reason, never had a kingdom in this world.* Of course, I must not be supposed to imply that the means to this end will be everywhere the same. *We know that special regard must be paid to the institutions, customs, and traditions of various lands; and we do not deny that there are certain countries, such as the United States and England, in which the workers may hope to secure their ends by peaceful means. If I mistake not, Holland belongs to the same category. Even so, we have to recognise that* in most Continental countries, *force will have to be the lever of the revolution.* It is to force that in due time the workers will have to appeal if the dominion of labour is at long last to be established.[5]

Marx also insisted that a historical stage could not be skipped—that a country could not move to socialism before it had passed through the stage of fully developed capitalism. To think otherwise, he held, was a utopian idea. It is true that he seemed to make an exception for Russia by saying the agricultural commune (*mir*) could be an instrument of socialization, but this exception was wrung from him by his followers in Russia, to whose agrarian populist sentiment he may have felt he must defer.

The Role of Idea, Initiative, and Leadership

What are the roles of ideas, human initiative, and leadership in the historical process? Marx believed in the significance of ideas. Men, being rational creatures, have to justify their actions, and the very act of justification becomes a force in the class struggle. However, he made a distinction between ideas that correspond to a particular economic situation and those that reflect an obsolete order. The latter he called *ideology* (using the term in a different sense from what it means today), by which he meant "false consciousness." Ideas that reflect a progressive order are "true" ideas. Being true, they are subject to scientific validation, and thus Marx considered his social philosophy scientific.

Changes in the social order require human initiative. People cannot simply wait for history to do the work. History provides only opportunities; it is human action that transforms opportunity into reality, and the historical role of socialism is enacted by the working class. Because it is the lowest class in society, its emancipation will be tantamount to the emancipation of society.

In order to fulfill this role, the working class needs leadership, in which, Marx stated, his followers must take a prominent part, though they have no right to claim a monopoly. In the Communist Manifesto, Marx and Engels note, "The Communists do not form a separate party opposed to other working-class parties. . . . They do not set up any sectarian principles of their own by which to shape and mold the proletarian movement."[6]

Dictatorship of the Proletariat and the Withering Away of the State

In its struggle to gain power, the working class must organize itself, and after becoming victorious must set up a dictatorship of the proletariat. (The phrase *dictatorship of the proletariat,* incidentally, does not occur in any of the major works of Marx, and appears only twice in his correspondence, but has given rise to a great amount of misunderstanding.) According to Marx, every government is a dictatorship by the very fact that it is a coercive authority, and the need for government is the result of the fact that many people have to compete for a limited amount of goods. This competition must be regulated by an authority that has powers of coercion, and hence the need for governments. But governments do not regulate this competition in a neutral fashion; they are, in effect, executive committees of the dominant class and regulate the competition in their favor. Every government, in short, is a dictatorship of the ruling class of the time. When the bourgeoisie is the ruling class, the government is a dictatorship of the bourgeoisie. The fact that people have equal voting rights is of little consequence since it is economic power that counts.

When the proletariat emerges as the dominant class, the government will be a dictatorship of the proletariat, but it will be more just than the previous one. In the bourgeois era, the dictatorship was one of the few over the many; in the proletariat era, it becomes a dictatorship of the many over the few. Ultimately, in the stage of fully developed communism, when there is an abundance of goods, a coercive authority will no longer be necessary. As the society moves from socialism toward communism the state starts to wither away.

Proletarian Internationalism

In its fight for control, the working class must act on an international basis. Three reasons were given for proletarian internationalism. (1) If the working class of any one country wants to be victorious, it must have the support of the working classes in other countries because the threatened bourgeoisie will receive the support of other national bourgeoisies. (2) For the working class, the nation-state is not the ultimate form of human organization. Every socioeconomic order creates its own form of political organization. Just as the feudal order gave rise to the feudal state, capitalism created the nation-state; but the nation-state does not serve the interests of the working class. In fact, the working class has no stake in it whatever. (This assumption, incidentally, was shared by Marx and the bourgeoisie of the nineteenth century. The bourgeoisie believed that only those who owned property should have the right to vote, because only property gave people a stake in the state. His position is therefore less revolutionary than it sounds.) (3) With the rise of an international economy, only a political authority that is coextensive with the worldwide operation of the economy can be a rational form of political organization.

It should be mentioned that Marx and Engels regarded the struggles for national emancipation during their time as not deserving of support. Only if the consequence of such a struggle was the undermining of the dominant class should it be supported by socialists. A case in point was the struggle for freedom in Ireland. To the extent that the Irish were successful, the exploitation of Ireland by the British would cease, and hence a source of economic power (particularly for the English artistocracy) would disappear as well. In contrast, Marx and Engels considered the emancipation struggle of the Austro-Hungarian Slavs in 1848 and 1849 contrary to the interests of the European working class.

Marx's Economic Theory

On what economic theory was Marx's proposition of the decline of capitalism and the rise of socialism based? It is best to start with his conception of *surplus value,* according to which the only value-producing factor is labor. In this Marx followed in the footsteps of the classical economists, particularly Ricardo. A commodity has value only because of the socially necessary labor time its production required. Socially necessary labor time is the production time required under normal conditions, using average skill and modern machinery. However, the worker does not receive the full value of what he has produced; instead, he receives a bare subsistence wage.

Let us assume that a man works for eight hours and during the first four hours earns his subsistence wage. Whatever value he produces in the next four hours—the surplus value—is appropriated by the capitalist. Thus the worker has been exploited.

Another line of thought sought to prove that the exploitation of workers is bound to increase as capital becomes concentrated in fewer and fewer hands. Marx divided capital into *constant* capital (machines) and *variable* capital (labor), and since it is only labor that produces value, it follows that the capitalist makes his profits from the exploitation of his labor force. But with progressing technology, the ratio of constant capital to variable capital becomes higher. And to the extent that constant capital improves the efficiency of labor, the capitalist is driven to accumulate more and more of it. Because of this process, capital becomes concentrated in fewer and fewer hands.

But as constant capital is accumulated, its share in the product increases and the share of labor decreases. Since labor is the source of profit, its decreasing share in the product leads to a falling rate of profit, and the capitalist therefore increases the pressure on the power that is available to absorb the ever-increasing volume of production and does a greater volume of business. Since more and more workers are being displaced by machines, insufficient purchasing power is available to absorb the ever increasing volume of production, and crises occur, which increase in severity as time goes on. Eventually, a large number of increasingly exploited workers is faced by a small group of capitalists, and the time of revolution is at hand.

Marx's theory of the worker's increasing misery is surrounded by much confusion. As popularly understood in the West, Marx meant that the absolute volume of goods and services available to the workers would decline. But the evidence indicates that he meant the workers' share in the rising national income would decline. Marx was aware that the worker would try to defend himself against exploitation by establishing trade unions, but—in line with his assumption that government is the executive committee of the ruling class—he believed that trade unions would not be permitted to play an important role.

MARXISM AS PHILOSOPHY AND IDEOLOGY

In viewing Marxism, one has to make a distinction between Marxism as a philosophical system and Marxism as an ideology. A philosophical system must be evaluated in terms of the validity of its propositions and its consistency, and an ideological system must be judged in terms of its inspirational significance—part of which is its ability to appeal to divergent groups in society. In this respect an ideology has much in common with religion. Although, from a philosophical point of view, many divergent themes represent a weakness in a system, from an ideological point of view this may represent strength. As Lewis S. Feuer has pointed out,

No society can last long unless it provides for the motives of diverse personalities, and no philosophical system can have a universal appeal unless it incorporates the most contrary themes. A consistent philosophy can never have more than a sectarian following.[7]

In this section we will be primarily concerned with Marxism as a philosophical system, and particularly with the validity of critiques of its propositions. Then, we will enumerate the many divergent themes that give strength to Marxism as an ideology.

The same criticism that has been made of Marxism as a philosophy of history can be made of historicism in general. Historicism assumes that history is not open-ended and contingent but follows a distinct pattern. Attacks on historicism have been particularly strong in recent years, but it seems fair to say that such criticism has derived from revulsion to the potential consequences of a fanatically held philosophy of history rather than from a genuine conviction that there is no sense in history. After all, if we start from the proposition that life is meaningful, we must also accept the proposition that the unfolding of social life must follow some kind of pattern. The question, then, is the degree to which this pattern is determined, and what accounts for it.

Marxist interpretation of history stresses the economic element. While the way people make a living certainly influences their social organization and cultural life, it is not always the determining factor. To interpret the medieval period in terms of economics and not religion would lead to highly dubious results; however, once people have shifted their attention from the beyond to the here and now, they must necessarily be concerned with the material bases for the good life on this earth. Indeed, an economic interpretation of the age of capitalism has much to commend it, but the qualification must be made that there is no linear relationship between an economic order and even the politics of a society. To neglect, for instance. the fact that European society was the inheritor of the age of feudalism, while the United States had no such inheritance, would be to ignore an important difference in development between the two societies. Yet after all is said and done, Marx's stress on the economic factor has been a significant contribution to our understanding of history.

In fairness to Marx and Engels, it should also be pointed out that their economic interpretation of history was not as rigid as some of their more eager followers made it appear. Engels said,

Marx and I are ourselves partly to blame for the fact that the younger people sometimes lay more stress on the economic side than is due to it. We had to emphasize the main principle vis-à-vis our adversaries, who denied it, and we had not always the time, the place, or the opportunity to give their due to the other elements involved in the interaction.[8]

Even with such qualifications, Marxism loses little of its originality, for as George Sabine points out:

The importance of Marx's economic interpretation of history can hardly be exaggerated. It brought to light the enormous weight of economic forces, such as technology, transportation, the supply of raw materials, the distribution of wealth, finance, and the formation of social classes, in past and present politics, in law, and in the formation of moral and social ideals. Whether he exaggerated the importance of economic factors is of little moment, for their importance is certainly great. His emphasis upon them closes once for all the gap between politics and economics left by the earlier liberal utilitarianism. It is probably not an exaggeration to say that, by his development of this suggestive hypothesis, Marx was the most important social philosopher in the whole of the nineteenth century.[9]

The major significance of Marx's economics is the direction of its concerns. While the orthodox economists have analyzed the forces that determine prices, resources, and allocations in a market economy geared to the maximization of profit, and have established models for perfect competition and the like, Marx devoted himself to the question of economic change, to what today would be called *growth economics,* or the interrelationship between economic change and other institutional changes. These topics are very much in the forefront of today's concerns, particularly with regard to the underdeveloped countries.

It is generally recognized that the theory of surplus value does not have a concrete operational value. How does one determine the socially necessary labor time? Furthermore, is it possible to express skilled labor in multiples of unskilled labor? Also, when capital is ignored as a factor of production, the cost of investment of capital over time is not given economic consideration, an omission that—as the Soviets found out—may lead to all kinds of irrational allocations.

But Marx's theory of surplus value does direct attention to the issue of the fair wage and to the connection between labor productivity and compensation. For classical economists, this question never arose; for them, the wages a competitive labor market assigned were the most rational form of compensation. Likewise, the needed equilibrium between the expansion of production and purchasing power was a novel thought. In this respect Marx can be considered the father of the business cycle theory.

Marx's theory of the relative impoverishment of the working class has not worked out in practice. Increases in wages have by and large kept pace with increases in labor productivity, though this was not achieved without bitter struggles on the labor front. And the issue of alienation, which Marx emphasized, applies not only to capitalist society but to every industrial society, as is even admitted today by many communist intellectuals in Eastern Europe.

Marx's prediction of the collapse of capitalism has remained unfulfilled, but this has been, at least in part, a result of the forces of change that Marxism unleashed. The rise of socialist parties in Europe and a powerful trade union movement in all Western countries transformed laissez-faire capitalism into welfare capitalism, which eliminated many of the sources of discontent Marx had assumed were ineradicable short of the changes he advocated. In some ways Marxism became a self-denying prophecy.

Marx's theory of government has a realistic starting point in the assertion that there is a dominant elite in every society and that, in a society based on private ownership of the means of production, the elite will be based on wealth or the management of wealth. This position provided a sound counterweight to the naive assumption of the liberal school that universal suffrage is tantamount to having an equal say in political affairs. The existence and acceptance of pressure groups reflect the fact that mere participation in the electoral process is an insufficient means of self-assertion, and particularly for those who are economically weak. But as labor obtained the rights of collective bargaining and striking, a check was put on the dominant elites.

Marx also exaggerated the problem of class in relationship to the individual. To take the position that problems of the individual are merely problems of the class to which he belongs has not been borne out by experience; there is an inherent tension between the individual and society, which results from the fact that society operates on the principle of conformity while the individual has a tendency toward freedom. This tension is also experienced by individuals who are members of the elite. However, it is true that where there is an absence of mobility in society the problems of the individuals of the lower class are basically the problems of their class.

Finally, the significance of Marxism's challenge to the nation-state is that it implies a basic truth: No form of human organization is permanent. To give a contemporary example, in a period in which economic decisions can no longer be entrusted to individual nation-states we have seen the creation of the European Economic Community. Marx's expectations of proletarian internationalism, however, have so far not materialized.

As an ideology Marxism has many divergent themes that have permitted it to become the fountainhead for numerous, often conflicting movements. Marxism makes for egalitarianism while acknowledging the need for leadership; it stresses the inevitability of historical development while at the same time calling on people to act. It calls for idealism and self-sacrifice, as well as appealing to peoples' material interests. It provides for both the self-respect of the lowly and the desire of upper-class intellectuals to identify with the needs of the lowly. It provides for discipline while holding out the promise of complete freedom in the higher stage of communism. It appeals to the scientific impulse in men by pointing out an anachronistic paradox: mankind, which is able to bend nature to its will, is unable to organize society in such a way as to eliminate suffering. It proclaims that poverty is not inevitable and exhorts people to work harder and harder to eliminate poverty. It emphasizes struggle and class warfare, but also points out that, under certain conditions, violence is unnecessary. It holds out the promise of transnational fellowship while suggesting that people make the best of the opportunities that are within a nation. Over the years and decades, the dominant themes of Marxist movements were determined by the social environments within which they arose and the changing world situation in general.

NOTES

1. Karl Marx, "A Contribution to the Critique of Political Economy," in *Marx and Engels: Basic Writings on Politics and Philosophy*, ed. Lewis S. Feuer (Garden City, N.Y.: Doubleday, 1959), p. 43.
2. Karl Marx, "Thesis on Feuerbach," in *ibid.*, p. 243.
3. Karl Marx and Friedrich Engels, "Manifesto of the Communist Party," in *ibid.*, p. 12.
4. Karl Marx, "A Contribution to the Critique of Political Economy," *op cit.*, pp. 43–44.
5. Karl Marx, "Speech to the Hague Congress," in G. M. Stekloff, *History of the First International* (London: Martin Laurence, 1928), pp. 240–41.
6. Karl Marx and Friedrich Engels, "Manifesto of the Communist Party," *op cit.*, p. 20.
7. Feuer, *op. cit.*, p. xi.
8. Friedrich Engels, "Letter to Joseph Bloch," in *ibid.*, pp. 399–400.
9. George H. Sabine, *A History of Political Theory* (New York: Holt, Rinehart and Winston, 1937), p. 703.

CHAPTER FOUR

CONSERVATISM

Conservatism is essentially an attitude that involves opposition to, or at least distrust of, social change. It assumes an ideological character only if the beneficiaries of a status quo defend it in the face of radical challenges. At such time the upholders of the status quo have to translate their sentiments into ideological propositions, or if the status quo they wish to defend is based on an obsolete radical ideology, they have to reassert its continued validity. Inasmuch as the status quo, as well as the forces that challenged it, have differed greatly in different times and places, the ideological defenses of social orders have shown equally great variation. The survey of conservatism that follows is therefore limited to Western Europe and the United States.

BACKGROUND OF EUROPEAN AND AMERICAN CONSERVATISM

Conservatism as an ideology first arose in Europe as a defense of the European aristocracy against the ideas of the French Revolution. Later, the upper bourgeoisie developed a conservative defense against the claims of socialism; but the situation of the European petty bourgeoisie was more complex. In France, the petty bourgeoisie was the carrier of the revolutionary tradition. In Great Britain, some elements of the petty bourgeoisie identified with the conservatism of the upper classes, while others supported the socialists, after the decline of the Liberal Party. In Germany, the petty bourgeoisie espoused a romantic conservatism, which became the breeding ground for Nazism.

In the United States, a conservatism similar to that of aristocratic Europe arose only in the antebellum South; otherwise, since the United States did not have an aristocratic past, its conservatism had a very different base than that of Europe. In the main, American conservatism represented a clinging to the notions of laissez faire long after time and events had made them meaningless. But there has been another form of conservatism in the United States, which arose in opposition to the emergence of corporate capitalism and the predominance of the city. This populist conservatism espoused the older virtues of economic individualism and the frontier. In more recent times, it was from the tradition of populist conservatism that right-wing politics in the U.S. arose.

Because of the differences between European and American conservatism, the two forms must be treated separately; however, some of the underlying principles of European conservatism have their counterparts in the United States. We do not refer here only to resistance to social change, which is common to all brands of conservatism, but to such attitudes as concern with private property and suspicion of intellectuals.

EUROPEAN CONSERVATISM

Conservatism regards the past as the anchor of the present and people as bound to tradition; if they are cut loose from it, they lose their moorings. In other words, the past teaches us lessons, and society inherits a collective wisdom; it is only at its peril that it neglects the experience accumulated over the centuries. This does not mean that our forefathers did not make errors, but that, over the generations, such errors have been largely eliminated through experience and we thereby receive a purified tradition. Conservatism points out that it is difficult to build but easy to destroy, and the injudicious act of those who constantly dream about reforming society might do irreparable harm.

The Organic Character of Society and the Aristocratic Tradition

To the conservative, society is not the sum of the individuals who compose it; it is an organic whole whose individual parts have special functions that have to be harmonized for the good of the whole. For many conservatives, an idealized picture of the Middle Ages is the model. They feel somewhat ill at ease in modern capitalist society, which is based on individualism and competition and where the relationship between men is based on the cash nexus.

The conservative has a suspicion of democracy; his ideal is the hierarchical society, which alone can give the proper style and dignity to living. Without it, society is a disoriented mass. Accordingly, the development of culture and the flowering of the arts depend on the existence of a secure upper class. If, nevertheless, democracy must be, the conservative expects the lower orders to defer to their betters. Whereas the liberal and the socialist believe in a fraternal relationship among men, the conservative believes in a paternal principle. The most congenial form of government for the conservative is authoritarian.

The Inequality of Men

The liberal and the socialist desire equality in social development, but the conservative believes that equality is a utopian goal and that people are different in their capacities—primarily in their capacity to exercise authority. This difference is largely determined by the milieu into which one is born; but the aristocratic conservative also feels (though he may not always express it) that inbreeding within the aristocracy has generally led to a higher type of man. Hence the emphasis of the conservative on the "good family," "breeding," and "good upbringing." He therefore believes in hereditary elites of nobility or wealth.

In his defense of private property, the conservative does not point to the enjoyment it may bring, or to the opportunities it provides for profitable investment, but to its function as a basis for a hierarchical order. Similarly, he is disturbed by the quest for equality because he sees that it is intimately connected with social mobility, and preoccupation with social mobility—in his view—is a constant source of undesirable restlessness.

Suspicion of Intellectualism and the Intellectual

The conservative's suspicion of intellectualism is based on a belief that the application of reason to human institutions is undesirable. Reason, in the form of critical reason, too easily dissolves those deeply buried fundamentals of society that by their very nature cannot be exposed to analysis without being harmed. Reason also is bound to dissolve the bonds among men whose only rationale is custom and tradition.

Furthermore, reason orients people toward grand utopias, which in the end leads only to disaster. In the construction of utopias, people overlook the old Adam and all the human limitations. Perfection is not given to man; the reach for perfection is an attempt to emulate God, and hence sinful. Inasmuch as there are no perfect solutions, moderation and compromise are the outstanding virtues for conservatives.

Conservatives distrust intellectuals because of their critical attitudes toward the roots of society and their dissemination of utopian schemes. Furthermore, they feel that the intellectuals' constant commerce with new ideas introduces elements of unrest in the body politic.

Attitude Toward Social Change

The conservative accepts social change if it has become inevitable, but he puts the full burden of proof of this inevitability on the new order and, in cases of doubt, espouses a presumption in favor of the old. If reform is to be accepted, it must be gradual and organic, for the conservative has a horror of revolution, especially of their great social cost. It is his position that, after such great expenditures of effort and emotion, and after all the great social dislocation involved in revolution, people are not very far advanced from where they started out. Had they only been more patient and wiser, they could have achieved the same goals with much less pain.

There is a great range of conservative attitudes toward reform. At one extreme are those who would stand pat in the face of the most urgent needs for reform; at the other extreme are those who do not object to moving along with the times, and if they do not necessarily welcome the new with open arms, at least accept it gracefully. The latter are often referred to as *liberal conservatives.*

The Conservative and Liberty

Liberty has no absolute value for the conservative; it is viewed as only one value among many and is often juxtaposed with loyalty. Some conservatives, especially of the German variety, even go so far as to define liberty in such a fashion as to negate it; liberty is more or less the opportunity to do one's duty. In a more moderate form, liberty is juxtaposed with order, as can be seen in the following passage from Edmund Burke.

I should therefore suspend my congratulations on the new liberty of France, until I was informed how it had been combined with government; with public force; with the discipline and obedience of armies; with the collection of an effective and well-distributed revenue; with morality and religion; with the solidity of property; with peace and order; with civil and social manners. All these (in their way) are good things too; and, without them, liberty is not a benefit whilst it lasts, and is not likely to continue long.[1]

Conservatism and the Petty Bourgeoisie

In those European countries where capitalism came late and developed unevenly, the social structure paired the traditional aristocracy and the upper-class bourgeoisie (as a junior ally) on one side with the working class on the other side. In between was the group of artisans and small businessmen that formed the lower or petty bourgeoisie, which, beset by status anxiety, developed an ideology all its own.

In Germany, for example, the petty bourgeoisie tried to find solace in dreaming of a past where it had been the backbone of society. Hence they romanticized the Middle Ages, when craftsmen fashioned their products from beginning to end and thus could take pride in their accomplishments, when materialism had not yet triumphed over spiritualism and men did not chase money but donated their labor to the building of great cathedrals. The petty bourgeoisie was anticapitalist, but in a particular way. If it had been truly anticapitalist, it would have had to identify with the working class and accept socialism, a horrendous alternative. To escape the dilemma, the petty bourgeoisie decided to be against a particular kind of capitalism that was allegedly connected with the Jews. There was a creative capitalism engaged in by gentiles and a rapacious one engaged in by Jews. As the German socialist August Bebel characterized the situation, "Anti-Semitism is the socialism of the fools."

Another important element in petty bourgeois conservatism was rabid nationalism. While the aristocracy retained a cosmopolitan outlook, the petty bourgeoisie made the nation its proprietary concern.

In the end, the petty bourgeoisie of Germany became the carrier of reaction. Under the impact of the great dislocations that followed the first World War, the petty bourgeoisie provided the fertile soil for Nazism.

AMERICAN CONSERVATISM

The Conservatism of the Business Class

The conservatism of the American business class represents the retention of the laissez-faire philosophy long after it had become obsolete. Nevertheless, by pointing to the originally liberal element in laissez faire the American conservative claims to be a true liberal. He is insistent on the notion that the essence of liberty is economic freedom, which in turn is based on private property. In contrast to the European conservative, the American conservative is egalitarian in theory, but his emphasis on private property and property rights contains important elements of inequality.

For a long time the American conservative rejected interference by government in the economy, considering the marketplace the natural arbiter of human activity. He accepted the business cycle as a God-given phenomenon that was designed to "shake out" the economy. Also, he was bitterly opposed to trade unions and collective bargaining. Today he accepts unionism but decries the power of the unions; he accepts the countercyclical interventions of government in the economy but complains that they are ineffectual. What reconciles the business conservative to the economic activities of the government is the fact that government has become an important customer, whose business he only too eagerly solicits.

Today, business conservatism is particularly challenged on its tendency to give precedence to property interests over human interests. The confrontation between property rights and human rights arises in such situations as tenants versus landlords and the interests of developers versus the aesthetic and recreational needs of the people.

An important difference between the American and the European conservative is the former's belief in technological development. While the American businessman may be conservative in a social sense, his conservatism does not extend to innovations in business techniques and technological change. At the same time, however, he is reluctant to see that technological change is connected with social change and that new technologies are bound to bring about new power relationships in society.

Populist Conservatism

Populist conservatism originated as a reaction against the rise of corporations, the concentration of wealth, and the economic power of cities. It was a hankering for an earlier, less complicated age, when the simple virtues flourished and were universally honored. It was egalitarian, antiintellectual, conformist. A historic strand in the American political tradition, populist conservatism emerges whenever there is a crisis whose complexity defies simple interpretations, let alone solutions.

Populist conservatism reflects the status anxiety of groups that feel they are losing their position in society. They react by trying to impose the older values that underlay the society of their day on all social groups. Strangely enough, not only groups whose status is threatened experience status anxiety but also groups "on the make," which try to assert themselves by espousing the older virtues vis-à-vis those who have been long established. They try to show that the established group has lost its roots in tradition and thus that its status is undeserved.

New Conservatism

New conservatism refers to a group of intellectuals who cluster around the *National Review* and identify with the conservatism espoused by Edmund Burke. They try to apply Burkean principles to the contemporary American scene, although the relevancy of these principles, which reflect England and its eighteenth-century monarchy, landed aristocracy, and established church in their fight against the challenges of the French Revolution, is more than questionable.

The new conservatives decry both the values of our business society and the policies of the welfare state—the former from the standpoint of antimaterialism, the latter from that of antistatism. They are against materialism, egalitarianism, and the individual's reliance on the state. But since the new conservatives find support for their antiwelfare position only among business conservatives, they have become in practice—whether they like it or not—supporters of business conservatism.

The Conservative and the Reactionary

The difference between the conservative and the reactionary is that the former comes to accept the new socioeconomic constellation, though he may have initially opposed the forces behind it, while the latter would like to reverse the process. The business conservative, for example, accepts the New Deal, though he wants to freeze its achievements, while the reactionary wants to undo it. But nowadays the reactionary is less a part of the business community and more a part of populist conservatism; he wants to go back to a past that he depicts in the most glowing terms. In his romanticized version of the past, all people were happy and no social group had legitimate grievances.

The major difficulty that the reactionary must overcome or explain is how a glorious past could have been transformed into an unhappy present. Having eliminated social grievances as levers of social change, he lays the blame on the operation of subversive forces that have confused the people. His favorite explanation for the sorry state of present affairs is that it is the work of agitators, who have fomented imaginary grievances in order to exploit them for their own ends. Today, the reactionary's special obsession is communism: any change is part of a communist conspiracy, including new methods of birth control and sex education.

NOTE

1. Edmund Burke, *Reflections on the Revolution in France* (London: J. M. Dent, 1910), p. 7.

CHAPTER FIVE

RACISM

The ideology of racism owes its existence to an odd combination of two factors: the necessity of finding a justification for discrimination that would hold up in the face of the rising tide of egalitarianism, and the availability of modern biology, which could appear to support such a purpose by providing a "scientific" rationale for discrimination. In the past, the subdivisions of mankind had various rationales: consanguinity in the case of tribes, religious beliefs in the case of theocratic communities, and language and culture in the case of nation-states. None of these divisions, however, was based on assumed genetic differences among men.

Strangely enough, modern biology helped create the myth of racism—that is, the belief that mankind could be divided into something called races, that such a division was meaningful because each race had certain ineradicable genetic characteristics that translated themselves into different mental and moral capacities, and that some races were superior to others because the immutable character of genetic structure made such superiority permanent. But certain vague notions about the significance of genetic differences preceded the rise of modern biology.

The breeding of improved strains of horses and cattle had gone on for centuries, and the idea of "blood" has had a mystical quality since ancient times. The usage of language carried this notion further, as when we say something is "in the blood," although what we really mean is that a certain tradition has become part of one's upbringing. Historically, hereditary elites made special claims about their capacities in order to justify the passing on of the right to rule from father to son without having to prove a special mental or psychological ability. Hence it was said that this right resided in the blood. And we still use *blue blood* to refer to people who make claims to special treatment merely on the basis of their descent. In short, the rise of modern biology encouraged people with ulterior motives to systematize the various beliefs about the significance of blood and physical appearance and produce the pseudo-science of racism.

Although it is true that various groups of men have genetic differences, these differences are meaningless; the only meaningful differences among men are cultural differences. And while at any point in time some cultures are more advanced than others, this has nothing to do with biological factors; it is a matter of historical circumstance. At the time of the ancient Roman Empire, the forefathers of today's highly civilized Frenchmen and British were culturally a sorry lot compared, for instance, with the Romans and Greeks, but this did not preclude their later advancement, even though their biological makeup was little changed.

The great length to which people went to "prove" the existence of races, and of course their inherent inequality, was a result of the need to counter increasing demands for equality with a basis for discrimination. The desire to discriminate has many sources: the need for a scapegoat as in anti-Semitism (with the decline in religious convictions, traditional or religious anti-Semitism was redefined along racial lines); the need for instant ego satisfaction, so that one is able to look down on somebody else without having to prove one's own worth; and the need to find a moral justification for the exploitation of groups. Racism provided a convenient rationale for the relationship between imperial powers and their colonial peoples and was similarly convenient in the U.S. for the relationship between whites and blacks.

Whatever their original sources, it is difficult to eradicate racist attitudes that become part of the cultural pattern of the dominant groups. Part of this pattern is a selective view of discriminated groups; only the negative aspects are perceived and the positive aspects ignored. Every group has its weaknesses, so that when one's perception is biased along negative lines there is never any great difficulty in finding grounds for hostility and even hatred. In turn, oppression creates certain disabilities among the oppressed, which give superficial plausibility to acts of discrimination.

In addition, a tendency toward mental inertia sustains people's prejudices effortlessly. Indeed, it sometimes seems that the most unnatural demand on *Homo sapiens* is thinking. Where changes in outlook would involve the admission that one had been wrong, a special problem exists. An admission of wrongness involves an admission of guilt, and since such feelings are damaging to the self, they are more often than not suppressed. But these feelings must have some outlet so that what happens is the very opposite of what rationally would be expected: there is a human tendency to hate those whom one has wronged.

Racial theories sprang up almost simultaneously in Europe and in the United States. In Europe they had their source in the aristocratic-conservative repudiation of the idea of equality. Joseph Arthur de Gobineau (1816–82), a French aristocrat who despised everything connected with the ideas of the French Revolution, was the first important racist theoretician. However, his treatise *The Inequality of Human Races* was essentially an indirect assertion of the inherent inequality of groups within a society in which some were born to rule and others to obey. When race theory was adopted in Germany, it lost its aristocratic implications. Racism was "democratized" in the sense that the "pure stock" of the common people was hailed as a redemptive force ("blood and soil"). In Germany, race became the common man's nobility, placing him above all other nations.

Both the aristocratic and the democratic form of racism victimized the Jew and capitalized on many centuries of religious anti-Semitism that had placed the Jew outside the pale of Christian society. Eventually, racism in Europe centered on the opposition of Jew and Aryan, and German race theorists made it their special business to assert that Germany represented the highest embodiment of Aryanism. Since the Aryans were the superior race, and since Germany was the highest representative of the Aryan race, it followed that under the leadership of Germany the Aryan race should dominate the rest of mankind.

In the United States, racism was an outgrowth of the institution of slavery, though, as we will see, European racist ideas were also taken over in the nineteenth and twentieth centuries, particularly when immigrants began pouring into the country.

Slavery

The ancient world accepted slavery as a matter of fact; it was a result of conquest and domination. But it would have been difficult to infer the racial inferiority of the slave because in many cases he belonged to the same ethnic group as his master, as was true, for example, in Greece. According to Homer, slavery was the fate that awaited the defeated Greeks of Troy at the hands of the victorious Greeks from the mainland. The story is also told that Plato, while on a trip from Syracuse to Greece, was taken prisoner and offered for sale in the slave market at Aegina, where he was purchased by a former pupil and restored to freedom. Despite these facts, Aristotle (384–22 B.C.) made a theoretical (but rather confused) defense of slavery in Book 7 of his *Politics*. However, he could not make up his mind whether a slave is inferior by nature or becomes inferior by being a slave. Still, he considered slavery natural because the dominant-subservient relationship is organic, as illustrated by the relationships between husband and wife and parents and children.

Later, St. Augustine (354–430) felt he had to defend the institution of slavery though it ran counter to the religion to which he was committed. His defense began with the statement that the equality of man is a principle that prevails only in the state of innocence, and the domination of man over man came into the world with the fall of man. Domination, as expressed in slavery, was therefore a result of man's sinfulness. But St. Augustine does not tell us why the general sinfulness of man should be permitted to express itself in the domination of a particular group that happens to be weak.

Preracist Slavery in the United States

Slavery was an issue in the United States when the Union was formed, but the Constitutional Convention decided that it was a matter to be handled by the individual states and did not come under the jurisdiction of the Union. Not until the 1820's did the great debate over slavery begin. According to William Sumner Jenkins, a number of reasons triggered a more "fundamental" defense of slavery on the part of slaveholders at that time:

Due to the fight over the admission of Missouri into the Union, the Charleston Insurrection of 1820, the enlarged scope of activity of the [African] Colonization Society, and the increased propaganda of the abolitionist groups, the South, for the first time, felt an imminent danger to the welfare of the slave system.[1]

Eminent men, such as John C. Calhoun, took up the defense of slavery, and the debate became an all-consuming interest of the nation as a whole. Proslavery arguments were based on constitutional, philosophical, and religious grounds, and ultimately on "scientific" proof. The arguments enumerated below are not designed to give a comprehensive view of the pro- and antislavery debate, but only to show the power of rationalization in the service of selfish causes, and to help explain the reasons why racism is so deeply embedded in the fabric of American society.

In regard to the constitutionality of slavery, the proslavery forces denied that the Declaration of Independence had legally binding power; they asserted that it merely represented a justification for independence to the outside world and dealt with the independence of nations rather than the position of individuals. Finally, they argued that its use of the words *men* and *citizens* did not apply to Negroes. In support of this position they referred to the Constitution, which in Article 1 (section 2, clause 3, and section 9, clause 1) and Article 4 (section 2, clause 3) either implicitly or explicitly recognizes slavery. Their argument was that the states had brought the institution of slavery into the Union and that therefore slavery was a matter for the states, and not for the Union.

As far as the constitutional guarantee of a republican form of government was concerned, the proslavery forces maintained that it involved only the right to self-government and had no bearing on the right to individual freedom. In this connection, they pointed out that the republican form of government was not considered diminished by the exclusion of certain categories of citizens, such as women, from participation in the political process.

Of particular interest is the defense of slavery on philosophical grounds, with eminent scholars providing part of the intellectual armory. It was pointed out that equality could mean only equality of condition among those who are equal in capacity, and of course the Negro was not equal in capacity to the white. An argument that indicated shrewd psychological insight pointed out that equality among whites was dependent on slavery. According to T. R. Cobb,

The mass of laborers not being recognized among citizens, every citizen feels that he belongs to an elevated class. It matters not that he is no slaveholder; he is not of the inferior race; he is a freeborn citizen; he engages in no menial occupation. The poorest meets the richest as an equal; sits at his table with him; salutes him as a neighbor; meets him in every public assembly, and stands on the same social platform. Hence, there is no war of classes. There is truthfully republican equality in the ruling class.[2]

Of course, Cobb did not mention the reactionary exploitation and manipulation to which the poor white can be subjected if he is told he is part of the ruling class. Thus racism has two subsidiary effects: the artificial self-esteem of the lower class of the dominant race and the consequent exploitation of the lower class by the upper class.

A complementary connection between freedom and slavery also was established, for it was said that the spirit of liberty in Greece and

Rome was derived from the very institution of slavery. Similarly, the fierce and proud sense of liberty and independence of the Southerner was said to be enhanced by the existence of slavery, for it is the feeling of being a master that creates such a spirit. It was also pointed out that slavery permitted the leisure that enabled slaveholders to devote themselves to the higher things in life, foremost among which was the practice of self-government. In addition, by excluding the most ignorant people from participation in politics, the institution of slavery made for a stability that the nonslave states could never achieve because their most ignorant people were fellow whites who had a full claim to participation in politics.

Biblical Justification

The religious or biblical argument deserves mention here because it shows the perversion to which religion can lend itself. There was, first of all, the question of how baptism affected the status of slaves. In settling this issue, one went back to an argument that had been made a hundred years earlier, in 1727, when the bishop of London had said that

Christianity, and the embracing of the Gospel, does not make the least Alteration in Civil Property, or in any of the Duties which belong to Civil Relations; but in all these Respects, it continues Persons just in the same State as it found them. The Freedom which Christianity gives, is a Freedom from the Bondage of Sin and Satan, and from the Dominion of Men's Lusts and Passions and inordinate Desires; but as to their outward Condition, whatever that was before, whether bond or free, their being baptised, and becoming Christians, makes no manner of Change in it.[3]

Biblical arguments for slavery made use of passages in the Old Testament that distinguished between Jews and non-Jews. Jews could be held in bondage for only six years, but for heathens there was no limitation (Leviticus 25:39–46). Slavery was accepted in the New Testament as a matter of course, and many passages exhorted slaves to be obedient to their masters. A frequently quoted passage was the epistle of St. Paul, in which the story is told about sending the slave Onesimus back to his master Philemon.

And finally, it was pointed out that slavery had beneficial effects on the Negro because it made possible his becoming civilized and a beneficiary of Christian salvation.

RACISM IN THE UNITED STATES

The real racial theories started some time in the 1850's and first revolved around questions of the unity of the human race. Whether the human race was considered to be unified or made up of a diversity of races, the inferiority of the Negro could be demonstrated. The proslavery ethnologist who accepted the unity of the human race had recourse to the biblical passage about the curse on Canaan: "And [Noah] said, Cursed be Canaan; a servant of servants shall he be unto his brethren" (Genesis 9:25). But by the 1850's, the plurality-of-origins theory had gained the ascendancy and become the chief weapon of the proslavery elements. Its main proponent was Josiah Clark Nott (1804–73) who in his *Types of Mankind* (1854) held that there is not a single human race but many different races, each with different capabilities. No race, it was argued, could transcend its genetic limitations, and the Negro race was inferior and would always remain so.

Racism in the United States was not confined, however, to the relationship between whites and blacks; it also lay behind the restrictive immigration legislation of the period 1917–24, and provided the rationale for the McCarran-Walter Act of 1952 which codified U.S. immigration laws. Only in the most recent immigration legislation have the racist overtones of the earlier statutes been abolished—at least on the surface.

Until quite recently, people from southern and eastern Europe were considered to be inferior to those from northern and western Europe. Oscar Handlin noted,

It . . . becomes a matter of considerable importance to ascertain how the conception originated and gained currency that the peoples of southern and eastern Europe were inferior to those of northern and western Europe. At root, this concept could be traced to the racist beliefs, freely expressed in the 1890's, that the peoples of the Mediterranean region were biologically different from those of northern and western Europe and that the difference sprang from an inferiority of blood and could be observed in certain social characteristics.[4]

Handlin goes on to tell of the enthusiastic reception given *The Passing of the Great Race* (1916) by Madison Grant, the distinguished anthropologist of the American Museum of Natural History. In it, Grant complained about the poor stock of these new immigrants, as compared with the earlier Nordic immigrants, and foresaw dire consequences for the United States. In a contemporary review, *Science* magazine called Grant's book "a work of solid merit."

The notion of the superiority of the Nordic European over the southern and eastern European was even maintained in an official document, the 1910 report of the Immigration Commission, which had been established in 1907 to study immigration and make recommendations to Congress. This report, which in part consisted of a dictionary of races, cataloged the racial characteristics that were considered decisive in their contribution to American life. The report even referred to the Japanese to "prove" the significance of race: Although all Japanese spoke the same language, racial differences did exist. The "fine" type of the aristocracy—the Japanese ideal, as distinct from the "coarse" type—they claimed, undoubtedly resulted from its descent from the Ainus, the earliest inhabitants of Japan, whom the report characterized as Caucasianlike people.

Up until the 1930's, racism was used as an ideology for purposes of discrimination. Later Nazism appropriated the ideology for the purpose of extermination. Its victims were, among others, six million Jews; but the outrages committed in the name of racism led to revulsion against racism as an ideology. Except for the apartheid doctrine of South Africa, racism is no longer overtly defended, although this does not mean that it does not exist. It has, so to speak, been driven underground, where it continues to shape public attitudes, though often unconsciously.

APARTHEID

Today, racism has been so discredited as an ideology that the proponents of apartheid try to camouflage it. Nevertheless, apartheid is the official ideology of the government of South Africa and has important international consequences.

Apartheid is the creation of the Afrikaners, the descendants of Dutch settlers who, during the seventeenth century, came to the Cape of Good Hope. Under the pressure of the British they moved into the interior and during the nineteenth century created three Boer (Dutch farmer) republics, leaving the Cape area to the British. The attitudes of the Boers and the British toward the natives were quite different, especially as the British were less color conscious than the

Boers. In fact, the British made political use of the natives in their fight against the Dutch. When the Boers moved northward, it was not merely the political and economic pressures of the British that induced them to do so but also the British policy of attempting to give legal equality to the natives.

The three Boer republics were surrounded by the native Bantus, who threatened their existence. At the same time, however, the Boers made increasing use of Bantu labor. Exploiting their superior technology and the intertribal dissensions among the Bantus, the Boers were able to make them into a caste of menials. In doing this, the Boers appropriated racist assumptions, citing the Bible as their source, as had the Southern slaveholders in the United States.

After the Boer republics were defeated by the British in the Boer War (1902) and the Union of South Africa was established (encompassing the Cape Colony and the three Boer republics), the most important issue was the nonwhite franchise. The British element in the Cape Colony supported a general franchise, limited only by "the level of civilization," it being understood that as the natives' level of civilization increased, increasing numbers of natives would become part of the electorate. The Afrikaner element objected to this; a compromise solution allowed each area to establish its own franchise.

Why were the British more liberal in their attitudes toward the natives? It had something to do with their being the industrial and commercial element, while the Afrikaners were predominantly rural. But the British and the Afrikaners also differed in that the former retained their loyalty to Britain—in fact, considered South Africa as simply an outpost of Great Britain to which they might return some day. The Afrikaners, in contrast, had no overseas loyalty; their country was their only home. As the British element came to accept South Africa as their country, and began to feel more threatened by the natives—a threat that became more ominous as more and more African colonies became independent—the British element, like the Boers, came to accept the separation of races as a desirable fact of life.

However, apartheid as an ideology is primarily the product of the Afrikaners and, curiously, of even the academic and intellectual Afrikaner communities. The ideologues of apartheid start from an organic interpretation of the community. Each community, or *volk,* represents a biosocial group and has a distinct personality, based on history and bonds of blood, and its own destiny. On the basis of this definition, the proponents of apartheid take the position that the whites in South Africa have nothing in common with the nonwhites; the nonwhites have their own communities—Bantu, Indian, and others. All these communities—white and nonwhite—can live together in the same state as long as they are vertically separated. They assert that apartheid does not necessarily involve the superiority or inferiority of communities; in reality, of course, this is not true.

South Africa, as a state, is dominated by the whites; nonwhites are excluded from political decisions. Whites also dominate the economy of South Africa, nonwhites being assigned functions of a low order with no chance of moving up the economic ladder. Therefore the political as well as the economic position of the nonwhites belies the assertion that apartheid does not necessarily involve relationships of dominance and subservience. All the policies of the South African government are based on the assumption, tacit or otherwise, that the nonwhites are permanently incapable of creating a modern civilization. Eugene Dvorin notes,

> *The implication of* [*apartheid*] *is that the existence of a "natural," "common," or "universal" man is denied and that men are conceived as only members of different races. . . .*
>
> *. . . The ideal is that of the* Herrenvolk, *or "master-race," a people with a common past, common language, and biological superiority . . . destined by physical and mental superiority to dominance over other races. . . .*[5]

Perhaps it is best to conclude this chapter on racism with a quotation from the UNESCO statement on race of July 1950:

> *According to present knowledge there is no proof that the groups of mankind differ in their innate mental characteristics, whether in respect to intelligence or temperament. The scientific evidence indicates that the range of mental capacities in all ethnic groups is much the same.*
>
> *. . . Historical and sociological studies support the view that genetic differences are not of importance in determining the social and cultural differences between different groups of* Homo sapiens; *and that the social and cultural* changes *in different groups have, in the main, been independent of* changes *in inborn constitution.*[6]

NOTES

1. William Sumner Jenkins, *Pro-Slavery Thought in the Old South* (Chapel Hill, N.C.: University of North Carolina Press, 1935), pp. 65–66.

2. Quoted in *ibid.*, p. 193.

3. Quoted in *ibid.*, p. 19.

4. Oscar Handlin, *Race and Nationality in American Life* (Boston: Little, Brown, 1957), p. 96.

5. Eugene Dvorin, *Racial Separation in South Africa: An Analysis of Apartheid Theory* (Chicago: University of Chicago Press, 1952), pp. 56–58.

6. Quoted in Ashley Montagu, *Man's Most Dangerous Myth: The Fallacy of Race* (Cleveland: World, 1964), p. 365.

PART TWO

IDEOLOGIES AND POLITICS

CHAPTER SIX

EUROPE: GREAT BRITAIN, FRANCE, AND GERMANY

Great Britain, France, and Germany, the three countries we have chosen to represent Europe, illustrate the extremely different answers to the question of what constitutes the good life and the good society that can arise, even within the same civilization. This very diversity permits us to look deeply into some of the most fundamental issues of social and political organization. By way of identification with the thinkers we encountered in Chapter 1, we may consider Great Britain as the country of Burke and Bentham, France as the country of Descartes and Rousseau, and Germany as the country of Hegel and Nietzsche. At the same time, all three countries have been influenced by socialism in varying degrees.

GREAT BRITAIN

Since the Glorious Revolution of 1688, Great Britain has been a stable society, where change was slow and steady and the new was organically integrated into the old. The British traditionally have been reverential toward established institutions, and, accepting man's conservatism, have preferred to dress the new in the cloth of the old. In matters of social organization, practicality has been favored over theorizing; fundamental questions have not been raised for fear of widening splits instead of narrowing them. Since 1688, it has been possible to focus emotions on the monarchy as an institution that has prestige but no political power, and thus separate the emotional and the irrational from politics.

The British have tended to take care of issues as they arise, not attempting to place them in larger frameworks. There is also a particular reluctance to follow abstractions. The spirit of the common law, with its emphasis on the specific case and its derivation of principles from the accumulation of precedents—its tendency to decide cases on their narrowest grounds without going into fundamentals—is the spirit of Great Britain.

The acceptance of the British aristocracy and its almost reverent cultivation made for a society in which status was accepted as a matter of course. The mass of people take it for granted that they have social "betters" and that they should not raise their voices on issues about which they know little. Groups with grievances have been slow to voice them and patient in awaiting their redress.

The weakness of royal power led to representative institutions and local government at an early date. The monarchy felt threatened by the power of the nobility and relied on the bourgeoisie as a counterweight, with the result that the bourgeoisie became accustomed to administering the state. In their fight against the monarchy, the aristocracy and the wealthy organized themselves into two competing parties, the Tories and the Whigs.

The process of democratization was slow and gradual, and because the new groups that received the franchise were small, there was no need to form parties other than the two already established. In 1832, the new voters added to the rolls were similar enough in wealth and status with those already enfranchised that they were accommodated in one of the two existing parties, with the Whigs and the Tories eagerly wooing the newcomers. The aristocracy's attitude toward the common people was that of noblesse oblige.

Democracy in Great Britain was thus elitist; but, at the same time the public attitude toward government was positive. Unlike the French who viewed the meaning of the democratic system as being a contest between the individual and the government, Britons interpreted democracy as participation in the political decision-making process, a contribution that was both a duty and an honor.

The positive attitude toward government was at least in part due to the tolerance that has characterized British public life. It was this tolerance which made possible the ready assimilation into the elite of individuals rising from the lower classes.

Aneurin Bevan, the former leader of the left wing of the British Labour Party, told a typical story of his initiation into the House of Commons. Coming from a Welsh miner's family, he had grown up to hate the establishment, and after his election to the House of Commons, seeing the portraits of the past leaders of Great Britain in Westminster Hall, had said to himself: "These are not my people." Since it is the custom that a newly elected member delivers his maiden speech with a member of the other party giving a formal reply, Bevan decided to attack the establishment and all it stood for in the most abusive form, looking forward with gleeful anticipation to "bringing the roof down." After excoriating the establishment, Bevan sat down and awaited the fulminations of the Conservative member. Instead, Bevan was assured that the House had followed his speech with great interest and hoped that it would have many more opportunities to hear from the new member. The Speaker thereupon called the next item on the agenda, and Bevan felt quite deflated.

It is this absorptive quality of the establishment that eventually also resulted in the nonrevolutionary transition from aristocratic rule to the rule of the bourgeoisie, or the "embourgeoisement" of the aristocracy. Toward the end of the nineteenth century, as many successful businessmen and bankers were ennobled, most members of the House of Lords came from bourgeois backgrounds. As the age of industrialization created a rather large working class, it was possible to resolve social conflict (comparatively speaking) without destroying the nation's social fabric.

FRANCE

In sharp contrast to those of Great Britain, French politics have always been polarized. Because there has rarely been a consensus on fundamentals, France has moved between the extremes of near anarchy and authoritarianism. Following in the tradition of Descartes the French seek clarity and tend to crystallize issues very sharply. Compromise has always been viewed as a betrayal of the intellect.

Cartesianism is also associated with skepticism, which never accepts a position as definite. Taken together, the desire for clearly defined issues and skepticism make politics argumentative and overly fluid. This combination defines the special character of French democracy. As Maurice Duverger, a prominent French political scientist, puts it:

Most people may not be aware that Descartes was one of the founders of French democracy. His attitude of systematic doubting, of mistrusting and resisting conventional ideas, which characterizes French mentality and tradition so deeply, is one of the cornerstones of French democracy; it is the belief that a doctrine must be questioned the very moment it begins to be established; that in order not to hamper the free movement of individual thought one has to destroy what has just been built so as to advance anew. . . .

This conception is very deeply rooted in the French, and it explains the role the university and the intellectuals have played throughout French history in the struggle for democracy. In most countries, the intellectuals participate in the struggle for freedom. But this participation is far more active in France than elsewhere, and involvement of the intellectual is more readily accepted there than in other countries.[1]

The role of the intellectual, it should be mentioned, was established prior to the struggle for democracy. The kings actively wooed artists and intellectuals and the splendor of the court was in part dependent on the brilliance of the artists and intellectuals the kings were able to attract. In assuming the patronage of the Académie Française in 1635, Cardinal Richelieu institutionalized the prestigious role of the intellectual, and even today this self-perpetuating body represents the pinnacle of a man's ambition in France. To become one of "the immortals," as the members of the academy are called, has meant more to a Frenchman than becoming president or prime minister of the republic. Given the prestige of the intellectual in France, his support for a political regime—or lack of it—has great significance. The collapse of the *ancien régime* was initiated by the desertion of the intellectuals, whose criticism eroded popular confidence in the regime and made the aristocracy and the court doubt their right to rule.

It must also be pointed out that the hallmark of democracy in France has been resistance to authority, whoever might represent this authority. As mentioned before, democracy in France does not mean the right to participate in political decision-making so much as the right to be left alone by the government. Thus there is a certain anarchic streak in French democracy. But this attitude is contradicted by an opposite tendency, the tradition of Rousseau, to see man not just as an individual, but as a part of society; man is a man only because he is also a citizen. Rousseau, as we have seen, believed in the existence of the general will, which is more than the will of the majority. It is above society; it has an objective existence; and it can be discovered, but once discovered it has to be followed. Jacob L. Talmon states,

In this way the general will is at the same time outside us and within us. Man is not invited to express his personal preferences. He is not asked for his approval. He is asked whether the given proposal is

or is not in conformity with the general will. "If my particular opinion had carried the day, I should have achieved the opposite of what was my will; and it is in that case that I should not have been free." For freedom is the capacity of ridding oneself of considerations, interests, preferences and prejudices, whether personal or collective, which obscure the objectively true and good, which, if I am true to my true nature, I am bound to will. What applies to the individual applies equally to the people. Man and people have to be brought to choose freedom, and if necessary to be forced to be free.[2]

Rousseau's view of the organic character of the community and his identification of democracy with virtue imply that interest groups cannot insert themselves between the state and the individual. Representative institutions themselves, such as parliaments, corrupt democracy. Talmon concludes, "Parliamentary institutions, the separation and balance of powers, were thus impossible as roads to social harmony. The various interests would be judges in their own cause. The clashes among them would paralyse the State." [3]

By implication, Rousseau called for the leader or leaders who stand above the contending forces. It is the democracy of the Jacobins and of the plebiscitary democracies of Napoleon III and Charles de Gaulle. But it is a form of democracy—if we want to call it that—that had appeal after the excesses of the Cartesian form had led the country to chaos. Thus the polarity between Descartes and Rousseau laid the foundation for the perennial tensions in French politics.

Generally, the two forms of democracy have coexisted. On the one hand, there is the excessive French individualism; on the other hand, there is the Rousseauan legacy of a strong central administration. On the one hand, France is a country of many regional differences; on the other hand, Paris *is* France—more so than any other capital in relationship to its country.

In some ways the French civil service has considered itself the embodiment of the general will—as serving the state and not the government. It has provided devoted services and many brilliant representatives, and carried on as governments come and go. Obviously, it is most itself while serving people like Charles de Gaulle, because it does not have to heed the dissonant voices of warring elective representatives but can implement that higher rationality which is based on expertise. It should be pointed out that, given this character and attitude of the civil service, instability has not been the result of revolving-door governments per se. When no severe social or political issues have confronted the nation, the civil service provided continuity. Problems arose when issues demanded new approaches, for political innovation is beyond the capacity of a civil service.

Part of the instability of France has been due to the sharp break with the past brought about by the French Revolution and the lack of a broad consensus on basic institutions during the nineteenth century. The battles of monarchy versus republic, church versus state, and army versus civilian control of the military were fought over and over again. When, by the twentieth century, these battles had been determined in favor of the republic, the separation of church and state, and civilian control over the army, social tensions between the bourgeoisie and the working class began to dominate the French political scene.

The sharp break between the *ancien régime* and the republic in which a strong monarchy was suddenly overthrown occurring at a time when the social problems of the industrial age already cast their shadow also helps explain the multiparty system in France. As we have seen, the slow process of democratization in Great Britain under a relatively weak monarchy permitted the gradual integration of new social strata into two preexisting aristocratic groupings. In France, no parties existed on the eve of the revolution; the Estates General—something of an aristocratic parliament—had not been called together since 1614. When the revolution opened the floodgates, all the different (and often minor) interests sought expression in politics. While in an earlier period of agricultural society social conflict could involve only peasants and landlords, the coming of the age of industrialization introduced a number of additional issues to complicate party politics.

The following table illustrates the instability of the French government and also provides orientation for the beginning student of French politics.

Dates	*Regime*
To 1789	*Ancien Régime*
1789–1792	French Revolution
1792–1799	First Republic

1799–1814	Napoleon (1799–1802, First Consul; 1802–1804, Lifetime Consul; 1804–1814, Emperor [First Empire])
1814–1830	Bourbon Restoration
1830	July Revolution
1830–1848	Monarchy of Louis Philippe (House of Orleans)
1848	February Revolution
1848–1852	Second Republic, with Louis Napoleon as President
1852–1870	Monarchy under Louis Napoleon III (Second Empire)
1870	Fall of the Monarchy
1871	Paris Commune
1870–1940	Third Republic
1940–1944	Vichy Regime
1944–1946	Provisional Government under Charles de Gaulle
1947–1958	Fourth Republic
1958–1969	Fifth Republic under Charles de Gaulle
1969–	Fifth Republic (Post de Gaulle Era)

GERMANY

Whereas the politics of Great Britain were those of common sense and the politics of France were the result of an unstable balance between rationalist individualism and romanticist collectivism, the spirit of German politics has been metaphysical and romanticist. Hegel's conception of history as the unfolding of the world spirit of which the highest manifestation is the state resulted in an abstruse view of the state not as a human institution devoted to human ends but as an entity in some sense apart from and above man. While Hegel did not make the state an end in itself, but rather established a reciprocal relationship between the individual and the state in the sense that the end of the state is the individual's liberty, this liberty was so defined as to make the state the judge of its meaning and limitation. Without the state, people "do not know what they will"; democracy has no place in such a conception. Hegel observes,

To hold that every single person should share in deliberating and deciding on political matters of general concern on the ground that

all individuals are members of the state, that its concerns are their concerns, and that it is their right that what is done should be done with their knowledge and volition, is tantamount to a proposal to put the democratic element without any rational form into the organism of the state, although it is only in virtue of the possession of such a form that the state is an organism at all.[4]

Hegel is, in effect, an advocate of the dynastic bureaucratic state, which, by the pretense that it speaks for all, makes it appear that it stands above the selfish conflicts of particular groups and individuals.

German political thought not only romanticized the state and what it stands for, but also the Folk within it. The *Folk* was, in essence, an almost metaphysical entity whose spirit was the matrix of art, culture, and law. It was the Teutonic Folk that gave rise to the German nation, and the German nation was vital only as long as it was faithful to its Teutonic spirit. As Ernest Barker pointed out, there has always been a haze about German political thought, which, if the Germans ever understood it, has certainly confounded non-Germans.

The romanticized Folk, just because it is made an entity, a being, and even a person, can readily be identified (at any rate by the synthetic mind) with the entity, being, or person of the State—that is to say with the Government—that is to say, when we come to the last resort, with the person of the Governor.[5]

Next to the apotheosis of Folk and state, German political tradition has had a particular preoccupation with power, and in this respect the writings of Nietzsche have had a major impact. For Nietzsche, the will to power was the core of life—man's ultimate horizon after he has realized that there is no God. Traditional morality—that is, Christianity—must be rejected, for it is a slave morality that makes weakness a virtue by dissolving man's urge to be master of his fate. But once man knows that religion and all philosophies are artificial creations, he becomes aware of his power. If there is no truth, man's possibilities for creative expression become limitless. Besides discarding religious belief, Nietzsche went beyond reason, as the tool only of the surface, or conscious, mind. Reality is apprehended only by the deeper recesses of the mind—in modern terminology, the unconscious.

Nietzsche formulated the future man as a "superman," who will be part poet, part philosopher, part saint; it is not clear whether he would be partly political. The solution of the crisis Nietzsche saw arising among Western men would involve beliefs in radical individualism for the few, while the many would continue to live an increasingly herdlike existence.

The political metaphysics of Hegel and the will-to-power doctrine of Nietzsche were bound to work havoc in the minds of semi-intellectuals of a romantic bent, of which Germany has had such an abundance. It is these pseudo-intellectuals, in contrast to the truly educated who unfortunately never deigned to descend into the arena of politics, who have greatly determined German politics.

The tragedy of political life is that power and wisdom are not natural companions. Those who crave power are seldom wise, and those who are wise usually do not seek power. The relationship between wisdom and power may vary from country to country, but nowhere has the separation between the two been greater than in Germany.

LATE NINETEENTH-CENTURY DEVELOPMENTS

Industrialism and the Rise of Socialism

The industrial age created a sense of internationalism that was based on economic interdependence, with the result that its social issues had an international dimension. This, however, is not to say that the different stages of economic development resulting from the uneven development of capitalism, as well as from different national contexts, did not lead to different approaches to these social problems and different solutions or attempted solutions. In Great Britain, a conservative country of pragmatic bent with functioning parliamentary institutions, socialism (in the sense of a broad movement of social reform along cooperative lines) found its expression in Fabianism, though an admixture of Marxism can be found, particularly in the left wing of the British Labour Party. France became the home of revolutionary action, as was exemplified by the Paris Commune. In Germany, although social backwardness precluded social action, the German tendency toward speculation provided fertile soil for the growth of theory, and thus Germany became the homeland of Marxist thought. In tracing the development of European socialism, we will give centrality to Marxism and discuss other forms of socialism in connection with it.

A decisive event in the development of European socialism was the establishment in 1864 of the International Working Men's Association, or the First International, which was supposed to be an international organization of European trade unions. Marx gave the inaugural address, drafted the preamble to the rules of the IWMA, and in general played a leading role in its development, although it was also composed of anarchists (led by Mikhail Bakunin) and revolutionaries (led by Louis Blanqui). In associating himself with the organization, Marx took a rather practical line; he eschewed revolutionism and revolutionary bombast. "After 1850 Marx had ceased to belong to the extreme Left of the revolutionary movement and had become acutely suspicious of mere *emeutism* (revolutionism) which he saw as presenting unnecessary opportunities to the enemy to destroy the workers' organization and deprive them of their leaders by imprisonment or exile." [6]

Marx, however, still expected a revolutionary situation that would make it possible for the working class to seize state power; but it would be incorrect to say that this thought preoccupied him. By the 1860's, Great Britain had found new social stability as a result of certain important social reforms, and Marx had earlier singled out Great Britain as the most promising country for a socialist revolution in view of her highly developed capitalism. In this connection, it should be recalled that Marx ultimately accepted the possibility of peaceful transition to socialism in the advanced Western countries and enunciated this belief in the last Congress of the First International.

The IWMA also contained a revolutionary left, however, made up of Louis Blanqui (1805–81) and his followers. They believed in conspiratorial politics and the organization of a small elite of committed revolutionaries who, at a propitious moment, would seize power by a *coup d'état* and through ruthless action sweep the mass of people into support of the revolution. But the mass itself would not be able to rule; this would fall to the elite. Though Blanqui had a socialist program of sorts, his chief concern was the revolution. Thus Marx and his followers took a dim view of Blanqui's position, which was devoid of any serious sociological and historical analysis. For them, it was sheer revolutionism.

The Paris Commune

The spirit of Blanqui, if not his elitist organizational ideas, was manifested in the Paris Commune in 1871. The commune holds an important place in the lore of socialism; the Russian revolutionaries of 1905, in setting up their soviets, invoked the Paris Commune as a model. Therefore,, a brief description of it is in order.

After the defeat of France under Napoleon III in the Franco-Prussian War of 1870–71 and the conclusion of the armistice, Prussian troops threw a ring around Paris; a provisional French government was formed and installed itself in Versailles; and the Parisians were left to fend for themselves. In this situation, the class antagonism between the Parisian proletariat and bourgeoisie became overt; a social revolution establishing a new type of society was to come. But given the low level of capitalist development and, consequently, the limited political consciousness of the workers, the notion of what this new society was to be was rather vague. The proletarians were mainly interested in the creation of new, revolutionary institutions. They assumed that once the revolution was undertaken it would in due course find its specific programatic content.

The Paris Commune was established as such a revolutionary institution; it was composed of representatives elected by the people by universal suffrage and subject to their recall. It combined all powers: legislative, executive, and judicial. The separation of powers was considered reactionary because, under the monarchy, the executive had been the state and had set itself above the people. Only by combining these powers could one be sure that officials would be responsible to the people.

Given the history of France, this was a sound position, for the existence of distinct executives (whatever their constitutional relationships to the legislature) had enabled them to overthrow regimes they disliked. Louis Napoleon had been elected President of the Second Republic, and having this executive power he could overthrow the republic and make himself an emperor. Similarly, our notion that the separation of powers is the best safeguard for the maintenance of democracy has important qualifications, the chief one being that it limits the executive only if he respects the constitution. A separate executive, if he wishes to use his *de facto* powers, can overthrow a government much more easily than if all officials in a government have both executive and legislative powers; that is, if these functions are intermixed. Whether a country can be run on such a basis is, of course, a different matter.

To demonstrate the universalist character of the commune, foreigners were elected to it: "The flag of the Commune is the flag of the World Republic." The egalitarian character of the commune was further manifested in the salaries of its officials, who received the same amount as the average Parisian worker. In reordering society, the commune decreed the separation of church and state, the elimination of all religious symbols from education, and the closing of pawnshops. The factories that had been closed by their owners were to be reopened and run by the workers as cooperatives, and all cooperatives were to be united in one syndicate.

The commune lasted from March 26 to May 17, 1871, when it was crushed by the Versailles government. The Versailles government, bourgeois and monarchical in its orientation, had at first only looked on the developments in Paris with misgivings, and at one point had even negotiated with the communards. But the revolutionary commitment of the latter and the conservative attitude of the government made compromise impossible. In a frenzy, the Versailles troops slaughtered thousands of Parisians and deported many others. The massacre that ended the commune surpassed by far that in the French Revolution.

Marx gave a glowing description of the commune in his *Civil War in France,* published in May 1871, but later had reservations which reflected his skepticism and nonrevolutionist tendency:

> . . . *Apart from the fact that this* [*the Paris Commune*] *was merely the rising of a city under exceptional conditions, the majority of the Commune was in no way socialist, nor could it be. With a modicum of common sense, however, it could have reached a compromise with Versailles useful to the whole mass of the people, the only thing that could be reached at the time.*[7]

As a result of the defeat of the Paris Commune, and also as a result of the quarrels between the followers of Marx and the anarchistic followers of Bakunin, the First International collapsed.

Social Democracy in Europe

With the collapse of the Paris Commune, the center of socialism shifted to Germany, where it became "purified" along Marxist lines.

The German socialists had maintained themselves against great odds, such as Bismarck's antisocialist laws, and in the end emerged stronger than before. Their principled stand, the thoroughness of their organization, and their successes in subsequent parliamentary elections could not fail to have impressed socialists abroad. Toward the end of the century, nearly every country in the world had a socialist party that looked to Germany for inspiration.

The socialist parties of Western Europe were reformist, accepted the parliamentary "game," and were nationalist in the sense that they considered themselves part of the political establishment of their respective countries. Indeed, working through the establishment, they had achieved various workers' demands. Bismarck, though he outlawed the Socialist Party, adopted a number of social welfare measures, such as public health care for wage earners. Moreover, as the socialist parties were successful in elections, they helped shape legislation that favored their interests. But as these parties played the political game, they were drawn into what we would call the establishment and they succumbed to its flatteries and other blandishments.

While it could be said that the laissez-faire state had left the worker out in the cold, the transformation of the laissez-faire state into the social welfare state gave the worker a home; it could no longer be said that the worker had no fatherland. However, there was enough internationalism left to demand the establishment of a new international union, the Second or Socialist International. Founded in 1889, it was nothing more than an association of social democratic parties, and its congresses adopted resolutions or recommendations that had no binding force.

The practical reformist tendencies that appeared in all socialist parties, including the German Social Democratic Party, gave rise to a sharp theoretical and ideological debate that was fought out—not surprisingly—in Germany. The "pope" of Marxism, Karl Kautsky, represented the orthodox viewpoint; Eduard Bernstein represented revisionism.

Karl Kautsky (1854–1938) accepted the class basis of socialism in full and rejected collaboration with other classes. Though advocating the revolutionary overthrow of capitalism, he conceived this revolution as peaceful. In his theoretical approach, he followed Marx to the letter, though the intervening years should have shown him that certain of Marx's expectations had failed to materialize. For instance, he continued to believe in the increasing misery of the working class, though even in relative terms the income of the workers had increased. Since he defended an interpretation of history along more extreme materialist lines, he was not an activist in the fullest sense. He believed that socialism would arise only in the wake of a fully developed capitalism, and only then would there be a chance to bring the majority over to the side of socialism. To do so prematurely would mean that a small group would have to seize power and maintain itself by force—a perversion of the socialist ideology. Later, Kautsky denounced the Bolshevik revolution on this issue and was bitterly attacked for it by Lenin.

Kautsky found a certain difficulty in dealing with the use of existing institutions for the betterment of the worker; in doing so he saw a risk of strengthening the state he was committed to overthrow. He therefore adopted a rather ambiguous position, according to which workers' participation in existing institutions would sharpen their political consciousness, and—given the fact that the gap between the workers' aspiration and satisfaction was bound to increase—their political consciousness would increasingly assume revolutionary character. Kautsky's references to revolution, however, were rendered somewhat meaningless by the fact that he was a pacifist, and as such abhorred the idea of a civil war.

Eduard Bernstein (1850–1932) was a pragmatic person who could not understand why socialists should engage in revolutionary talk when all the developments pointed toward the gradual evolution of socialism. He denied that class conflict had increased and that capitalism faced imminent collapse. He objected to those ideologues who, on the basis of the dream of the coming revolution, would forego serious efforts for social improvement that were both possible and sought after by the workers. He held that socialism would not be attained by the implementation of a detailed blueprint but as the result of accumulated piecemeal measures of social improvement and economic change. Bernstein also attacked the notion that the worker had no fatherland; he pointed out that the worker had received a stake in the state and that the German worker should not be ashamed of being a German patriot.

The problem with Bernstein's position was that it did not include a grand design for the future—something that may be necessary for any movement devoted to radical change. It could be argued that only such a design would exert the necessary pull on people's imagination and tell them whether they were on the right course. It alone could provide the necessary differentiation that would prevent their sliding into sheer opportunism. Furthermore, since only a country deeply committed to democracy would permit the accumulation of those piecemeal changes that in the end would lead to a different socio-economic system, what was to be done in countries that were not so committed to democracy?

In short, the German Social Democratic Party condemned Bernstein and supported Kautsky, though in practice it lived by Bernstein's precepts. It thus chose the worst of both worlds. Its revolutionary words antagonized the lower middle classes, some of whose members would perhaps have been won over to socialism, while its lack of revolutionary drive prevented it from being taken seriously by the imperial regime.

While these theoretical and ideological disputes were engaged in with passion and determination within the German Social Democratic Party, they were irrelevant in Great Britain and had only a minor echo in France. In Great Britain for the greater part of the nineteenth century, socialists were political appendages to the Liberal Party. Various attempts were made to form distinct socialist parties, but it was only in 1906 that the British Labour Party was able to rally all socialist forces. The spirit of the British Labour Party was "Fabian"; that is, it more or less followed the principles of the Fabian Society, which was founded in 1883–84 by a number of prominent intellectuals and reformers, such as Sidney and Beatrice Webb, and George Bernard Shaw. The purpose of the society was to help reconstruct society "in accordance with the highest moral possibilities." The society took its name from Fabius Cunctator, "the Hesitator," a Roman general in the war against Carthage who, by refusing to give battle, exhausted the enemy's strength and finally defeated his superior forces.

The Fabians' philosophy was a determinist view of history based on economics, but they did not believe that history makes great leaps; they assumed that it was the result of small, cumulative adjustments. Thus social changes result from the adaptation of people to new conditions, and the driving force in change is not necessarily the class struggle but man's general tendency to adapt to new demands. In bringing about change, one can appeal to man's rationality and moral conscience outside any narrow class context. In contrast to the German socialists, the British brought practice and theory into line, and thus could appeal to more strata of the population than just the working class. The Fabians, through their educational activities, were able to bring socialist ideas to the attention of what we would call opinion leaders, such as clergymen, teachers, and civil servants.

Although Marxism had a greater impact in France than in Great Britain, it did not have the socialist field to itself, as in Germany. In France, Marxism had to compete with syndicalism, a revolutionary labor movement that advocated the overthrow of the capitalist order by the direct action of industrial workers and the establishment of an autonomous association of workers, that would engage in the mutual exchange of products. Socialists wanted to capture the state, either through parliamentary or revolutionary means, but syndicalists were antistatist and hence somewhat anarchist. According to the syndicalist viewpoint, to put the state in charge of the economy would mean to exchange one set of rulers for another, and because the state requires a bureaucracy for the running of its affairs, workers could end up being ruled by bureaucrats who by definition are unimaginative, used to routine, and hostile to any kind of innovation. Syndicalists rejected political action not only because they rejected the state, but also because they believed that the solidarity of workers is based only on working conditions and economic exploitation. Outside the workshop, workers' interests differ; they may have different views on religion and even on the politics of the day. To get them to engage in revolutionary action, one must appeal to their position in industry, not involve them in political action and useless controversies. The weapon of the workers is the strike, and after they have been educated in a number of smaller strikes, the general strike will lead to the triumph of their cause.

Thus a certain lore developed around the idea of the general strike that made it less a rational weapon for the labor struggle than a myth designed to galvanize workers. George Sorel (1847–1922), in his *Reflections on Violence,* espoused the creative roles of violence and the "social myth." For him, violence meant being engaged in an unending struggle in which victory was not necessarily the goal; the goal was the fight itself. Fighting brings out the best in man whereas compromise means softness and decay. When he spoke about the social myth, he accepted the psychological interpretation that men do not act purposefully because of intellectual convictions but because of their faith in a particular destiny.

Syndicalism was strong in France between 1900 and 1914, but

it declined after the First World War. Trade unions, which had been syndicalist, became political, and the largest of them—the Confédération Générale du Travail—attached itself to the Communist Party. Syndicalism had also found a home in Spain, where in the interwar period there was an unending battle between syndicalists and communists. This battle continued into the Spanish Civil War, in which both were on the same side, but their historical antagonisms hampered the common effort.

THE FIRST WORLD WAR AND THE FATE OF SOCIALISM

As we have seen, the rise of the welfare state deradicalized socialism and at the same time "nationalized" it. One issue, however, was thought by socialists all over the world to require international co-operation. This was the war issue.

The special responsibility which socialists felt they had in this regard was due to their belief that it was capitalism that breeds war. To make things worse, many socialists had the uneasy awareness that the very success of welfare capitalism would increase rather than decrease international tensions. For by being committed to the welfare of the worker the state would have to become more urgently concerned with its economic successes which under conditions of capitalist production involved access to foreign markets, sources of raw material, cheap native labor. Since all capitalist nations would have to pursue the same goals, conflicts among them would become inevitable. The paradox that had arisen was that while the socialization of the nation had made proletarian internationalism for purposes of economic betterment of the working classes largely superfluous, it had made proletarian internationalism for the purpose of preventing wars more urgent.[8]

Various congresses of the Second International dealt with the issue. At the Stuttgart Congress of 1907, a rather innocuous resolution was adopted that everybody could interpret as he wished. But when the First World War broke out, most socialist parties rallied to the causes of their countries using all kinds of arguments to rationalize their decisions. There were, however, small left-wing groups that did not go along with the majority. These groups were not concerned, as were the center groups of their respective parties, with the speedy ending of the war; their aim was the transformation of the imperialist war into an international civil war. With Lenin as the leader, these groups later formed the nuclei of the emerging communist parties. The socialist Second International collapsed with the outbreak of the war, although it was revived after the war.

Socialist and Communist Parties After the War

The interwar period up to 1935 was characterized by bitter antagonism between communists and social democrats. This antagonism was particularly bitter in Germany because the social democrats had cooperated with the traditionalists in suppressing a number of communist uprisings. According to the communists, defeated Germany was the most propitious place for a proletarian revolution, and it was due only to the treachery of the social democrats that this had not come to pass. Socialists were called "social fascists" and were considered by the communists to be their chief enemies. The struggles between socialists and communists left the working class in such disarray that it was unable to cope with the rising threat of Hitler.

In France during the interwar period, the working class moved gradually into the communist camp, as mentioned earlier, and the largest trade union, the Confédération Générale du Travail, came under communist domination. The French Socialist Party had become a petty bourgeois party—the party of white-collar workers, teachers, small businessmen, and so forth—but the hostility between socialists and communists was less intense in France than in Germany.

In Great Britain the interwar years saw the formation of two Labour governments, 1923–24 and 1929–31, both of which collapsed because of the social and economic crises of the times. In 1931 the Labour Party was split from top to bottom when its leader Ramsay MacDonald deserted the party and decided to form a National Government composed of Labourites who had followed him, Conservatives, and Liberals. MacDonald lasted as Prime Minister until 1935.

In 1935, after Hitler had taken over Germany and the Soviet Union had to face up to the Nazi threat, Stalin ordered communists to come to terms with the socialists, and he espoused the cause of the "popular front." Popular front governments, with communist support, were established in France and in Spain. The French popular front collapsed because of its inability to cope with the great unrest that gripped France at the time. Rent internally because of its inability to take a stand on the civil war in Spain, it adopted a neutral stance, which made it a radical government only by self-designation. The popular front in Spain collapsed with the victory of Franco in 1938.

Thus Western Europe was characterized during the interwar period not by reform but by reaction. In Italy, reaction took the form of fascism, and in Germany, Nazism.

Fascism and Nazism

Reaction in Europe after the war was the result of wartime exhaustion and the disappointment that victors and vanquished alike experienced after such exhaustion. The war had brought great economic dislocations, and the huge reparations imposed on the defeated Central Powers meant that, since they could pay only through the export of their goods, they were bound to disturb international markets. Inflation wiped out savings, the typical form of financial security of the middle class. Though an impoverished middle class should have found its natural ally in the working class, the chronic contempt with which even the lower middle class in Germany looked on the worker made such an alliance impossible. That the upper classes, fearful for their privileges, would exploit this attitude of the middle classes for the purpose of forming a broad antisocialist front, is only too understandable.

Italy, though nominally a victor, was in consequence of the war a defeated country. It was treated by France and Great Britain as a minor ally, and felt that it was regarded with condescension, if not contempt. The immediate postwar years brought rampant inflation and unemployment, and large groups of people became alienated from the system. The peasants, as always, were the forgotten people in Italian politics; the small shopkeepers and artisans were driven to the verge of ruin; and the returning soldiers were left to fend for themselves. The purported victory, with all the territory it brought, was of no use to them. In such a desolate position, they had nothing to hold on to but the glory of the country, and thus nationalism became a substitute for more tangible benefits. The great landowners and industrialists also felt endangered. Fearful of socialists and communists, they looked about for some form of insurance. Benito Mussolini (1883–1945), a political adventurer, became the rallying point for an authoritarian movement of social peace, national honor, and Roman greatness. Mussolini began as an antiwar left-wing socialist, became a right-wing socialist who supported the war, and in the end was expelled from the Socialist Party. Possessing the flamboyance that appealed to many Italians, he was able to attract wide attention and to organize fascism as a mass movement.

Given the heterogeneous character of its followers and the fact that it had to hide its counterrevolutionary tendencies, fascism did not develop any theory worthy of the name. Fascist theory consisted of little more than a set of platitudes, developed after Mussolini's seizure of power, that tried to rationalize events. But since Marxism was considered the chief enemy of fascism, fascists embraced opposite tenets from those espoused by Marxists.

Since the Marxists regarded the antagonism of economic classes as a permanent and inescapable factor in a capitalist society, fascism must assert the conciliation of class-interests in the organic totality of nation and state. The secondary enemy, political liberalism and the defense of individual freedom, could equally well be met by the same type of national idealism. To equate freedom with caprice, to condemn both as egoism, and to represent the pursuits of happiness as a mean desire of selfish advantages have been stock arguments with idealist hero-worshippers since the days of Thomas Carlyle.[9]

While these ideas may perhaps have provided a basis for what could be called fascist theory, they were stated in such ambiguous language as to be all things to all men. And in many ways they were contradictory, as indicated by Alfredo Rocco (1875–1935), the chief theoretician of fascism:

We, too, maintain the necessity of safeguarding the conditions that make for the free development of the individual; we, too, believe that the oppression of individual personality can find no place in the modern state. . . . Our concept of liberty is that the individual must be allowed to develop his personality in behalf of the state. . . .[10]

But if the state is to determine the direction of individual development, how can one at the same time assert that individual personality should not be oppressed? Rocco goes on to say "Fascism does not look upon the doctrine of economic liberty as an absolute dogma. . . . But Fascism maintains that in the ordinary run of events economic liberty serves the social purposes best; . . ."[11] The latter statement must have pleased the Italian industrialists who had generously financed Mussolini. In fact, it was designed to reassure them that the fascists would serve as their savior from socialism and communism.

But Rocco continued to contradict himself:

Fascism insists that the government be entrusted to men capable of rising above their own private interests. . . . It also proclaims that the great mass of citizens is not a suitable advocate of social interests for the reason that the capacity to ignore individual private interests in favor of the higher demands of society and of history is a very rare gift and the privilege of the chosen few. . . . This must not however be construed to mean that the masses are not to be allowed to exercise any influence on the life of the state. On the contrary, among peoples with a great history and with noble traditions, even the lowest elements of society possess an instinctive discernment of what is necessary for the welfare of the race. . . .[12]

We may assume that the fascist leaders, including Mussolini, did not believe in this synthetic combination of contradictions. In line with Sorel, whom Mussolini greatly admired, they assumed that the essence of an ideology (or in this case myth) is its ability to galvanize the masses into action. But it was doubtful whether the masses cared for fascist ideology. Nationalism, and a flamboyant leader who could repair Italy's international prestige, most probably sufficed to rally them to fascism.

Although Italian fascism had a comparatively light note, Nazism was completely humorless and morbid. Charitably, we may view fascism as a political manifestation of the tradition of irrationalism, but there is a strong demarcation between this tradition and sheer madness—a line that was crossed by the Nazis.

POST–SECOND WORLD WAR CONSERVATISM

The post–Second World War era in Europe was characterized by conservatism. Immediately after the war there was a possibility of a communist takeover in France and in Italy, but this possibility was thwarted, certainly in part, by the Marshall Plan. That the countries of Western Europe, after the traumatic experiences of the war, would have wanted to settle back into a rather placid life is understandable. But this desire did not necessarily lead to political stability.

Up to 1958, France was managed (but never really governed)

by center coalitions. In 1958 a severe political crisis, provoked particularly by the war in Algeria, led to the reemergence of General de Gaulle. He brought the war in Algeria to an end by recognizing the independence of Algeria and introduced important constitutional reforms, changing France from a parliamentary to a presidential system. After his resignation in 1969, Georges Pompidou became President, leading a conservative government.

In the postwar period Germany and Italy were ruled by the conservative Christian Democratic parties. The Italians in 1962 undertook "an opening to the left" which, however, did not lead to stability. Subsequently, left-center coalitions have interchanged with right-center coalitions reflecting the unsettled political conditions of the country.

In Germany, after a long rule by Christian Democrats, the Socialists came into office in 1969 in coalition with the small liberal party, commanding only a slim majority. The policy of reconciliation with the East, pursued by Chancellor Willy Brandt, found wide support with the result that the government was reelected in 1972 by a comfortable majority.

In Britain, the Labour Party came to power in 1945 on a program of extensive social reform. The program included the nationalization of some major industries and the establishment of a public health service. The social reforms, many of which were long overdue, helped to heal social cleavages that had been tolerated for many years. Thus the British Labour Party was instrumental in strengthening the stability of Great Britain as a middle-class society. Subsequently, the British electorate has swung back and forth between the Socialists and the Conservatives; the Conservatives have been in office since 1970.

The conservatism of Western Europe has also enveloped the communist parties, transforming them into revisionist parties. A detailed discussion of this topic will follow in a later chapter.

NOTES

1. Maurice Duverger, "The Development of Democracy in France," in *Democracy in a Changing Society,* ed. Henry W. Ehrmann (New York: Praeger, 1964), pp. 70–71.

2. Jacob L. Talmon, *The Origins of Totalitarian Democracy* (New York: Praeger, 1961), pp. 41–42.

3. *Ibid.*, p. 45.

4. G. W. F. Hegel, *Philosophy of Right,* tr. T. M. Knox (Oxford, Eng.: Clarendon Press, 1942), p. 200.

5. Ernest Barker, *Principles of Social and Political Theory* (New York: Oxford University Press, 1951), p. 20.

6. G. D. H. Cole, *A History of Socialist Thought,* Vol. II, *Socialist Thought: Marxism and Anarchism 1850–1890* (London: Macmillan, 1957), p. 92.

7. Karl Marx, Letter to F. Domela-Nieuwenhuis, February 22, 1881, cited in *Marx and Engels: Basic Writings on Politics and Philosophy,* ed. Lewis S. Feuer (Garden City, N.Y.: Doubleday, 1959), p. 391.

8. Max Mark, *Beyond Sovereignty* (Washington, D.C.: Public Affairs Press, 1965), p. 34.

9. George H. Sabine, *A History of Political Theory* (New York: Holt, Rinehart and Winston, 1937), p. 748.

10. *Communism, Fascism, and Democracy: The Theoretical Foundations,* ed. Carl Cohen (New York: Random House, 1962), p. 344.

11. *Ibid.*, pp. 344–45.

12. *Ibid.*, pp. 345–46.

CHAPTER SEVEN

THE UNITED STATES

The United States has been the Lockean country par excellence. While in the older British society Locke was part of an historical stream within which a liberal-bourgeois order had to contend with a conservative-aristocratic tradition, the United States started out as a bourgeois country; it had no aristocratic past. Furthermore, the British bourgeoisie had barely arisen as the dominant class when the strong voices of social reform made themselves heard, and Locke was quickly superseded by Bentham and the utilitarians. In the United States, extensive social reforms came only with the New Deal.

In ascribing a dominant role for Locke's theories in the course of American history, we do not mean to give the impression that they were not challenged; they were often challenged severely. Throughout American history there was something of a dialectic process between Lockean thought and its opponents. However, Locke's ideas never lost favor more than temporarily. Indeed, Locke has been the ideologue of the American businessman, and while at times in our history the businessman was challenged and even discredited, in the end he has always managed to come out on top. Thus, the long reign of Lockean thought has made it part of American intellectual folklore, which has been an additional factor in its resilience.

At the time of the founding of the United States, Thomas Jefferson (1743–1826) and the Jeffersonians were the chief disciples of Locke; Alexander Hamilton (1757–1804) and the Federalists were aristocratic in outlook and temperament. The Jeffersonians were optimistic about man and praised his rationality; the Federalists, following Hobbes, believed that fear and self-interest, not human reason, were the driving forces in history. One had to be ever suspicious of the majority because it threatened the rights of the well-born and well-to-do natural leaders.

How did the Federalists guard against these dangers? Having united the colonies in a federal government, they made sure that this government could not be used by the many against the few. They provided for the separation of legislative, executive, and judicial powers, with checks and balances; they fixed the federal character of the government, with its strong upper house; and they determined that the Senate was to be elected indirectly.

The Federalists wanted the government to be strong enough to serve the interests of business, but at the same time they feared its takeover by the lower classes. If a strong government, one that had wide-ranging functions, were to be captured by the masses, it would be a better instrument for assaults on the privileges of the few than if it had been weak. But this contradiction was partly resolved after various basic business interests had been taken care of (through the instrumentality of a strong federal government) and the order of laissez faire became generally accepted.

The Jeffersonians had always been in favor of a weak federal government and laissez faire. The Jeffersonians were also not majoritarians. While the antimajoritarian bias of the Federalists was based on their fears for the privileges of the minority, the antimajoritarian position of the Jeffersonians was based on their concern for the rights of the individual. In the Lockean spirit, they were concerned lest a majority encroach on the inalienable rights of the individual. Even a minority of one must be protected.

That Jefferson, for all his belief in the goodness and rationality of man, was not a majoritarian became clear in his first inaugural address (March 4, 1801): "This [is a] sacred principle, that though the will of the majority is in all cases to prevail, that will, to be rightful, must be reasonable; that the minority possess their equal rights, which equal laws must protect, and to violate which would be oppression."[1] Since property came to be accepted as an inalienable right (though Jefferson considered it not a natural right but a civil right), its protection had both a conservative and a liberal foundation. In fact, since the liberal foundation proved to be so strong, there was no need to invoke elitist principles in the defense of property.

This concurrence on property was made possible by the opportunities available in a country with apparently unlimited frontiers. There was, in contrast to Europe, social mobility (except for the slaves). The indentured servant, who was brought to America by his well-to-do master, would eventually be free to become a farmer or craftsman. The man who could not make a good living in the East could move West, and by mixing his sweat with the soil could bear out Locke's proposition on the origin and meaning of property.

The coexistence of farmer and businessman worked well up to the period of the Civil War. First of all, the country was overwhelmingly rural. In 1860, only 16.1 percent of the total population resided in urban centers of 8,000 people or more (not until 1920 did the majority of Americans live in cities). Business up to the time of the Civil War was on a small scale, and industry consisted mostly of handicrafts. There were a few craft unions in the 1850's and 1860's, but they were of no great importance. It was only after the Civil War that the interests of industry and agriculture diverged and the working class began to feel deeply aggrieved.

SOCIAL DARWINISM

The post–Civil War period saw the rise of the great entrepreneur—John D. Rockefeller, Cornelius Vanderbilt, Andrew Mellon, and a host of lesser figures—and the ruthlessness with which some of them proceeded to amass their fortunes required (because of the resentment of those who suffered in the process) an ideological justification. There was also the problem of defending the assertion that laissez faire worked in the interest of all when, in fact, so many were falling by the wayside. The ideas of Charles Darwin (1809–82) and Herbert Spencer (1820–1903) provided good rationalizations, and the notion of the survival of the fittest was taken over as the explanation for the workings of society. Progress, like evolution, was inevitable, but a price had to be paid: the elimination of the unfit. It was not difficult to make a further connection between social evolution and moral evolution. Spencer, following the laissez-faire school, believed that the growth of society must not be impeded by state interference, and that governmental social welfare programs must be rejected because they would reward unfitness. All that the unfit should expect was charity. John D. Rockefeller expressed the spirit of the age in the following terms:

The growth of a large business is merely a survival of the fittest. . . . The American Beauty rose can be produced in the splendor and fragrance which bring cheer to its beholder only by sacrificing the early buds which grow up around it. This is not an evil tendency in business. It is merely the working-out of a law of nature and a law of God.[2]

In the American academic community, committed as its economists were to laissez faire, social Darwinism found a sympathetic reception. One of the foremost sociologists of the period, William Graham Sumner (1840–1910), wholeheartedly embraced its assumptions: "Let it be understood that we cannot go outside of this alternative: liberty, inequality, survival of the fittest; not liberty, equality, survival of the unfittest. The former carries society forward and favors all its best members; the latter carries society downwards and favors all its worst members." [3]

Later generations are amazed to note how naively fitness was equated, even by academics, with success in business—as if business acumen was the very embodiment of human creativity. Under this equation, Mozart would be considered an unfit member of the human species because he ended up in a pauper's grave.

However, the position of Sumner and those who thought along the same line was challenged by some of their fellow intellectuals. Their most outstanding critic was Lester Frank Ward (1841–1913), who objected to the transfer of theories from the realm of natural science to social science, insisting that, though nature has no purpose, social action is purposeful, and that nature obeys blind forces, while man can be master of his fate. Ward also rejected the idea that economic success was identical with merit. Nevertheless, Ward's position was not as popular as Sumner's and even within academia his views were shared by only a few.

The effect of social Darwinism was that it helped retard social welfare legislation. The British Parliament had begun to pass such legislation in the 1830's and 1840's—before the time of Darwinism—but in this country social welfare legislation was neglected until the twentieth century. While the emergence of the industrial tycoon created resentment among many, such individuals were also accorded a great deal of admiration. The new men of wealth had in most cases risen from rags to riches, so that most Americans in modest circumstances could vicariously participate in the success of the tycoons and perhaps dream about becoming one. In addition, the life styles of the new men of wealth provided drama on the American scene, and thus the tycoons filled the roles played in other countries by a court and aristocracy. Attacks on the conspicuous consumption of the moneyed elite did not find a particularly wide response.

Thorstein Veblen (1857–1929), a critic of the gilded age, and the man who coined the expression *conspicuous consumption,* made a distinction between productive interests and pecuniary interests. He identified the former with those creative activities that lead to technological development, and the latter with those profit-seeking activities for which technological development is a means for further profit and remains subordinate to it. In making this distinction, he tried to undermine the ethic on which business rested. However, a radical movement in a broader sense resulted from the rise of the corporation.

In contrast to the robber baron, the corporation appeared as an anonymous, sinister force with which it was difficult to come to grips. Emerging at the end of the 1870's, the corporation came to represent enormous concentrations of capital and, over the years, monopolization. In the case of widely dispersed stock, the corporate structure made it possible even for holders of small blocks of stock to wield a disproportionate amount of power; control by stockholders became increasingly nominal. Thus two developments had successively taken place: the separation of labor from ownership (after the small shop became obsolete) and then the separation of management from ownership (as management became the controlling force).

POPULISM

The rise of industry, and particularly monopolies, became a severe irritant to the farmer. His feeling of importance as the provider to society was deeply shaken by the awareness that he was being relegated to a lesser status, that a new era had arisen in which the city was becoming dominant and industry was replacing agriculture as the main sector of the economy. At the same time, the farmer felt victimized by forces beyond his control—high interest rates, deflation (which appreciated his debts), high elevator charges, and discriminatory freight rates. Politically, this discontent became known as *populism,* which was in many ways a romantic ideology. Populists looked back with nostalgia at the time when the United States was a country of small freeholders, proud of their independence and conscious of their role in society. But in a progressive way, populists demanded repossession by the government of the unused land given to the railroads, government ownership of the railroads, telegraph, and telephone, and a graduated income tax.

Like every romantic movement, populism had its conservative

and reactionary aspects. It was nativist in the sense that it was suspicious of things foreign; it was antiintellectual; it was racist, chiefly in the sense that it was anti-Semitic—though it has been disputed whether populists were different in this respect from the general cross section of Americans. Hostile to new immigrants, populists were particularly concerned with the "moral corruption" they believed was being imported. In general, they were suspicious of all values that appeared different from those traditionally associated with Yankee Protestantism.

PROGRESSIVISM

The progressive movement at the turn of the century arose from (to borrow a phrase from Russian history) the "conscience stricken" urban middle class. It represented an attempt at self-reform and was based on a belief in economic individualism and a more direct form of democracy. Later, it was directed against corporations and the corrupt party machines that dominated the cities. Its slogan for the city was "good government," in the sense that governments should be run by properly trained managers.

While people in the progressive era could not help but admit that the country had made enormous strides economically and that it was more prosperous than ever before, there was a feeling among many that America was losing its soul. Because Americans were accustomed to view progress in terms of competition and individual initiative, they looked on the corporation as the very antithesis of this American tradition. Obviously, at a time of rapid technological advance, individual entrepreneurship was eliminated from those industries that required large sums of investment, such as steel. If the word *alienation* had been in vogue at that time it would have expressed the general sentiment—the feeling that people were being divorced from entrepreneurship. Woodrow Wilson (1856–1924), who formulated these misgivings most eloquently, believed that success had to be based on merit to be justified, and merit in turn was bound up with individual competitive enterprise. He admitted that the middle class shared in the prosperity the new economic organization made possible, but he was alarmed that the middle class no longer originated prosperity.

The progressives were not concerned only with the new economic forces, they were also concerned about the discontent of the lower classes, who suffered most in the economic depressions that were part of the general upward trend of the American economy. The progressives feared the radicalization of the masses, and on the whole had little sympathy for socialism. They believed in "the system" (as one would say today); they thought it was flexible enough to accommodate change and thus prevent disruption. The progressives were not interested in abstract schemes and blueprints but in practical solutions to concrete problems.

The upshot of the progressive movement was a number of important pieces of legislation for the regulation of business, such as the Interstate Commerce Act of 1887, the Sherman Act of 1890, and the Clayton Act of 1914. In regulating the management of currency, the establishment of the Federal Reserve System in 1913 was a milestone. In the same period, a great number of statutes dealing with social policy were enacted, though social legislation had rough sailing on the federal level because of the attitude of the Supreme Court. In interpreting the Fourteenth Amendment, the court considered all such legislation unconstitutional on the grounds that it violated freedom of contract.

The child labor law of 1916, which forbade the interstate transportation of goods that had been produced with child labor, was struck down by the Supreme Court in 1918, and similar obstacles were encountered in laws calling for federal control of the hours of work. Only with the coming of the New Deal, and the change in attitude of the Supreme Court in 1937, did broad economic and social regulation become possible. However, the progressive era started to move the country away from laissez faire. But in saying this it should be made clear that the historic commitment of the country to private property was in no way shaken.

SOCIALISM IN THE UNITED STATES

Socialism was a foreign import into the United States, and socialist parties have always remained marginal to the American scene, which is not to deny that many of their ideas were taken over by other members of the traditional American establishment. In 1893, Engels acknowledged the difficulty of establishing a strong socialist party in the United States in a letter he wrote to Friedrich Sorge, who had been secretary of the First International when in 1872 it transferred its headquarters to New York.

It is not to be denied that American conditions involve very great and peculiar difficulties for a steady development of a workers' party.

First, the Constitution [*is*] *based as in England upon party government which causes every vote for a candidate not put up by one of the two governing parties to appear to be lost. And the American, like the Englishman, wants to influence his state; he does not throw his vote away.*

Then, and more especially, [*there is*] *immigration which divides the workers into two groups: the native born and the foreigners, and the latter in turn into (1) the Irish, (2) the Germans, (3) the many small groups, each of which understands only itself: Czechs, Poles, Italians, Scandinavians, etc. And then the Negroes. To form a single party out of these requires unusually powerful incentives. Often there is a sudden violent elan, but the bourgeois need only wait passively and the dissimilar elements of the working class fall apart.*

Third, through the protective tariff system and the steadily growing domestic market the workers must have been exposed to a prosperity no trace of which has been seen here in Europe for years now.[4]

Since the success of socialist parties has been minimal in the U.S. we will limit ourselves to a brief discussion of two socialist parties that are still on the American scene: the Socialist Labor Party and the American Socialist Party. (The Socialist Workers' Party will be discussed in connection with communism in the United States.) And since at various stages there was a close interrelationship between socialism and the labor movement, a brief sketch of the latter is also in order.

The first important labor organization, the Noble Order of the Knights of Labor (founded in 1869), believed in one big union; it enrolled only individuals, and was not a federation of separate unions. It was strongest in those industries where craft unionism was nonexistent. It saw its task as promoting unity among workers in preparation for a society in which the means of production would be used in their interest. Its program was mildly socialistic, but it did not have an action program for the transformation of society. The Knights achieved their greatest success in the 1870's and 1880's, after which their strength declined because of their defeats in a number of labor disputes and of a split within their ranks as a result of the Haymarket affair.* Some of the leaders condemned the execution of the anarchists; others welcomed it as a necessary move in stamping out anarchism. Other factors contributing to the decline of the Knights of Labor were its insistence on the idea of a single union and its dependence on the unskilled worker, who at that time represented no power whatsoever.

Of more practical significance for labor were the activities of Samuel Gompers (1850–1924), who in 1890 established the American Federation of Labor as an organization of craft unions interested strictly in bread-and-butter issues. Up to the time of the New Deal, the AFL was the dominant force in labor.

A most exciting movement at the end of the nineteenth century was syndicalist in origin. It was a trade union movement that sprang up among miners in the West and in 1893 resulted in the creation of the Western Federation of Miners, under the direction of William D. ("Big Bill") Haywood (1869–1928). It was anti-AFL and tried to set up a separate labor organization in the West. With better education for the miner as a goal, leaders of the WFM, along with dissident elements of the AFL and leaders of the Socialist Labor Party and the American Socialist Party, founded the Industrial Workers of the World (the IWW or "Wobblies") in 1905. After many splits, the IWW became an anachro-syndicalist organization whose slogans were direct action and the general strike. Though committed Marxists could not accept this position, the spirit of action appealed to them. The left wing of American socialism was influenced by both the IWW and Marxism. The right wing was trade union oriented and gradualist, and ultimately greatly influenced by Bernstein's maxim: "The goal of socialism is nothing, the movement everything."

Socialists were also affected by the utopian thought of several philosophers of the day. During the comparative heyday of the Knights of Labor, Henry George (1839–97) attacked the unjustified en-

*On May 3, 1886, a clash occurred in Chicago between strikers at the McCormick Harvesting Machine Company and scab laborers. The police intervened, and in the ensuing confusion six men were killed. A protest meeting was called by anarchists the next day; when a large force of police officers ordered the crowd to disperse, a bomb was thrown. Seven policemen were killed and many others were injured, but the bomb thrower was never identified. Under the pressure of aroused public opinion, the anarchist leaders were indicted, tried, and found guilty. Seven were sentenced to death and an eighth was sentenced to life imprisonment. In the end, four were hanged.

richment of landowners that resulted from the expansion of cities and the closing of the frontier, elaborating his critique in his writings, the best known of which is *Progress and Poverty* (1879). George, critical of the unearned increment landowners received from the rising price of land, demanded that this increment be appropriated by the state through taxation. His position was that if unearned increments accrued to the state, no other taxes would be needed; hence his proposal became known as the single tax. Though he was attacked by some as a dangerous radical, his ideas were only mildly radical, and he was not a socialist. He did not believe in the common ownership of land—he believed that capital had its own distinct claim to a return, similar to that of labor. At one time George was close to the Socialist Labor Party, which, jointly with another socialist group, urged him to run for mayor of New York. He was willing to join the socialists on a few issues, such as the nationalization of railroads and public utilities, but not on their overall program. Inevitably, he broke with them.

Edward Bellamy (1850–98) was a utopian socialist who in *Looking Backward* (1887) advocated full economic equality within a system of state socialism. Thus he favored state ownership and economic planning. A peculiar twist was his idea that labor should be organized as an "industrial army" in the service of all the people. He argued that inasmuch as the organization of the people into armies for destructive purposes was generally accepted, there was no reason why people should not be organized in an army for peaceful and productive purposes. Daniel De Leon (1852–1914) was an early supporter of Bellamy, but left him for the Socialist Labor Party, and subsequently Bellamy's main support came from middle-class liberals.

The Socialist Parties

The first socialist party on a national scale was the Socialist Labor Party, which started out as the Workingmen's Party in 1874 (it took the name Socialist Labor Party in 1877). Under the leadership of De Leon, it became a radical Marxist party, more radical than the European social democratic parties. De Leon regarded a militant working-class organization as indispensable for the overthrow of capitalism. For him, political action was not a means of gaining advantages but of undermining the capitalist order. He tried to create an uncompromising socialist trade union movement, and all his life relentlessly fought the conservative, reformist trade unionism of Samuel

Gompers. As far as tactics were concerned, De Leon was not a violent revolutionary; he believed in a peaceful changeover. De Leon's personality generated a wider appeal for the party than it otherwise might have had; after his death it became a purely sectarian organization and has continued as such to this day.

The man who founded the American Socialist Party, modeled after the Western European social democratic parties, was Eugene V. Debs (1855–1926). Originally a railway fireman, Debs organized the American Railway Union as an industrial union in 1893. He led a Pullman Company strike, disobeyed a court injunction, was sentenced to six months in jail for defying it, and became a convert to socialism. In 1893 he organized a rival party to De Leon's Socialist Labor Party, the Social Democratic Party, and in 1901 joined forces with a dissident wing of the SLP, which resented the autocratic leadership of De Leon and his hostility to the AFL. Out of this alliance the American Socialist Party was born. The ASP was a heterogeneous mix of Marxists, Christian socialists, native and immigrant radicals, trade union people, and well-to-do parlor socialists.

The high point of American socialism came in 1912 when Debs polled 897,000 votes in the presidential election (5.2 percent of the total). The subsequent decline of the American Socialist Party came partly as a result of the First World War. Socialist parties throughout the world suffered in this period because, contrary to their earlier commitments, they had supported the war efforts of their respective countries. In contrast, the American Socialist Party suffered because its majority rejected American participation in the war and even during the war conducted an antiwar campaign. However, many prominent members opposed this stance and subsequently left the party.

After the war the ASP, except for its left wing which turned to communism, increasingly developed into a middle-class party of reform that saw its role as educational rather than politically activist. Under Norman Thomas (1884–1968), "the respectable rebel," it became, partly as a result of his personality, purely a party of social conscience. He himself was accepted and even regarded with indulgence by the traditional establishment.

THE PERIOD OF NORMALCY

The United States had entered the First World War to make the world safe for democracy—to win the war that would end all wars.

The American ideology, as proclaimed by President Wilson, was characterized by political idealism, which did not accept the proposition that the game of power politics was inherent in a system of sovereign states. Instead, borrowing a concept from the philosophy of laissez faire, Wilsonian idealists assumed a harmony of interests among nations. Under an international laissez-faire system, each nation would specialize in the production of those commodities for which it was best equipped. And since all nations were interested in mutually beneficial exchanges, there would be no rational basis for war. If one further assumes that people are basically peaceful, war can result only from bad governments, national oppression, or misunderstanding. The spread of democracy, the granting of independence to oppressed nationalities, and the creation of a forum for settling misunderstandings would assure lasting peace.

Such idealistic expectations were bound to be unattainable. The United States was confronted at Versailles by political realists from the other Allied countries, for whom the name of the game was power. Their behavior created disillusionment in the United States and, having entered the war reluctantly in the first place, Americans were only too glad to wash their hands of international responsibilities. Turning its back on the League of Nations, the United States embraced isolationist "normalcy" and "business as usual" with a near religious fervor. As Calvin Coolidge (1872–1933) expressed it: "The business of the United States is business. . . . He who builds a factory builds a temple."

The 1920's were the golden age of American business, when prosperity was assumed to be never ending. The businessman was a greater hero than ever before. But the "Roaring Twenties" ended with the crash of 1929, the great watershed year in American history. American self-confidence was deeply shaken, and it would take a long time to recover it.

THE IDEOLOGIES OF PROTEST

The collapse of the economy in the Great Depression provided unique opportunities for radical ideologies, especially communism and its various derivatives. American communism had its roots in those radical socialists who had represented the left wing of the American Socialist Party. They split with the socialists and established the American Communist Party primarily as the result of the First World War and the Bolshevik Revolution. As the war went on, social unrest grew within American society. One indication of these social cleavages was the strikes that broke out. Though not hampering the war effort, the strikes were considered subversive and were consequently suppressed. Various antiwar figures were arrested and sent to prison. All this was confirmation to the left wing that the war was both imperialistic and a means of suppressing dissent.

The significance of the Communist Party emerged only during the Depression; and it was through the intellectuals whom it recruited (either as members or fellow travelers) that the Communist Party exerted influence on the American scene. At the same time, it was influential in a number of trade unions. Its appeal to intellectuals is well stated by Irving Howe and Lewis Coser:

The belief in some ultimate Reality that the Communists alone had been able to penetrate; the implicit assumption that by adopting the pose of ruthlessness the party was proving its claim to a deeper seriousness; the impulse to self-abasement ("down with us") that so many intellectuals felt in the presence of the working class or, more frequently, a caricature of the working class in the person of a party functionary—all these are central to the experience of the thirties. . . .

. . . The depression had done more than disturb [*the intellectuals'*] *lives; it had ripped apart the fabric of their values and beliefs, leaving them cold and shivering in the winds of uncertainty. Intellectuals may deal professionally with ideas, that is, with problems, but like the rest of humanity they find it hard to refrain from the narcotic of certainty: not many are able to suffer a prolonged acceptance of a mode of life that is inherently problematic.*[5]

In the end, however, the imposition of a doctrinaire line could only disillusion many intellectuals. Earlier, the fallout between Stalin and Trotsky had led to the emergence of a number of Trotskyite groups, among which the Socialist Workers' Party was the most important. (The party continues to this day and runs candidates for elective public offices in many states.) Further disaffection with the Communist Party followed the Moscow show trials, which were perceived by many intellectuals for what they really were: fabricated charges of the Stalinists. A commission of inquiry, set up by anti-Stalinists and headed by John Dewey, found Trotsky and the other defendants not guilty.

Disaffection and schism were continual occurrences, and the success of the New Deal further diminished the influence of the Communist Party. For many radicals, practical achievement won out over ideological commitment. Finally, the Soviet-Nazi pact of 1939 inflicted a shattering blow. In 1940, however, when the Soviet Union became an ally of the United States, the fortunes of the party revived. The accomplishments of the Soviet army made many Americans admirers of the Soviet Union, from which the Communist Party could only profit.

But the outbreak of the Cold War reversed this trend. Since Stalin's brand of communism required loyalty to the Soviet Union, being a communist in the United States was doubly provocative in a period of conflict with the Soviet Union. Anticommunism now became a broad national policy in the United States. Unfortunately, however, it also became a political football and in many cases a ploy for demagogic exploitation. Outstanding in this connection were the antics of Senator Joseph McCarthy. In addition, the breast beating of many ex-communists and their approach to anticommunism (which was often as totalitarian as had been their original commitment to communism) could not help but keep the public temper at a high pitch.

Though repression had its impact on the Communist Party, its ultimate disintegration in the United States was a result of Khrushchev's revelations about Stalin, thc suppression of the Hungarian uprising, and the treatment of Soviet intellectuals. In general, the party has been bypassed by events so that today the radicals of the New Left consider it irrelevant.

THE NEW DEAL

The New Deal represented an abandonment of laissez faire and the adoption of Benthamite ideas, but in a qualified sense. The New Deal still assumed that the public interest was nothing more than the sum of private interests. Hence, the New Deal put together a broad coalition that only in our day seems to be falling apart—a coalition of ethnic groups as represented by the big-city political machines, farmers, workers, the South, and intellectuals. There was something for all: social welfare for all who needed it, price support programs for the farmer, better opportunities for labor to organize and bargain collectively, and excitement for the intellectual in participating in a great social experiment.

There was initial hostility toward the New Deal only by sectors of the business community that thought the New Deal was socialistic, but in fact it was designed to bolster the capitalist system. There was concern that if government was to be effective in mastering the economy—if organizations such as the TVA were to be successful—the free enterprise system would be undermined. The free enterprise system was based on the assumption that only private business is efficient and that government, by definition, is wasteful, inefficient, and bureaucratic.

Just as it was assumed that the public interest is the sum of all private interests, it was also assumed that the problems of society are the sum of the problems of these individual interests. Hence it was taken for granted that social problems could be attacked by piecemeal social engineering; and such an approach was eminently congenial to the pragmatic American temper.

The economic theory that came to dominate the New Deal was that of John Maynard Keynes (1883–1946), who believed that an economy could be kept going on a high level if, as the need arose, increased government spending made up for declines in private spending. Such government spending would of necessity involve deficit financing; but this should be accepted as a matter of course. Keynesian economics became known as the "new economics," in contrast to classical economics with its emphasis on balanced budgets, but the term has since become ambiguous because it also applies to post-Keynesian economics. Keynesians are somewhat divided between two different tendencies: the liberals want fiscal policies that increase purchasing power; the conservatives advocate fiscal policies that encourage investments. Nevertheless, liberal Keynesians do not believe that the public sector has an autonomous claim on resources according to some principle of priority; spending in the public sector is engaged in only to support the private sector, with the result that it cannot be based on long-range planning and hence has a rather unorganized and accidental character. Basically, the Keynesian assumption is that public needs are identical with private demands, for which there is, of course, no qualitative yardstick. A demand for pop music, for example, is no more desirable or undesirable than a demand for housing. It therefore follows that economic progress is seen as the steady increase of the gross national product and not the utility of the products produced. (It is post-Keynesian economics which is concerned with the latter issue.)

In short, the New Deal adopted Keynesian economics and attacked problems as they presented themselves—though the major problem, unemployment, disappeared only with the coming of the Second World War, when the economy, geared to warfare, needed every able-bodied man. The post–Second World War period was one of more or less sustained prosperity, with occasional minor recessions; full employment was taken for granted, though there was a hard core of unemployed due to a decline in the demand for unskilled labor because of technological developments. Even under conditions of sustained prosperity there is significant unemployment among unskilled people, which particularly affects the black community.

THE SITUATION TODAY

A number of additional issues came to the fore in the 1960's, foremost of which was the vigorous fight of blacks for equality. Blacks rejected their limited opportunities for advancement in American society, their living conditions, their lack of access to good education. In connection with the blacks' struggle has come an awareness of the extent to which poverty still exists in the United States and of the fact that poverty involves not only people out of work but also people who are poorly paid.

Since the problems of poverty, slums, and inadequate schools have centered on the city, they have been subsumed under the heading of urban problems. Unfortunately, the solutions that have been applied thus far have been piecemeal and uncoordinated, viewing each problem as separate and unrelated to the others. For example, programs designed to improve urban education did not take into account the effect of slum environments on children's motivation to learn; instead, they attempted to improve schooling through a series of educational "innovations." As one innovation failed it was followed by another, similarly condemned to failure. When a program failed no fundamental questions were asked; the blame was placed either on the purported inadequacies of the beneficiaries or on administrative deficiencies, the latter to be dealt with by administrative reorganization.

Comprehensive social planning is not completely without advocates, however. Many post-Keynesians take the position that the increase of the GNP is no longer as important as is its better use in social terms. They criticize the fact that many commodities are produced with built-in obsolescence, and maintain that if goods were produced that had a longer life span, more resources could be saved for taking care of social needs. These post-Keynesians take the position that even if the economy were to move full blast on the basis of private demand, there would still be crying public needs that require government action.

Given the ideological commitment of the country, it is improbable that social problems in the U.S. will be solved along the lines outlined above. Instead, the attempt will be made to include the poor in the consumer orbit by the establishment of a guaranteed annual income. The so-called negative income tax has been propounded by conservative economists, foremost of whom is Milton Friedman of the University of Chicago. The idea is conservative in its implications because it does not lead to a diminishing private sector or involve the government in business; it would turn the lower strata of the population (who have no purchasing power) into consumers, and thereby into additional sources for the creation of effective demand.

While the conception of the guaranteed annual income is conservative, liberals, increasingly frustrated by the poor showing of federal programs, are coming around to the idea of the guaranteed income. It will not, of course, provide a solution to the problem of social integration, or the problem of the quality of life. All it can do is create the preconditions for attacking these problems.

NOTES

1. *Great Americans Speak: Short Speeches That Have Shaped Our Destiny,* ed. Frederick G. Packard, Jr. (New York: Scribner's, 1951), p. 20.

2. Quoted in Richard Hofstadter, *Social Darwinism in American Thought,* rev. ed. (New York: Braziller, 1959), p. 45.

3. *Ibid.,* p. 51.

4. Friedrich Engels, Letter to Friedrich Sorge, December 2, 1893, in *Marx and Engels: Basic Writings on Politics and Philosophy,* ed. Lewis S. Feuer (Garden City, N.Y.: Doubleday, 1959), p. 458.

5. Irving Howe and Lewis Coser, *The American Communist Party: A Critical History* (New York: Praeger, 1957), pp. 280–81, 283.

CHAPTER EIGHT

RUSSIA AND COMMUNISM PRIOR TO THE REVOLUTION

RUSSIA UNDER THE CZARS

When Marxism came to Russia toward the end of the nineteenth century, it found a very different environment from that of Western Europe; Russia had remained backward under outdated social and political institutions. In many ways, an unhappy history and an unfortunate geographical location seemed to have predisposed Russia to its backwardness. At a time when the Renaissance had liberated man in Western Europe from the shackles of dogma and unquestioning subservience to authority, Russia was dominated by the Mongols, whose willing tools the Russian princes had become. These Russian princes eagerly copied the Mongol ways in their relationship with their own subjects. The Byzantine form of Christianity, with its emphasis on submission to authority and its rituals of self-debasement, also became a powerful element in the establishment and maintenance of autocracy. During its expansion, which began in the eighteenth century, Russia moved chiefly into Asia and conquered even less advanced peoples. She was thereby deprived of the benefits of many other conquering nations, which became more civilized by being exposed to the superior cultures of those whom they came to dominate physically.

Up to 1861, three-fourths of the Russians were serfs, and the landowners were parasitic noblemen. Earlier, the nobility had to serve the state, but by the beginning of the nineteenth century the administration of the country was in the hands of a bureaucracy recruited chiefly from the middle class. At the same time, the commercial and industrial bourgeoisie remained small and unassertive. Industrialization in Russia began at a later date than in Western countries, and developed much more quickly. Almost immediately a relatively high level of technology that required substantial investments was achieved. The late arrival of industrialization in Russia necessitated as a matter of economic rationality the immediate establishment of large-scale enterprises. Since large investment funds were not available to private sources in Russia, economic development, like the building of railroads or factories for armaments, was undertaken by the government. Many other enterprises came into being as a result of foreign investment. While this form of economic development creates a native proletariat, it does not create a widespread native bourgeoisie.

Thus by the end of the nineteenth century, a working class that was relatively large in comparison to the bourgeoisie had arisen. Many were second or even third generation workers, quite literate, and mostly male (which is important from the standpoint of the revolutionary potential). They were concentrated in a few cities reaching from St. Petersburg (Leningrad) to Baku and to the southern Ukraine in the west (in the Civil War the cities were used by the Bolsheviks as fortresses in conquering the countryside).

The condition of the peasants before and after their emancipation in 1861 also deserves mention because it was their primitiveness that supported the backward political regime. The Russian serf was exposed to the arbitrary will of his master, who had legal authority to have him flogged as often and as severely as he wished. While some masters were humane and seldom used these legal rights, others were cruel and oppressive. Donald Mackenzie Wallace divided the oppressive landowners into four categories: (1) those who managed their own estate and oppressed simply for the purpose of increasing their revenues; (2) retired army officers who established order and discipline by employing the barbarous methods used in the army; (3) absentees who lived beyond their means and used the threat of army recruitment to demand from the stewards a much greater yearly sum than their estates could reasonably be expected to yield; and (4) those, in the latter years of serfdom, who bought estates as a mercantile speculation and made as much money out of them as possible in the shortest time. Of these, the speculators were the most severe. Utterly indifferent to the welfare of the serfs and the ultimate fate of the property, they cut all the timber, sold the cattle, and exacted heavy money dues under the same threat of army recruitment. As these threats were realized the military authorities were provided with a greater number of conscripts than was required, and thus the speculators could sell conscription receipts to merchants and burghers who were liable to conscription but did not wish to serve.

While serfs were attached to the property of their masters, they also cultivated communal lands controlled by an ancient institution known as the *mir* (a village community). In other words, the land cultivated by a serf and his family did not belong to them. Each family received allotments whose location may have differed from year to year.

In 1861 the emancipation decree of Czar Alexander II (1818–81) lifted the juridical authority of the masters and redistributed part of the land on the basis of a certain allotment per emancipated male, which in many cases was not greater than the preemancipation holding. But the regime was terrified by the thought of a mobile peasantry. Therefore, it gave the land to the *mirs,* with each peasant household being something of a shareholder, and required that in order to travel, a peasant needed the permission of the village elders, who in turn were controlled by the local bureaucracy. Furthermore, the peasants now bore the new burden of paying for the land. The emancipation, then, not only did not satisfy the peasants, it further embittered them because it quashed a hope they had held for ages; namely, that one day all the land would belong to them. What made things still worse was that the increase in population over the next few decades led to a shrinkage of the allotments, from 5 acres in 1877 to 3.8 acres in 1910.

After emancipation, the peasantry was restive and sometimes sullen. Its cultural level did not improve, and the peasant remained ignorant and full of superstitions, in whose maintenance the village priests had their full share. Indeed, because the cultural level of these priests was in most cases not much higher than that of the peasants, we should understand that the communists' later attacks on religion were not necessarily conducted solely on an ideological basis. They were, in part, attacks on a particular form of religion and its misuse for obscurantist purposes.

Russian society was presided over by an autocracy that appropriated to itself the right to be the source of all judicial, legislative, executive, and religious authority. Its motto, in the words of Nicholas I (1796–1855), was orthodoxy, nationalism, and autocracy. Constitutional reforms were always presented to the people as a gift from the Czar and not as rights the people had inherently. Whatever reforms were made were made under pressure, grudgingly, and often, when possible, were rescinded.

The Intelligentsia

The intelligentsia, who were the carriers of reform and ultimately of revolution, were an interesting class. But before we deal with this group we should make a distinction among intellectuals, professional people, and the intelligentsia. An intellectual is a person who thinks that ideas are of prime importance; he deals with ideas critically and has a running discourse (so to speak) with the events and problems of the day. In doing so, he goes beyond the assumptions that underlie his society. An intellectual, then, is a critic of society. A professional person, in contrast, is somebody who renders services on the basis of his expertise and whether he is also an intellectual depends on his concerns. The lawyer who is exclusively concerned with drawing up contracts, advising clients on wills and estates, and the like is a professional; but the lawyer who is interested in civil rights or reforming criminal justice, and devotes considerable thought to these things, is an intellectual. In a sense, the writer is a most characteristic intellectual. Whether he is a commentator on contemporary affairs or a writer of fiction, he is in contact with the whole range of the individual and social problems of his times.

The term *intelligentsia* originated in the 1860's in Russia, and connotes intellectuals who feel compelled to enter the political arena or to become activists. An intelligentsia arises under special conditions: in societies of uneven development, in societies in the process of formation, or in societies in crisis. In the case of Russia, uneven development was the background; while Russia was in general socially and politically backward, there was a group of knowledgable and creative people who were the equals of the best that Western Europe had to offer. This group, having felt the repressiveness of the autocracy's censorship, exile system, and heavy-handed bureaucracy most severely, was aware that such a regime could exist only because of the backwardness of the masses. Not only was raising the level of the masses in the best interest of the intelligentsia, the plight of the peasant also appealed to the conscience of the intelligentsia.

The nineteenth-century ferment among intellectuals began with an attempted coup in December, 1825, by a group of officers who belonged to the conscience-stricken aristocracy—the people who, though materially beneficiaries of the regime, suffered morally under it. These officers had been to France as part of the campaign against Napoleon, and had seen the enormous difference between the West and Russia; when they came home they decided to attempt to transform the absolutist monarchy into a constitutional one. The attempt failed, the ringleaders were executed, and the rest were banished to Siberia.

The repressive measures of the government, by stifling any independent social and philosophical thought, were responsible for transforming generations of intellectuals into revolutionaries. In order to understand the development of revolutionary thought in Russia, an exploration of the intellectual orientation of nineteenth-century Russia is necessary.

INTELLECTUAL CURRENTS

By the beginning of the nineteenth century two broad streams of thought had evolved: that of the Slavophiles and that of the Westernizers. The Westernizers took the position that only a Western orientation could save Russia; the Slavophiles believed that Russia had a special mission to fulfill, that she had nothing to learn from the West, and that the West had no spiritual values. They espoused the *mir,* which they invested with a particular spirituality and came to see as the nucleus for a reorganization of society along lines of agrarian socialism. Two recurring themes of the Slavophiles were the youth of Russia and the decadence of the West; it would be on account of Russia that the West would be "saved." The political programs of nineteenth-century Russia were always a mixture of Westernism and Slavophilism; Western thought was adapted to the Russian experience, while this experience more often than not was presented as both peculiarly Russian and also of universal significance.

But the limited influence of the West on Russia is most apparent in the fact that capitalism and laissez-faire liberalism found no roots in Russia; the Russian intellectuals had only contempt for Western bourgeois democracy and capitalism. Russians traveling in the West were witnesses to the misery of early industrialization and to what they considered the petty reckoning of profit and loss of capitalist enterprises (which they contrasted with the expansiveness of the Russian soul and the generosity of the Russian people). Their accounts thus provided little encouragement for a belief in bourgeois democracy.

One of the persons who observed capitalism and bourgeois institutions at close range was Alexander Herzen (1812–70), whose experience with the bourgeois monarchy of Louis Philippe was characterized by the exclamation of a deputy in the French Chamber, "Enrich yourselves!" Needless to say, he was somewhat disillusioned.

The revolution of 1848, in which the bourgeoisie used the working class to overthrow the monarchy and then turned against it, filled him with bitterness and hatred. He considered Europe sick and believed that the United States and Russia would become the carriers of the civilization of the future.

I do not believe that the destinies of humanity and its future are fixed and nailed to western Europe. If Europe does not succeed in recovering herself by a social transformation, other countries will transform themselves. There are some already prepared for this movement, others which are preparing. One is known—I mean the States of North America; the other [*Russia*], *full of vigour, also full of barbarity, is known little and badly.*

Speaking about the United States, he had this to say:

This young and enterprising people, more active than intelligent, is so much occupied with the material ordering of its life that it knows none of our torturing pains. . . . The sturdy race of English colonists multiplies exceedingly; and if it comes to the top, the people belonging to it will be, I will not say happier, but more contented. Their contentment will be poorer, more commonplace, more sapless than that which was dreamed of in the ideals of romantic Europe; but it will bring with it no Tsars, no centralization, perhaps no hunger. He who can put off the old European Adam and put on the new Jonathan, let him take the first steamer to—somewhere in Wisconsin or Kansas. He will be better off there than in decaying Europe.[1]

Concerned primarily with his own country which was composed of a majority of peasants, and rejecting Western capitalism, Herzen turned to agrarian socialism. He saw the *mir* as the prototype of the future agricultural commune, and thus began the populist movement in Russia (*narodniki*). It would find both its high point and the beginning of its decline in the 1870's, when the students and intellectuals would "go to the common people."

If a government is moderately bad, the prevailing thought will be to improve it; but if it is intolerably bad, it may occur to some people that if there were no government, governments would have no chance to be oppressive. Unrealistic as such a position is, it is psychologically understandable, and this psychological basis explains the impact of anarchism on Russia. While anarchism is an old ideology, Mikhail Bakunin (1814–76) gave it a new thrust and style. Bakunin advocated the

destruction of all the religious, political, juridical, economic, and social institutions that constitute the present bourgeois order of things.

We have complete faith in the instincts of the masses and understand Revolution as an organized outburst *of what is called* revolutionary passion *and as a destruction of that which in bourgeois language is called* social order.

. . . *We want radical destruction, complete annihilation of that empire of Russia which is a menace for the freedom of the world, a shameful prison for all the peoples subject to it, a violent and systematic negation of everything called human right, justice, humanity.*[2]

Bakunin wanted a free association of producer cooperatives to replace the forced organization of people by government. The leaders of his revolution were supposed to be an elite, and individual acts of terrorism were to prepare the way for the downfall of government. While this thesis was followed for a short time by a branch of the *narodniki* movement, it was rejected by Lenin as petty bourgeois romanticism. However, the idea of the professional revolutionary was taken over by the Bolsheviks and was a tenet in the organization of the Communist Party. It is for providing the idea of the professional revolutionary, then, that anarchism is significant.

Philosophically, Hegelian thought dominated Russian intellectual life up to the middle of the nineteenth century. But as the pulse of revolutionary action quickened, there was a shift from Hegelian idealism to the materialism of Feuerbach. Hegel had conveyed the comfortable view that since ideas define reality, thought somehow translates itself into action. Hegel's metaphysical bent also appealed to people who liked to talk about God and the world. Feuerbach's materialism, in contrast, made short shrift of religious speculation and provided a utilitarian basis for morality. Also, contrary to Hegel's philosophy, it made social thought a function of social conditions.

The new generation, armed with a materialist philosophy and the activist thought of a professional revolutionary, was ready to go to battle, and what is nowadays called a generation gap resulted. The younger generation scandalized the older generation by its wholesale rejection of everything Russian. This situation is skillfully portrayed in Ivan Turgenev's novel *Fathers and Sons* (1862), in which youth is represented by Bazarov, who is rude, arrogant, and unlovable —except by the common people. The fathers, represented chiefly by his friend's uncle, are kindly and gracious but ineffectual. Bazarov —"a man who does not bow down before any authority, who does not take any principle on faith, whatever reverence that principle may be enshrined in"—is called a nihilist by the elders, who seem to believe that one who does not accept their assumptions denies all assumptions. Bazarov, however, has a firm belief in the critical intellect; what he rejects is the falsity of romantic attitudes, sentimentality, and "flabbiness." Nevertheless, he believes that what should be put in its place is beside the point; first the rubble has to be cleared away.

The "go to the people" movement of the 1870's represented the culmination of *narodniki* agitation, as students and professional people descended on the villages. They tried to be helpful in many ways, at the same time agitating among the peasantry for reform. Some tried to prepare the peasants for a general uprising; others espoused a new partition of the land. But they were received by the peasants with great suspicion and were turned over by them to the police in droves. This short spell of activity turned out to be a total fiasco.

RUSSIAN MARXISM

It seemed now to many intellectuals that to base a revolution on support from the peasantry was a forlorn hope; the peasantry was not, by itself, a revolutionary class. They therefore turned to Marxism, with its emphasis on the proletariat as the class destined to make the revolution. A Marxist study circle was established in 1883 under the leadership of a disillusioned *narodnik,* George Plekhanov (1857–1918), who became the father of Russian Marxism. Later, the Russian Social Democratic Party was founded in 1898 in the presence of a young man of twenty-eight, Vladimir Ilich Ulyanov, who was later known as Nikolai Lenin (1870–1924).

After the foundation of the party a fight immediately arose among its leaders over theory and tactics. At the party congress of 1903, the party divided into two wings: the Bolsheviks (led by Lenin) and the Mensheviks. The names resulted from the fact that the followers of Lenin had an accidental majority at the congress (*bolshinstivo* means majority in Russian) and their opponents were in the minority (*menshinstivo* means minority). However, it was only in 1912 that the Russian Social Democratic Party officially split apart.

The first and ultimately the most important difference between the two factions was in tactics. The Mensheviks wanted to establish a party on the West European pattern; that is, a democratic party based on broad participation in the decision-making process. Political activity was still not permitted in Russia, but the Mensheviks espoused this course in anticipation of the changes that seemed to be in the air. The Bolsheviks, led by Lenin, had very different ideas.

Lenin

Lenin challenged the Mensheviks' notions on both fundamental and tactical grounds. He reversed the relationship between leadership and the masses described by classical Marxism. According to Marx, it was the proletariat that made the revolution; the leadership was merely an exponent of the masses. Lenin took the position that, by its own efforts, the working class could develop only a trade union consciousness, that is, a consciousness that accepts the capitalist order and seeks improvements under it, such as shorter hours, higher wages, and so forth. Only the intellectual could conceive of a society different from the one into which he was born.

The history of all countries shows that the working class, exclusively by its own effort, is able to develop only trade-union consciousness, i.e., *it may itself realise the necessity of combining in unions, for fighting against the employers and for striving to compel the government to pass necessary labour legislation, etc. The theory of socialism, however, grew out of the philosophic, historical and economic theories that were elaborated by the educated representatives of the propertied classes, the intellectuals. The founders of modern scientific socialism, Marx and Engels, themselves belonged to the bourgeois intelligentsia. Similarly, in Russia, the theoretical doctrine of Social-Democracy arose quite independently of the spontaneous growth of the labour movement; it arose as a natural and inevitable outcome of the development of ideas among the revolutionary socialist intelligentsia.*[3]

In this formulation the working class is less a carrier of revolution than a tool for making it. Philosophically speaking, giving the intellectuals such a role amounted to making consciousness more than a reflection of material circumstances; it added an idealist element.

Not only did Lenin assign the intellectuals the role of creating a revolutionary consciousness, when it came to determining the tactics of the party he advocated an organization that was based on a group of professional revolutionaries—a tightly knit group of people under strict discipline. This group would make the revolution and draw the working class into it. He thus came close to assigning a revolutionary will—independent of adequate socioeconomic forces—a rather decisive role. Such a position on the role of will is referred to as *voluntarism,* and thus Lenin added both an idealist and voluntarist dimension to Marxism.

If we begin with the solid foundation of a strong organisation of revolutionaries, we can guarantee the stability of the movement as a whole and carry out the aims of both Social-Democracy and of trade unionism. If, however, we begin with a wide workers' organisation, supposed to be most "accessible" to the masses, when as a matter of fact it will be most accessible to the gendarmes and will make the revolutionaries most accessible to the police, we shall neither achieve the aims of Social-Democracy nor of trade unionism. . . .

. . . It is far more difficult to catch a dozen wise men than it is to catch a hundred fools. And this position I shall defend no matter how much you instigate the crowd against me for my "anti-democratic" views, etc. As I have already said, by "wise men," in connection with organisation I mean professional revolutionaries.[4]

The question that confronted Bolsheviks and Mensheviks alike was the character of the coming revolution. Both were classical Marxists, in that they assumed that the next revolution would have to be a bourgeois revolution, since one could not skip a stage. However, Lenin thought that the bourgeoisie was too weak to make its own revolution and that, therefore, the proletariat would have to take the lead. The Mensheviks, in contrast, believed that it was up to the bourgeoisie to make its own revolution, and that in this enterprise the proletariat should be only a junior ally.

Another difference between Bolsheviks and Mensheviks was their attitude toward the peasantry. Lenin's position was that the peasantry should be considered an ally of the working class; the Mensheviks thought that since the peasantry wanted more private property, it was a counterrevolutionary force. Lenin's answer was that this might very well be so in the long run, but in the short run the peasantry was a revolutionary force and therefore a good ally of the working class.

Bolsheviks and Mensheviks also differed in their estimates of the length of the bourgeois stage. The Mensheviks believed that socialism could come only after a fully developed stage of capitalism, but Lenin did not commit himself to such a view. He spoke of the possibility of the "growing over" of the bourgeois revolution into a socialist revolution, although his thoughts at that time were rather vague. Later, in 1916, in *Imperialism: The Highest Stage of Capitalism,* Lenin provided a theoretical basis for what amounted to skipping the stage of capitalism in Russia.

Trotsky

Leon Trotsky (1879–1940) in 1905 developed (in conjunction with the German socialist A. L. Parvus) a well-thought-out theory for achieving a socialist revolution in a capitalistically underdeveloped country—the theory of permanent revolution. The permanent revolution, which would end only when class society had been completely liquidated, was to make no compromises with any single form of class rule; every new stage of the revolution was to be rooted in the preceding stage.

Since capitalism had come late to Russia, with the result that its industry had to be built by state and foreign investments, the Russian bourgeoisie was weak in comparison to the proletariat. The bourgeoisie was interested in a bourgeois revolution, the proletariat in a socialist one. However, since the bourgeoisie was weak and would not be able to consolidate its revolutionary gains, a revolutionary situation would continue to exist and the working class, through continuous struggle, would be able to move the revolution into the socialist stage. (The telescoping of stages in countries of uneven development was formulated by Trotsky into a general law: the law of uneven and combined development.)

Having won its revolutionary struggle, the proletariat would establish its own government. But, unless foreign revolutionaries came to its assistance, such a government could be quickly overthrown by the petty bourgeois majority. Belief that such assistance would be forthcoming was a second aspect of Trotsky's theory. He believed that, sparked by a Russian revolution, revolutions in the advanced countries would be undertaken by the workers who formed a majority of the people. Thus, successful revolutions in the advanced countries would help secure the gains of the Russian revolution.

The debates on revolutionary theory and tactics took place against a background of deep discontent. The autocracy had entered the twentieth century unchanged, although through a process of erosion it had lost the confidence of the majority of the people. This, together with international complications, made the regime unsure of itself, and the catalyst was the Russo-Japanese War of 1904–05. The Russian reverses in the war increased the general discontent and revolution was in the air. The government, through promises of amnesty for political prisoners and the granting of civil liberties, tried to maintain the regime, but all these attempts came to naught when the police fired on a crowd of harmless demonstrators in front of the Winter Palace.

RUSSIAN REVOLUTION

The Revolution of 1905

The Winter Palace incident set in motion a train of events that led to a general strike toward the end of October, 1905. Although the strike lasted only a few days it paralyzed the country. A council (soviet) of Workers Deputies was set up in St. Petersburg to coordinate the strike (a conscious parallel to the Paris Commune of 1871). Similar soviets sprang up in other cities. The executive committee of the St. Petersburg soviet was headed by Leon Trotsky, who on account of this position and what was to follow became a national hero. The soviet in St. Petersburg lasted for fifty days, and not only ran the city but was something of a national government. During this time the Czar was out of the city and his government was unable to cope with the situation.

In a desperate attempt to stop the revolution, the Czar had on October 30 issued a manifesto that legalized political activity, and promised civil liberties and a parliament (the Duma). But this parliament was to be elected on the basis of an unequal and in some cases indirect franchise as a guarantee of majorities that would be favorable to the regime or at least would not threaten it. The October manifesto had its greatest impact on the bourgeoisie, which had become frightened by the "outrageous" demands of the workers, such as the eight-hour day, a raise in wages, and the legalization of unions. The soviets were ultimately suppressed; its leaders, including Trotsky, went on trial; and the revolution subsided.

When the first Duma opened, in spite of the rigged franchise, parties opposed to the regime were in the majority, even though the socialist parties—the Social Democrats and the Socialist Revolutionaries (the successors of the *narodniki*)—did not participate. The leading party was the Constitutional Democrat (Cadet) Party, which advocated the expropriation of the large estates with compensation. This idea did not sit well with the government, and the first Duma was dissolved. When the second Duma proved similarly obnoxious, the election laws were changed so as to give the third Duma a more conservative composition.

The restlessness of the country at this time is conveyed by the fact that in 1906 troops had to be called out 2,559 times to suppress major or minor riots, and that 782 people were executed in 1908 for "political crimes." On the eve of the First World War, the country was on the brink of revolution, and it is hard to say whether the war postponed or hastened it.

Toward the Bolshevik Revolution

We have already mentioned the betrayal of proletarian internationalism by the socialist parties when the First World War broke out. Lenin, who at the time lived in Switzerland, was dumbfounded when this happened and gave considerable thought to the reasons why the parties succumbed to patriotic propaganda. He reevaluated the proposition that the revolution would first have to break out in the most highly developed capitalist countries, in *Imperialism: The Highest Stage of Capitalism* (1916).* He argued that Marx had viewed the contradictions of capitalism only within national frameworks—that he was able to view these contradictions in terms of the conflict between a particular national bourgeoisie and its own prole-

* Lenin identified five features of imperialism: (1) the concentration of production and capital developed to such a high stage that it created monopolies, which play a decisive role in economic life; (2) the merger of bank capital with industrial capital created the "finance capital" of a "financial oligarchy"; (3) the export of capital had become extremely important, as distinguished from the export of commodities; (4) the international capitalist monopolies now shared the world among themselves; (5) the territorial division of the whole world among the greatest capitalist powers had been completed.

tariat. Under the circumstances of his time, Marx had been correct in assuming that the revolution would be closest where these contradictions were sharpest—in the most highly developed capitalist countries. But by the twentieth century monopoly capitalism had appeared, had burst the national frameworks, and had become international capitalism.

Unable to maintain themselves internally because of the ever-increasing disparity between the amount of production and the purchasing power of the workers, the capitalists in the various countries had looked abroad for sources of raw material and cheap native labor. The contradictions of capitalism now led to struggles between national bourgeoisies. At the same time, the conflict between the national bourgeoisies and their proletariats was mitigated because as the bourgeoisie achieved success abroad it was able to appease its workers with better working conditions and better wages. In a world divided up as a result of capitalist expansion, change was possible only as one colony or sphere of influence passed from the hands of one power into the hands of another. Thus, economic competition became military conflict.

The First World War, according to Lenin, was such an imperialist conflict. He argued that the highly technological character of the war would put a greater strain on the less developed capitalist countries than on those that were highly developed. To use Stalin's words in interpreting Lenin: "the capitalist chain was bound to break at its weakest link which was Russia." Still, Lenin believed that though the revolution might come first in Russia, it would be unable to maintain itself unless it was followed by similar revolutions in the Western European countries.

The March 1917 Revolution *

After initial successes against Germany and Austria-Hungary, the Russian army suffered defeat after defeat; more importantly, however,

* Up to February 1918 Russia operated under the Julian calendar ("Old Style") which in the twentieth century was thirteen days behind the Gregorian (Western) calendar ("New Style"). To avoid chronological confusion for the twentieth century, the dates of events before February, 1918, have been converted to the Western (N.S.) calendar. Hence, the *March* 1917 Revolution (N.S.) instead of the February 1917 Revolution (O.S.) and the November 1917 Revolution (N.S.) instead of the October 1917 Revolution (O.S.)

the home front crumbled. Inflation and a scarcity of goods undermined the morale of the people, and the impression of ineptitude in high places added to the general malaise. As a nationalist deputy put it:

The trouble was that in all that huge city [*Petrograd*] *it was not possible to find a few hundred people sympathetic toward the Government. Even that's not all. The trouble was the Government didn't feel sympathetic toward itself. In fact there was not a single minister who believed in himself and in what he was doing.*[5]

Matters came to a head when the Duma established a provisional committee in February, 1917, which became the forerunner of the provisional government. At the same time, a Petrograd soviet of workers' and soldiers' deputies was established whose executive committee challenged, first, the provisional committee of the Duma and then, after the Czar abdicated, the provisional government. There was from the beginning a dual authority, with the soviets gradually moving into the ascendancy.

The difficulty of the provisional government, which came under the leadership of Alexander Kerensky (1881–1970), was twofold: its commitment to the prosecution of an unpopular war and its narrow social base. This liberal bourgeois government in a country in which the bourgeoisie had not been a powerful force was beset by difficulties from both the right and the left. To those on the right, Kerensky, a moderate socialist, was not very different from Lenin. The left, particularly the Bolsheviks, saw no reason to support him; they were by that time committed to move the bourgeois revolution into the socialist stage. The climax came when the right, under the leadership of General Kornilov, tried to oust Kerensky by force and he had to rely on the left, including the Bolsheviks, who some time before had been outlawed by him. It is interesting to note how often revolutionaries have their best allies in the reactionaries.

State and Revolution

During the summer of 1917 Lenin felt he had to work up a theoretical defense for the coming Bolshevik coup. This defense was undertaken with the Western European social democrats especially in mind, whom Lenin considered his most important opponents because he knew it was with them that he would be engaged on the international level in the struggle for the loyalty of the working class. At the same time, Lenin also saw the need to provide a vision of the society that was to emerge after the Bolshevik Revolution. This was the origin of his *State and Revolution.*

In contrast to the position of the social democrats that the existing state machinery could be used for the transition from capitalism to socialism, Lenin took the position that the state is an organ of class oppression; therefore, it was not a neutral instrument that could be used for radical social change. Under the rule of the bourgeoisie, the state was a bourgeois state. The socialist state, in contrast, would be an instrument of the rule of the proletariat, the majority, over the bourgeoisie, which is and always has been a minority.

Inasmuch as the proletariat was the lowest class in society, its rise to power would bring in its train the abolition of classes. This, in turn, would lead to the withering away of the state, since there would no longer be the opportunity for class rule. "The substitution of the proletarian state for the bourgeois state is impossible without a violent revolution. The abolition of the proletarian state, *i.e.,* of the state in general, is impossible except through the process of withering away.' "[6] The withering away would have to be a rather long process, however. Though the proletariat would have achieved power, there would not yet be equality between people, for in this state (henceforth called socialism) the motto would be "From each according to his ability, to each according to his work." The claim of an individual to remuneration in accordance with his contribution is bourgeois in essence.

The state withers away in so far as there are no longer any capitalists, any classes, and consequently, no class *can be* suppressed.

But the state has not yet completely withered away, since there still remains the protection of "bourgeois right" which sanctifies actual inequality. For the complete withering away of the state, complete communism is necessary.[7]

Lenin was also forced to try to discredit democracy in the Western countries because the social democrats were relying on this democracy in their efforts to move toward socialism.

If we look more closely into the mechanism of capitalist democracy, everywhere, both in the "petty"—so-called petty—details of the suffrage (residential qualification, exclusion of women, etc.), and in the technique of the representative institutions, in the actual obstacles to the right of assembly (public buildings are not for "beggars"!), in the purely capitalist organisation of the daily press, etc., etc.—on all sides we see restriction after restriction upon democracy. These restrictions, exceptions, exclusions, obstacles for the poor, seem slight, especially in the eyes of one who has never known want himself and has never been in close contact with the oppressed classes in their mass life (and nine-tenths, if not ninety-nine hundredths, of the bourgeois publicists and politicians are of this category); but in their sum total these restrictions exclude and squeeze out the poor from politics, from taking an active part in democracy.[8]

As far as the changes after the revolution are concerned, Lenin's anticipations, in the light of actual developments, read as sheer irony.

All *citizens become employees and workers of a* single *national state "syndicate." All that is required is that they should work equally—do their proper share of work—and get paid equally* [*for equal work*]. *The accounting and control necessary for this have been so utterly* simplified *by capitalism that they have become the extraordinarily simple operations of checking, recording and issuing receipts, which anyone who can read and write and who knows the first four rules of arithmetic can perform.*[9]

Lenin foresaw that, ultimately, all people will have learned to manage, and will actually manage, production by themselves. This, in turn, will open the door to the transition to the higher phase of communism wherein each receives according to his need.

The November 1917 Revolution

Finally in November, 1917, the Petrograd soviets were captured by the Bolsheviks, whose agitation, under the slogan "peace at any price, all land to the peasant, all powers to the soviet," had won them wide support. Not all of Lenin's associates backed the coup, but his boldness, and the assistance of Trotsky, were most responsible for its success. The Bolsheviks were also aided by demoralization of the country, the dissolution of the army (with the peasant soldiers rushing home to get their share in the land distribution), and the division among their political opponents—conditions that allowed a determined minority to seize state power. Even so, Lenin could muster the courage to make the coup only because he believed the revolution in Russia would trigger a general revolution in Europe.

The most immediate problem that confronted the Bolsheviks was to conclude peace with Germany, which they did under very harsh terms in March, 1918. But hardly had peace been established with Germany than the Civil War broke out, accompanied by interventions by many countries, including the United States. After much bitter fighting, the Communists * emerged victorious in 1920, though the last foreign troops (Japanese) did not leave the country until 1922.

The end of the Civil War left the country completely exhausted. In 1920, Russia's industrial production was only 13 percent of the 1913 volume. The prewar consumption of textiles per individual had been equivalent to 6.77 gold rubles, but in 1920 it was equivalent to only 0.9 gold rubles. The 1916 harvest had been 75 million tons of grain; in 1919 it was only 30 million tons. In the famine of 1920–21 (caused by a severe drought), 5 million people lost their lives. An American relief mission, under Herbert Hoover's direction, contributed $61 million to alleviate the situation.

During this period of strain and stress the Third, or the Communist, International was created. Lenin had considered its formation from the day he found out that the European socialist parties had reneged on their internationalism and become supporters of their respective countries in the war, and in March, 1919, he convened the founding congress of the new international. The platform called for the destruction of the capitalist order on an international front and for a link-up of the struggle against the international bourgeoisie with the aspirations of the people suffering under colonialism. "Colonial slaves in Asia and Africa! The hour of proletarian dictatorship in Europe will also be the hour of your own liberation."

When the Communist International was founded there still seemed to be hope that other countries would follow suit by having their own communist revolutions. Under this assumption, the international was supposed to be something of a coordinating agency for the international revolution, but within a year or two it became clear that the Soviet Union would remain the only communist country.

* In March, 1918, the Bolsheviks had changed the name of their party from the Russian Social Democratic Labor Party to the Russian Communist Party.

From this point on, the Communist International became an instrument of Soviet foreign policy.

NOTES

1. Quoted in Edward Hallett Carr, *Studies in Revolution* (London: Macmillan, 1950), pp. 63–64.
2. Quoted in Jesse D. Clarkson, *A History of Russia,* 2nd ed. (New York: Random House, 1969), pp. 324–25.
3. V. I. Lenin, "What Is to Be Done?" *Selected Works,* Vol. II (New York: International Publishers, 1945), p. 53.
4. *Ibid.,* pp. 134, 138.
5. Quoted in Clarkson, *op cit.,* p. 431.
6. V. I. Lenin, "The State and Revolution," *Selected Works, op. cit.,* pp. 21–22.
7. *Ibid.,* p. 87.
8. *Ibid.,* p. 80.
9. *Ibid.,* pp. 92–93.

CHAPTER NINE

THE SOVIET UNION UNDER STALIN

The second phase of Soviet development represented in many ways a retreat from earlier held positions. In order to retain firm political control, the Communist Party had to make some concessions to capitalism. In 1920 after the Civil War, the Soviet leadership had to accept the fact that the majority of its people were peasants who owned small plots of land; in dealing with the social system it had to make use of scarce professional talent. Also, small-scale private enterprise had to be readmitted as part of the New Economic Policy (NEP), which lasted from 1921 to 1927. The party's control was further strengthened by general belief that the regime would, in addition to its economic concessions, eventually also have to make concessions in its political stance. This belief made people who were dissatisfied with Communist rule bide their time and remain quiescent.

THE SUCCESSION CRISIS

In 1924, when Lenin died, a succession crisis arose. Lenin's leadership had been undisputed; he had gotten his way not by threats of force but through threats that he would resign—the highest tribute paid to a leader. The question of who would succeed him was complicated by an unresolved problem: Lenin had undertaken the Bolshevik Revolution in anticipation of a general European uprising which had not materialized, and the question was what would now be the direction of the Communist Party.

At the time of Lenin's death the Politburo consisted of Trotsky, Stalin, Zinoviev, Kamenev, Rykov, and Tomsky. Stalin, Zinoviev, and Kamenev formed a triumvirate against Trotsky, who as the great commander in the Civil War was the most popular leader; but Zinoviev and Kamenev also had distinguished records, and Stalin, as Secretary General of the party, had by that time established a well-organized machine that was loyal to him. The succession struggle centered at first on Trotsky's attacks on the bureaucratization of the party and the high-handedness of Stalin in particular, and then on Stalin's "socialism in one country" versus Trotsky's "permanent revolution."

"Socialism in One Country" Versus "Permanent Revolution"

By 1924 Joseph Stalin (1879–1953) had in a sense drawn the correct lessons from the failure of the world revolution. He took the position that capitalism had consolidated itself in the world at large—that, because of the existence of the Soviet regime, the frightened national bourgeoisies had banded together in an informal mutual assistance pact against revolution. Thus the Soviet Union would for a long time remain the only socialist country. But given the size of her territory and her vast resources, she could build socialism by herself. At the beginning of 1924, in his *Foundations of Leninism,* Stalin wrote about the Soviet Union's capacity to build socialism. At the end of 1924, in his *Problems of Leninism,* he spoke about her capacity to complete the building of socialism. In discussing this question, the relationship between the proletariat and the peasantry was of prime importance. At first, Stalin thought the peasantry would be an obstacle to the completion of socialism, but he later reversed himself.

Stalin also redefined the relationship between the Soviet Union and the international communist movement. The Soviet Union would no longer be merely a part of the international communist movement; on the contrary, the international movement would become an extension of the Soviet Union. According to Stalin, the consolidation of capitalism made it impossible for a country to launch its own communist revolution; therefore, it would be the state power of the Soviet Union that would bring these revolutions about.

Trotsky, in contrast, remained an internationalist; he refused to see the Bolshevik Revolution as anything more than one event, however important, in an international revolutionary movement. He denied that the Soviet Union could build socialism if she continued to be the only communist power, and believed that she would have to assume the character of a besieged fortress, which would play havoc with the development toward a "popular democracy." The discipline made necessary by the capitalist siege would lead to authoritarianism and a general debasement of socialist values.

The Victory of Stalin

But Stalin won out. His idea of socialism in one country appealed both to the patriotic pride of the Soviet people and to the need for a consolidation of the movement. Trotsky's ideas seemed to denigrate the capacities of the Russian people and urge them along the road of international adventures. The upshot was that in 1925 Trotsky lost his position as commissar of war.

Zinoviev and Kamenev, now afraid of Stalin, joined Trotsky in forming the so-called left opposition, which advocated rapid industrialization and elimination of the power of the rich peasants. At the other end of the spectrum, a group of people formed around Bukharin, Rykov, and Tomsky that advocated going slow on industrialization and minimized the threat of an independent peasantry. Having obtained Stalin's qualified support, it defeated the left opposition. In 1926 Trotsky lost his position in the Politburo; in 1927 he was expelled from the party and banished to Alma Ata. In 1929 Trotsky was banished from the Soviet Union and went to Turkey, then to Norway, and later to Mexico, when in 1940 he was assassinated, probably by an agent of the Soviet secret police. Zinoviev and Kamenev recanted in 1928, but lost their lives in the great purges of the 1930's.

In 1928 Stalin denounced Bukharin, Rykov, and Tomsky and their associates, whom he had used against the left opposition. They were tagged as the right opposition and lost their influence, though they continued in various party positions. Tomsky committed suicide in 1928, and Bukharin and Rykov were executed in the great purges. Thus by 1928 Stalin had emerged as the undisputed leader, though not as the absolute dictator he would become a few years later. On assuming full control of the party and the government, he instituted the very same measures for which he had denounced the left opposition. The great agricultural collectivization drive was started, together with rapid industrialization, under the First Five-Year Plan.

PARTY AND GOVERNMENT UNDER STALIN

Prior to Stalin's ascendancy, as we have seen, the Communist Party arose as a group of professional revolutionaries who were Marxist in orientation. The party purported to speak for the proletariat, which it asserted was unable to see its own best interests. Given the assumption that the working class could develop only a trade union consciousness, and the fact that the working class could not be a numerical force, the party—both as a dispenser of doctrine and a political organization—substituted itself for the proletariat. The right of the party to do so was derived from the conviction that Marxism, and later Marxism-Leninism, represented scientific truth and understanding about society and its laws of development. It enabled one to analyze events correctly and to discern future trends.

After the revolution, two issues had to be settled: the status of competing parties and the relationship of the Communist Party to the government. The Bolshevik leaders soon decided that the Communist Party should have a monopoly of legality; it was maintained, and is still maintained, that since the revolution had resulted in a society composed of only one class,* the proletariat, there was logically place for only one party. The multiparty system, in other words, reflected a multiclass society. The argument that democracy, irrespective of class content, requires competition for power has never been accepted by Soviet communists.

The relationship between the party and the government was stated by Zinoviev at the Eighth Party Congress in 1919:

Fundamental questions of policy, international and domestic, must be decided by the central committee of our party, i.e., the Communist Party, which thus carries these decisions through the Soviet organs. It carries them, of course, cleverly and tactfully, not in such a way as to tread on the toes of Sovnarkom and other Soviet institutions.[1]

The party retained its elitist character even after the revolution, for admission was on a rather selective basis. Up to the 1930's, admission was extended in consideration of the revolutionary services a person had rendered, such as his participation on the side of the Bolsheviks in the Civil War. Later, an applicant's professional standing became the chief consideration. The party wanted to become a cross section of the most able people in each profession and occupation, no matter how humble they might be.

In its internal organization the party was, and is, based on the principles of monolithic unity, democratic centralism, and criticism and self-criticism. *Monolithic unity* means that factionalism is not permitted—with the result that a person who achieves a slight advantage over his opponents can convert it into a complete victory. *Democratic centralism* means that the decision of the majority is

* Actually there were two classes in the Soviet Union—the proletariat and the peasantry—but the latter was considered a friendly ally of the proletariat.

binding on the minority; the minority must help execute the decision as eagerly as if it had been part of the majority. Also, a decision by a higher party organ is binding on a lower party organ, which makes the party structure a pyramid in which decisions come down from the top. *Criticism* and *self-criticism* connote a similar pattern: those on top can criticize those below, but not vice versa, and those who have been criticized are called on to repent.

It is obvious that such a party organization was a ready-made instrument by which a person of great manipulative skill and ruthlessness could establish himself as the absolute ruler of the party and thereby of the country. In a sense, we can also see the development of the governing system as the reverse of democratization. After the party had substituted itself for the proletariat, the Central Committee substituted itself for the party, the Politburo substituted itself for the Central Committee, and finally Stalin superseded the Politburo.

It should also be made clear that the government and the party represent two formal and distinct hierarchies, though it is true that in general there is a union of personnel at the top. The government was based on the idea of soviets, and when in 1917 the Bolsheviks seized power, they did so in the name of the soviets of workers', peasants', and soldiers' deputies. The soviets, originally revolutionary grass-root committees, were political entities as early as the revolution of 1905, and had their antecedents in the Paris Commune of 1871. The soviet was supposed to be an organization through which the people could participate directly in political life. In fact, the soviets became, instead, instruments of the party.

Each territorial unit in the Soviet Union has its own soviet, which serves as the local government. Each republic in the union also has a soviet that is comparable in the U.S. to a state legislature. At the national level is a bicameral federal legislature, called the Supreme Soviet of the U.S.S.R.; one chamber, the Council of Nationalities, represents the nationalities and the other, the Council of the Union, represents the citizens according to numbers.

In theory, the Supreme Soviet of the U.S.S.R. elects the executive, but, in practice, the party controls the selection process. To ensure proper control of the government by the party, the apparatus of the Central Committee—that is, the highest civil service of the party—parallels that of the executive branch of the government. For example, the Ministry of Agriculture has its counterpart in the Department of Agriculture of the Central Committee.

During the Stalinist era, both government and party were instruments of Stalin's dictatorship, and his third lever of power was the secret police. It was his special ability to play off the party hierarchy against the secret police that made it possible for him to keep his rivals off balance. But the hallmark of Stalin's politics was the use of terror, not only against members of the former aristocracy and bourgeoisie but also against his associates. A prime example was the mass purges of the 1930's, in which the victims were often chosen purely by chance.

In a way, terror was built into the party by the very fact that a small minority had taken it upon itself to reshape a recalcitrant majority; and in this respect every revolution poses a very fundamental question. Is the revolution a breakthrough to values that have been long in the making and are now shared by a substantial number of people (perhaps a majority), or is the revolution undertaken by a minority acting on behalf of its own values? In the first case, terror is used against a minority, the defenders of the old order, to ensure the survival of the new order; in the second case the terror is directed against the majority as a method of bringing about the development of the new order.

The American and the French revolutions belong in the first category. It may be assumed that, by the time of the adoption of the Declaration of Independence, the majority of Americans either supported independence or were not hostile to it. The minority—an assumed one-third of the American people—were loyalists, and they were victims of terror. The French Revolution likewise had broad support. But since the French Revolution was a social revolution—in contrast to the American Revolution, which represented a political separation only—terror in France was more extensive than in America.

The French Revolution differed from the Bolshevik Revolution in that the former represented the political consummation of an economic and social change that had occurred earlier, in the womb of the old order. Because capitalism and the bourgeoisie had arisen within the old order, the French Revolution represented the political breakthrough of the bourgeoisie. Classical Marxists assumed that the socialist revolution would take place along the lines of the French Revolution. The development of capitalism would produce a large proletariat whose values would be socialist; the revolution would represent the breakthrough of the proletariat to political power.

Once the Bolsheviks took the position that there was no chance for capitalism to develop in Russia, the process of revolution was reversed. The Bolsheviks seized political power and used it to initiate the economic and social revolutions that would bring forth both the proletariat and socialist values. Thus political revolution was not the end product but the starting point, and terror represented not merely the birth pangs of a new order but a long drawn-out process accompanying the development of that order. Once terror is built into a system in such a way, it must, in some form or other, affect those who direct it, and some paranoia is inevitable. Only a paranoic streak in Stalin can explain the great purges in which many powerless, and therefore harmless, Bolsheviks perished.

THE ECONOMY

Economic planning is central to communist ideology. But even though Marx had deplored the anarchic character of capitalist production, he had not dealt with the techniques of planning; therefore, when the Bolsheviks came to power there was no blueprint for the organization of a planned economy. However, they soon established a state planning commission to prepare for the time when the economy had progressed to the point where planning would be possible. It was not until 1928 that the First Five-Year Plan was put into operation. But before we discuss the operation of the planned economy as it emerged under Stalin, we should examine what a planned economy implies.

In a socialist society, which is based on public ownership of the means of production, a blueprint is made of what goals are to be achieved and what resources (human and material) are available in order to achieve these goals. The location of raw materials, their transportation, the synchronization of the activities of the various enterprises are included in the blueprint so that there will be a smooth flow of commodities from each unit to the next. Next, the surplus is calculated on a national basis and its distribution is determined; where to invest it and how much to return to the people in the form of wages are decided. The investment program determines what enterprises must be subsidized out of the general budget before they are self-supporting. Planning is not, therefore, the same as forecasting, which deals with uncontrollable trends.

In the Soviet Union, the Council of Ministers determines in a general way what the goals should be, what industries should be expanded, and so forth, and then directs the State Planning Commission to work out the plan within these guidelines. This procedure is comparable in the U.S. to the President's relationship with the Bureau of the Budget: the President tells the bureau what his plans are, how much should be spent for armaments, how much for social services, and so forth, and within these guidelines the budget is worked out. Of course, in order to become law the budget needs the approval of Congress, which may, and does, make changes.

In working out the details, the State Planning Commission is supposed to work closely with individual enterprises in order to determine their capacity for production and expansion. (Only too often, however, this cooperation is lacking, with the result that the plans are not quite realistic.) After the commission has worked out the overall plan, it is submitted to the Council of Ministers, and with their approval it becomes law. Each enterprise then receives its individual plan which has the force of law. Supervision for the fulfillment of the plans lies with the ministries in charge of the various branches of the economy.

An individual plan details the production goal, the sources of supply, the time and place of delivery, and the price at which the commodities are to be delivered. Prices are based on the assumed costs of raw material and labor, a fixed profit, and the relevant turnover tax. For example, if the price at which the commodity is to be delivered is 100, the plan assumed that the cost would be 70, the profit 15, and the turnover tax 15. However, the enterprise was exhorted to make a profit above the plan, which means that it was encouraged to save on material costs and to increase labor efficiency. If it were to be successful in this respect, the cost might be 60, and the profit would then be 25. The incentive for making an above-plan profit is that an enterprise, though it must contribute most of the planned profit to the general fund of the ministry, retains the bulk of the above-plan profit for investment and the improvement of social services.

During the Stalinist era, however, the emphasis was on the quantity of production, and bonuses were based chiefly on the overfulfillment of plans. The result was that capital was often wasted and goods were often shoddy. But if the Soviet economy was to be built up rapidly, quantity was needed at any price. A parallel situation occurred in the United States during the Second World War when the government needed airplanes quickly. It could not seek the lowest bids because the firms that could produce the planes most cheaply were not able to produce the quantity that was needed. Contracts were awarded on a cost-plus basis, with the result that planes of the same performance level carried different price tags.

To avoid stagnancy, every economy has to produce a surplus; in capitalist countries this surplus takes the form of profits that accrue to the investors. In the Soviet Union, surplus is "captured" in the form of the turnover tax, but is also expressed in the form of profit. The purpose of profit—and here we are referring to above-plan profit—is to encourage efficiency. Profits that are not used for investment accrue to the workers. Since in the Stalinist era emphasis was on quantity and not efficiency, profit was not particularly stressed, but as we will see later, post-Stalinist reforms have shifted the emphasis from quantity to efficiency, and hence profit has become more important.

For a number of reasons, the management of the economy under Stalin was characterized by a high degree of centralization. As long as few well-trained people were available, the most rational procedure was to concentrate them in one place and have them give explicit and detailed orders to the various managers. However cumbersome such a procedure might be, it was better than having inexperienced people make decisions on the local level. A highly centralized economy also made the shifting of scarce resources much easier.

As the economic history of the Soviet Union shows, planning was successful. After a number of five-year plans the Soviet Union had climbed into second place (after the United States) in industrial production. It is true, however, that its economic development was uneven; the production of capital goods was emphasized and the production of consumer goods was neglected.

Agriculture

The Soviet regime has experienced its greatest difficulties in dealing with the agricultural problem. In 1928, Stalin embarked on his collectivization drive that brought the country (as he later confided to Winston Churchill) to the brink of disaster. After the land decree of 1917, the peasants acquired land in a disorganized and often arbitrary fashion, and an inequitable distribution of land resulted. Moreover, during the NEP some peasants fared better than others: out of 25 million private farmers, 5–8 million were poor, 1.5–2 million were rich, and the rest were somewhere in between. In the collectivization drive, the regime could rely only on the cooperation of the poor peasants; the rich peasants were bitterly opposed to the plan and those in the middle were either sullen or hostile. Nevertheless, the collectivization drive was pursued with utter ruthlessness; whole villages were deported and many people perished.

In the development of the Soviet economy the agricultural sector was given low priority. In fact, the policy of the regime was to "starve" the agricultural sector in favor of the industrial sector. The industrialization of the Soviet Union came basically at the expense of the peasantry.

Collectives and State Farms

A collective (*kolkhoz*) represented a pooling of land by the people who used to own it, and the size of a particular collective was a matter of administrative discretion. The peasants who were now part of a collective worked the fields in organized units and had to deliver a certain percentage (15–25 percent) of their crops to the state at a price that, during Stalin's time, was so low as to be nominal. In fact, the state's share of the crops was tantamount to a tax. The remainder (after various deductions for seeds, insurance payments, and so forth) was distributed among the peasants on the basis of the number of labor days they had invested. The labor day is an accounting unit in which an actual workday is evaluated by the quality of work performed and can be equivalent to as little as one half labor day or as much as two-and-one-half labor days.

In addition to their share in a collective's production, peasants can receive income from the small, individual plots they are assigned and permitted to cultivate, and which they tend with great care. What the peasants do not use for their own consumption they can sell on the collective's market at prices that are set by offer and demand. Thus the Soviet citizen has two sources of food supply: the state stores and the collective markets.

On the face of it, the organization of the collectives is quite democratic: an executive committee is elected and a manager appointed at a general meeting of the membership. In fact, however, the managers are usually appointed by the government and are in full control of the collectives. A second type of agricultural organization is the state farm (*sovkhoz*), which was established on lands that formerly belonged to the czars and newly opened lands and which is operated like a factory. People who work on the state farms are agricultural workers and hence members of the proletariat.* The *sovkhoz* is considered a higher form of agricultural organization than the *kolkhoz.*

SOCIAL CONDITIONS

The Soviet Union under Stalin was a police state; there was neither individual freedom nor personal security. But in spite of these conditions, social gains were achieved on some fronts. A literate population was created, a new professional class came into being, free medical care was introduced, and access to higher education was made available to the talented.

The fact that Stalin continued to emphasize the fundamental equality of men (though he honored this more in the breach than in the observance) introduced a dynamism into the system whereby what originally was only pretense may be moving slowly and tortuously toward reality. Stalin's constitution of 1936, with its guarantee of civil rights and civil liberties, was farcical when it was promulgated but has proved to be of some use to the dissenters of the post-Stalinist era.

STALIN AND INTERNATIONAL COMMUNISM

As mentioned before, the victory of Stalin's theory of "socialism in one country" meant, in effect, that international communism became an instrument of Soviet foreign policy. Foreign communists were called on to transfer their loyalty from their own countries to the Soviet Union. International communism was pictured as comparable to an international political army; communist parties outside the Soviet Union were considered field armies with the Soviet Union as their high command. It was understood that the first duty of every communist was to follow the orders coming from Moscow unquestioningly, and foreign communists also were supposed to observe all the twists and turns of Soviet foreign policy.

At one time it was the policy of the Soviet Union to weaken the governments of the Western powers, and the communist parties in

* As noted earlier, the peasants in the collectives are not considered part of the proletariat since they can sell their surplus on a free market.

those countries were ordered to help in the process. Later, the Soviet Union found it expedient to cultivate these governments, as happened when Hitler came to power. Parallel with these changes were changes in the communist parties vis-à-vis the social democratic parties, which at one time were considered the chief enemies and referred to as social fascist traitors of the working class. However, when Hitler came to power the communists advocated forming popular front governments with these very same "traitors." When the Second World War broke out, it was referred to as a war among imperialist powers, but when the Soviet Union was attacked, the war was transformed into an antifascist war and the Western Allies were dubbed fellow fighters for democracy. This long process of treating foreign communist parties as often expendable appendages of the Soviet Union was thus a contributing factor in the decline of international communism.

NOTE

1. Quoted in Edward Hallett Carr, *The Bolshevik Revolution 1917–1923,* Vol. I (London: Macmillan, 1951–52), p. 219.

CHAPTER TEN

COMMUNIST CHINA

Communism was introduced into China under conditions that were vastly different from those in Russia. For more than three millennia China had nourished its separate cultural evolution with its own intellectual and psychological resources. It considered itself the center of the world and the possessor of the only valid culture; the rest of the world was inferior. This self-centeredness and sense of superiority, a result of the fact that China had never been challenged by equal civilizations, made it difficult for China to copy the ways of the West, even in order to defeat it. Her attitude toward foreigners has always been one of condescension, if not contempt. Having the self-assurance of an old civilization that has been able to absorb many people throughout the course of her history, China developed a form of nationalism (if this term is appropriate for the pre-twentieth-century era) that was not aggressive but matter of fact: the Chinese felt secure in the expectation that their ways would ultimately prevail.

TRADITIONAL CHINA

When the West "discovered" China, the country had been stagnant for several centuries—encrusted in its social structure and its ideology. Chinese society was agrarian and bureaucratic; the bulk of the people were peasants, either tenant farmers or poor private farmers, while the remainder made up the gentry. The major difference between the peasantry and the gentry was that the latter did not need to work (though by European standards many of its members were quite poor). If work is regarded as drudgery, we can understand that the highest good is leisure. Thus the gentleman was a man of leisure, and Chinese culture was the product of the leisure class.

The Chinese felt loyalty only to the family; there was no loyalty to a central authority. The emperor was considered the mediator between people and nature, distant beyond any possibility of identification. He was the "son of heaven," whose task was to harmonize the work of mankind with the heavenly world through right conduct. The religious attitude of China contained little that can be called metaphysical; it was earthly success that determined who was to be the son of heaven. If one dynasty was displaced by another, the new emperors were accorded the same religious respect as their predecessors.

China, in contrast to India, never had a caste system, and the country was administered by a bureaucracy that was drawn from the gentry. In principle, everybody could compete in the examinations for admission to the civil service, but only the sons of the gentry had the opportunity to spend the many years required to learn a most difficult form of writing, to absorb the classics, and to develop the literary style that was a precondition for even writing the exams. The ideology of the bureaucracy was Confucianism, which was also the ideology of the people; it was authoritarian and espoused a hierarchically ordered society. People were treated according to their status—there was no idea of equality before the law.

Treatment according to status meant that two identical actions, if performed by people of a different status, had a different significance; and this attitude carried over into modern times. If, for example, a speeding car was stopped by a policeman and its only occupant was a chauffeur, the chauffeur would be scolded or arrested. But if an important person was riding in the car, the policeman would apologize for having interfered. In Chinese tradition, the regulator of conduct was not an abstraction such as law, but the example set by the gentleman. If a gentleman misbehaved, his only penalty would be the knowledge that he had dishonored himself.

The bureaucracy, of course, was not responsible to the people, and was responsible to the emperor only in a limited sense; its duty was merely the maintenance of peace and order. There was no fiscal accountability to the court beyond the delivery of what was expected in taxes, with the result that the bureaucracy could use its position for financial gain.

The merchant class was not of high prestige, and it had no independent power. Since the economy was run by the state, along something like mercantilist lines, the merchant could do business only with the cooperation of the bureaucrat, with the result that the bureaucrat more often than not became a silent partner in business transactions.

THE COMING OF THE WEST

During the nineteenth century the West entered China, and as a result of two wars (the Opium War of 1840–42, fought by the British, and the Anglo-French War against China in 1866), transformed China into a semicolony with Britain as the dominant power. Hong Kong was ceded to Britain outright in 1842, and enclaves (so-called territorial concessions) were established within a number of other Chinese cities. The Chinese had no jurisdiction within the enclaves, which were governed by the consuls of countries to whom the enclaves belonged. Westerners, even those who lived outside these enclaves, were not subject to Chinese law; any cases involving them were also handled by the consul courts. Furthermore, China was not allowed to set her own tariff rates; the 5 percent tariff that was set was insufficient for the protection of infant industries. To add insult to injury, even the customs' administration was placed under foreign control. Westerners led the typical colonial life in China, with their own clubs, places of entertainment, and the like. They treated the Chinese with undisguised contempt.

The coming of the West to China coincided with a severe internal crisis. While the peasants' lot throughout Chinese history was unenviable, the doubling of the population from 200 million in the middle of the eighteenth century to 400 million in the middle of the nineteenth century created enormous pressures on the land. Today the bulk of the 650 million people of China inhabit an area that is only half as large as the inhabited part of the United States.

The Taiping Rebellion

The greatest internal upheaval, the Taiping Rebellion, started in 1850. It was basically an uprising born of the economic misery of the peasant, although there were a number of other contributing elements. The decline of the ruling dynasty created the fear of unsettling dynastic changes and the impact of Christian ideals of equality and brotherhood (though restricted to comparatively few people) had a revolutionary influence.

The leader of the uprising was Hung Hsiu-chuan, a onetime village schoolteacher who had failed in the provincial examinations for office, and who had subsequently become a Christian, and had been imbued with the conviction that he had a divine mission. He ultimately linked this mission with an attempt to create a new dynasty, the Taiping ("Great Peace") Dynasty. Hung's gospel of brotherhood and an egalitarian society attracted a mass following among the peasants, who believed that it meant the elimination of the landlords. The landlords and officials were, of course, bitter enemies of the Taiping movement. For fifteen years the Taipings kept China in turmoil, and for a few years were masters of Central China. They were finally defeated by a combination of landlord armies, Manchu troops, and foreign mercenaries. The socioeconomic program of the Taipings is of special interest because it provided for a primitive kind of communism. Units of twenty-five households were to be formed that would work in the fields and enjoy the fruits of their labor in common, pooling even their money and clothing as communal property. Other points in their program included the banning of opium, arbitrary punishment, footbinding, and concubinage. Christianity, as understood by Hung, was to be the official religion.

The ultimate defeat of the Taipings was not simply the result of superior force; there were three inherent failings in the movement. First, their program of primitive communism was not viable. Second, they lacked competent administrators because they did not appeal to the scholar-official class. And third, their attempts to perpetuate dynastic aspirations in the traditional style were not compatible with an uprooting of traditional society. Yet the defeat of the Taipings did not end their influence on China; their ideas were perpetuated in the folklore of the countryside. In his boyhood, Sun Yat-sen listened to the stories of one of the rebels who lived in his village and in his imagination identified himself with their fights.

Yet, while the Taiping Rebellion left its revolutionary lore, it was only toward the end of the nineteenth century that the educational, scientific, and economic impact of the West created the conditions for the modernization process of China. Imperialism characteristically imposes a revolution from the outside, but at the same time, as we will see, it does not allow the revolution to run its full course.

The Impact of the West

The presence of the West in China created a native bourgeoisie and intelligentsia. Western businessmen, not knowing the language and customs, needed Chinese intermediaries—people who at first were hired to serve in capacities such as cooks, houseboys, and messengers. Although outcasts from traditional Chinese society, in due time they entered the business of their masters and became independent middlemen, and over many years acquired great wealth. Eventually the former middlemen were so successful that there was no need for foreign businessmen in China. Many members of the new Chinese bourgeoisie became interested in the industrialization of China, particularly in light industry, but China's lack of tariff autonomy made this difficult. Thus all the economic elements that make for nationalism were brought together.

Similarly, through missionary schools, the establishment of native universities, and opportunities to study abroad, the Chinese were brought into contact with Western learning, including its political thought. Chinese intellectuals studied Locke, Bentham, Marx, and later Lenin. In trying to modernize their country, they were similar to the Russian intelligentsia, but they had the additional motivation of the need to rid their country of foreigners.

THE OVERTHROW OF THE MONARCHY AND ITS AFTERMATH

The combination of the new bourgeoisie and the new intelligentsia, assisted by overseas Chinese, brought about the overthrow of the Manchu Dynasty and the establishment of the republic in 1911. The leader was Sun Yat-sen (1866–1925), who came from a well-to-do peasant family near Macao. At the age of fourteen he went to Honolulu to join his elder brother and studied there, returning home three years later to scandalize his village by destroying the idols in the local temple. He studied medicine in Hong Kong but could not practice in Macao because he did not have a Portuguese diploma. He then embarked on a revolutionary career. Placed on the wanted list by the Manchu government, he was held captive by the Chinese legation in London and was about to be shipped to China when, as a result of the attendant worldwide publicity, he was released. Overnight, he had become an international celebrity.

While Sun and his followers were able to overthrow the monarchy, organizing a Republican China was a different matter. In line with the prevailing liberal thought in the West, Sun assumed that political institutions determined social and economic developments, and though he was concerned with improving the people's condition, he did not institute any direct reforms nor call on the peasants to rebel. Thus, as far as the mass of people were concerned, there was no change in their daily lives. Tenant farmers had to pay the same high rent as before; the other farmers eked out the same meager living and in the event of even a small calamity were as likely to lose their land as ever. In fact, in many ways the situation had become worse. The imperial court had provided a measure of unity; with the removal of the emperor the country had lapsed into anarchy. A long, dark era of warlordism ensued, which ended only in 1928.

In 1912, Sun Yat-sen, who had become the first president of the republic, was deposed and removed from public office. But his aspirations were undiminished. China had been an ally (though unwillingly) of the Western powers in the First World War. Thinking that the West would be interested in the democratic evolution of their former ally, Sun appealed in 1922 to Great Britain and the United States for assistance in unifying China under his leadership. But he was ignored. Sun then approached the Soviet Union with greater success.

The Entry of the Soviet Union

In 1923, after preliminary talks, a high-powered Soviet mission was sent to Canton, where Sun had been able to establish himself. The Chinese Communist Party had been founded in 1921, though it consisted of only a handful of intellectuals, among whom was Mao Tse-tung (1893–), at that time a librarian in Peking. Sun and the Soviets had agreed that Sun's party, the Kuomintang (Nationalist People's Party), would be considered the official vehicle of political action, but communists would be permitted to join it as individuals. The Soviet mission then helped reorganize the Kuomintang along the lines of the Soviet Communist Party.

Chiang Kai-shek

Chiang Kai-shek (1886–), a man who came from a moderately well-to-do gentry family and decided to make the military his career, had been drawn into the revolutionary struggle against the Manchu Dynasty. Following the First World War he had joined Sun's party and, after some seasoning at the military academy in Moscow, had become commander of the new Chinese army whose task it would be to defeat the warlords and unify the country.

On the death of Sun Yat-sen in 1926, Chiang, because of his

control of the army, became the most powerful figure. He turned against the communists and drove them underground, sent the Soviet mission packing, and in 1927 set out to finally subdue the warlords and unify the country. Unification was completed in a formal way: local leaders who swore allegiance to the national government headed by Chiang retained some power and were permitted to be independent satraps in some respects. In 1928, Chiang set up his government in Nanking.

THE CHINESE COMMUNISTS

Prior to Chiang's suppression of the Chinese communists, the party was managed from Moscow, specifically by Stalin. Under Stalin's order, the executive of the Communist International had instructed the Chinese communists to join the Kuomintang and submit to its discipline in the interests of a "united front" against Western imperialism. Stalin even went so far as to make Chiang an honorary member of the executive of the Communist International.

Stalin felt that China was not ripe for a socialist revolution and that the revolution that occurred would pit the bourgeoisie against landlords and foreign imperialism. The resultant government would have to rest on a coalition of four classes: the national bourgeoisie, the petty urban bourgeoisie, the workers, and the peasants; and it would be headed by representatives of the "progressive" bourgeoisie. In the eyes of Stalin, Chiang represented the "progressive" bourgeoisie, and therefore had to be courted to obtain a favorable position for the communists. Trotsky opposed this course. He took the position that a socialist revolution was possible in China. Although there is no way of substantiating Trotsky's position, Stalin's actions certainly led to a fiasco. The underground Chinese communists were now on their own as far as Moscow was concerned.

Facing suppression by Chiang and the Nationalist government, a small group of communists moved to Kiangsi Province in the southeast and tried to capture some cities in pursuance of the "proletarian" strategy. But all these attempts ended in defeat, which opened the way for Mao Tse-tung and his peasant strategy. China at that time had hardly any proletariat worth mentioning, because industry in China was almost nonexistent, consisting mostly of small artisan shops that employed a few people and were run on a paternalistic pattern. The only exception was the production of cotton goods by fairly modern spinning mills in the port cities, which, however, employed mostly women. Thus, there was no opportunity for the organization of workers for revolutionary action.

But by concentrating on peasant support, the communists were able to create an army that by 1932 numbered 100,000 men. They were constantly harassed by Chiang's troops, but they held out for a few years in the southeast in a relatively inaccessible area. Then, because of the increased pressure by the nationalists, they had to give up their position and in October, 1934, embarked on the long trek to the northwest. In 1935 they established themselves in Shensi Province, in a remote area bordering the Mongolian steppe. The gradual buildup of the strength of the communists was a result of their agricultural policy: wherever they got a hold, the landlords were driven out or eliminated and the peasants were told to divide the land among themselves.

The Three-way War

In 1931 the Japanese invaded Manchuria and tore it from China, which later led to the Chinese-Japanese War in 1937. During the war the Japanese occupied the whole coast of China and inland to a depth of a few hundred miles, including Nanking; the Nationalist government moved to Chungking. While at Nanking, the Nationalist government had been influenced by the more enlightened Chinese business interests but in Chungking it fell under the sway of a most backward landlord class, which greatly contributed to its demoralization.

During the Chinese-Japanese War, which the nationalists and the communists fought separately, a civil war was simultaneously waged between the two Chinese factions. Despite the Japanese presence, or perhaps because of it, the Chinese communists were able to expand their area of control. The nationalist officials and the more prosperous people fled toward Chungking in the face of the advancing Japanese army. But since the war involved many seesaw battles, the Japanese often had to give up their position due to pressure on their flanks or the overextension of their lines of supply and communication. When they left an area, communist scouts would enter, tell the peasants to take the vacated land of the landlords, and organize the villages. When the war ended, the communists had increased the area under their control eightfold.

The end of the Chinese-Japanese War also saw the expansion of the civil war over broad fronts. The nationalists received aid from the United States, the communists from the Soviet Union; but the outcome was in a sense determined by the peasant armies that fought on both sides. Chiang Kai-shek stated that land reform would have to await victory over the communists, but the communists undertook land reform while they fought. In 1949 the communists emerged victorious and Chiang was driven to Taiwan.

The Roots of Chinese Communism—Soviet Theory for Colonial Countries

The ideology of Chinese communism is the body of thought of one man: Mao Tse-tung. But Chinese communism was built on the Marxist-Leninist heritage, though again this heritage was modified to fit the needs and aspirations of the Chinese. The content of what was, in more realistic terms, a Leninist heritage was Lenin's theory for colonial peoples, which after the Soviet debacle in China was further elaborated by Stalin.

According to Lenin, imperialism means the control over sources of raw material and markets in foreign countries, and this control is political and economic. Political control means the denial of self-government to the natives, and economic control means, in essence, suppression of the possibility of industrialization.

Essentially, the dominant class in colonial countries, the landlord class, is not adversely affected by this control; it has no interest in industrialization. It continues to thrive on the exploitation of its peasantry, and foreign political control represents a guarantee for the maintenance of the existing order. But gradually members of the merchant class, and occasionally members of the landlord class, seeing the opportunities industrialization would offer, start to resent foreign rule. This incipient bourgeoisie now raises the cry for national liberation, and this cry finds an echo in the intelligentsia, in the incipient proletariat, and later in the peasantry. Only the traditional landlord class, afraid of the political awakening of the peasants that goes hand in hand with a national liberation movement, does not join in. An alliance between the bourgeoisie, the intelligentsia, and the proletariat is established whose aim is a struggle for national unification against foreign imperialism and backward landlordism.

The latter fight opens the way for the agrarian revolution. In the fight against foreign rule, the more successful among the bourgeoisie gain control over an important sector of the economy. Having done so, this "big bourgeoisie" through the use of monopolistic practices excludes others from gaining access to positions of economic significance. As a result of the industrialization undertaken by the big bourgeoisie, a proletariat arises that at some point challenges the position of its employers. Afraid of a takeover, the big bourgeoisie joins the landlord class and the foreign imperialists, and together they exploit the people.

The more numerous members of the middle and petty bourgeoisie (the storekeepers and artisans), not being as successful as the big bourgeoisie, resent the latter's activities and misuse of economic power, and therefore remain loyal to the alliance with the proletariat and the peasantry. In this alliance, the working class must assume the leading role and carry the revolution to the countryside. The landlords are expropriated, and the proletariat ultimately leads the peasants to collectivization. According to the Soviet theory, the revolution in the colonial countries cannot be successful without the help of the proletariat of the more advanced countries (that is, the Soviet Union): "No lasting victory can be achieved in colonial and dependent countries unless a real bond is established between the movement for emancipation in these countries and the proletarian movement in the advanced countries of the West." [1]

To the extent that national liberation struggles are successful and formerly colonial countries become independent, the position of the advanced capitalist countries is economically undermined and the ultimate showdown between the Soviet Union and these countries is greatly facilitated. But the Soviet Union must control the national liberation movements, and her timetable must be respected; that is, the interests of the national liberation movements must remain subordinated to the interests of the Soviet Union. In Stalin's words:

Cases occur when the national movements in certain oppressed countries come into conflict with the interests of the development of the proletarian movement. In such cases, of course, support is entirely out of the question. The rights of nations are not an isolated and self-contained question, but part of the general question of the proletarian revolution, a part which is subordinate to the whole and which must be dealt with from the point of view of the whole.[2]

To sum up: The center of the revolutionary struggle is in the West, and because the national liberation struggle is an auxiliary to the proletarian revolution, it is therefore subordinate to the main theater of conflict. Since only one country in the West has had a successful revolution, it is obviously the leader for all the other countries. It follows, then, that the Chinese Revolution is subsidiary to the Russian Revolution.

MAO TSE-TUNG'S COMMUNISM

Mao Tse-tung's communism involved both a strategy for victory and a program for action after victory. His strategy was unconventional warfare—that is, guerrilla warfare—an original contribution to communism that has been imitated and elaborated on by (among others) General Giap of North Vietnam and Che Guevara in Latin America. Guerrilla warfare is more than military tactics; it is also a form of political schooling and a means of creating an effective communist party. According to a 1939 editorial in the party newspaper *The Communist*:

What is guerrilla warfare? It is, in a backward country, in a big semicolonial country, and for a long period of time, the inevitable and therefore the best form of struggle for the people's armed forces to overcome the armed enemy and create their own strongholds. For eighteen years the political line and the building of our Party have been closely linked with this form of struggle. Apart from armed struggle, apart from guerrilla warfare, it is impossible to understand our political line and, consequently, to understand our Party-building. . . . We know that in China there would be no place for the proletariat, no place for the people, no place for the Communist Party, and no victory for the revolution without armed struggle. For eighteen years the development, consolidation, and Bolshevization of our Party have been undertaken in the midst of revolutionary wars and have been inseparable from guerrilla warfare. *Without armed struggle,* without guerrilla warfare, *there would not have been such a Communist Party as exists today. Comrades throughout the Party must never forget this experience gained at the cost of blood.*[3]

The following quotations from Mao Tse-tung explain both the relationship between guerrilla warfare and political objectives and the tactics of guerrilla warfare.

Without a political goal, guerrilla warfare must fail, as it must if its political objectives do not coincide with the aspirations of the people and their sympathy, cooperation and assistance cannot be gained. The essence of guerrilla warfare is thus revolutionary in character.

On the other hand, in a war of counter-revolutionary nature, there is no place for guerrilla hostilities. Because guerrilla warfare basically derives from the masses and is supported by them, it can neither exist nor flourish if it separates itself from their sympathies and cooperation. . . .

There is also a unity of spirit that should exist between troops and local inhabitants. The [*Communist*] *Eighth Route Army put into practice a code known as "Three Rules and Eight Remarks":*

Rules—*All actions are subject to command; do not steal from the people; be neither selfish nor unjust.*

Remarks—*Replace the door when you leave the house; roll up the bedding in which you have slept; be courteous; be honest in your transactions; return what you borrow; replace what you break; do not bathe in the presence of women; do not without authority search the pocketbooks of those you arrest. . . .*

The primary functions of guerrillas are three: first, to conduct a war on exterior lines, that is, in the rear of the enemy; secondly, to establish bases; lastly, to extend the war areas. Thus guerrilla participation in the war is not merely a matter of purely local guerrilla tactics, but involves strategic considerations.

What is basic guerrilla strategy? Guerrilla strategy must primarily be based on alertness, mobility and attack. It must be adjusted to the enemy situation, the terrain, the existing lines of communication, the relative strength, the weather and the situation of the people.

In guerrilla warfare select the tactic of seeming to come from the east and attacking from the west; avoid the solid, attack the hollow; attack; withdraw; deliver a lightning blow, seek a lightning decision. When guerrillas engage a stronger enemy they withdraw when he advances, harass him when he stops; strike him when he is weary; pursue him when he withdraws. In guerrilla strategy the enemy's rear, flanks and other vulnerable spots are his vital points, and there he must be harassed, attacked, dispersed, exhausted and annihilated.[4]

Mao's political ideology swung from a mildly revolutionary position in the 1940's to an extreme revolutionary position in the present day. It is interesting to note that in 1949 shortly before the communist takeover of China, the organ of the Indian Communist Party, at that time under the control of Moscow, denounced Mao Tse-tung as a Titoist. Now Mao denounces the Soviet Union in the same terms.

Mao's thoughts in the 1940's are found in his *On the New Democracy,* in which he visualized two stages in the evolution of communism in China: that of the New Democracy, followed by the stage of socialism. New Democracy referred to the bourgeois-democratic revolution, which was "new" because as a result of the Russian Revolution it had become a part of the world proletarian revolution. China's bourgeois revolution was under the leadership of a communist party and the bourgeois stage, while unavoidable, was not to be a goal but a means for moving toward socialism. The New Democracy also included a revolution against imperialism, feudalism, and bureaucratic capitalism. The forces behind this revolution were an alliance of workers, peasants, the intelligentsia, and the national bourgeoisie.

According to Mao, in the New Democracy, all big banks, big industries, and big commercial establishments would be state owned. All other enterprises would be permitted to remain in private hands, a necessary step because of the backwardness of China's economy. The ownership of land was to be readjusted, not with a view to building up socialist agriculture but in order to turn the land into peasant property.

How long would this stage last? Mao answered that "the first step will take quite a long time and can by no means be accomplished overnight. We are not utopians, and we cannot depart from the actual conditions confronting us." [5]

Once the Communists gained power, however, this program was quickly abandoned. The peasants, for example, were urged to form mutual-aid teams and producers' cooperatives. Then, in 1955, the collectivization of agriculture was undertaken. Compared with the upheaval in connection with collectivization in Russia, the operation in China was not too disruptive. Because of the scarcity of land, the plots that were given to individual peasant families were small, and the living they eked out was not far above subsistence, but the collectives at least provided a guarantee against starvation.

But the regime did not stop with collectivization; in 1959 the communes were established. Communes were made coextensive with political districts; hence the governmental functions of a district and the economic management of its commune were placed under a single authority. In contrast to the collective, the commune is a multipurpose economic organization. The major problem of the agricultural collective, in the case of overpopulated countries, is the waste of human resources. Agricultural work does not provide sufficient employment. The commune, however, permits the use of labor for both agricultural and nonagricultural purposes. People are employed in the building of roads and dams, in simple industrial work, and so on.

The establishment of the communes was hailed as the advent of communism: there was no differentiated pay and the essential services were free. The Chinese claimed that the communes showed that the stage of socialism could be skipped. Soviet leaders denounced this interpretation, insisting that the stage of socialism could not be bypassed and that the nondifferentiated pay in the communes was possible only because of the primitiveness of the work involved. How could one differentiate between a person who dug a ditch and another who made low-grade iron in a backyard furnace? The Chinese at this point were not yet ready to defy the Soviet Union openly, and so there were some modifications of the Chinese claim. However, in light of the Cultural Revolution, there is no doubt that Mao considered the bypassing of the stage of socialism a real and important achievement.

The Meaning of the Cultural Revolution

The development of China, if it had been permitted to take its "natural" course, would probably have followed the Soviet model: a long socialist stage, with emphasis on industrialization and centralized planning; political control in the hands of the party bureaucracy; and differentiated rewards and statuses on the basis of type of work and scarcity of talent. But this development seems to have been unacceptable to Mao, and three factors can be credited with having roused his antagonism: his personal outlook, shaped during the long struggle for communist victory; his fear of the impact of tradition, which would deform the revolution; and his interpretation of developments in the Soviet Union.

Some of the most revealing insights into Mao's thinking can be obtained from the interviews he gave to André Malraux in 1966. According to Mao:

In the Soviet Union, it was the party which made the Red Army; here, it seems as if often it was the liberation army which developed the party. . . .

If revolution can only be brought about by the workers, obviously we couldn't bring about revolution. The Russians' friendly feelings were for Chiang Kai-shek. When he escaped from China, the Soviet ambassador was the last to wish him goodbye. The cities fell like ripe fruit. . . .

Neither the agricultural nor the industrial problem is solved. Still less the youth problem. Revolution and children have to be trained if they are to be properly brought up. . . .

Youth must be put to the test. . . .

The revisionism of the Soviet Union may not make it lose votes, but it will make it lose teeth. As a party, it is against us. Like all the others, apart from Albania. They have become social-democratic parties of a new type.

. . . Humanity left to its own devices does not necessarily reestablish capitalism, . . . but it does reestablish inequality. The forces tending toward the creation of new classes are powerful. . . .

. . . The young are not Red by birth; they have not known Revolution. . . .

. . . Thought, culture, customs, must be born of struggle, and the struggle must continue for as long as there is still a danger of a return to the past. Fifty years is not a long time; barely a lifetime—our customs must become as different from the traditional customs as yours are from feudal customs. . . .

What is expressed in that commonplace term "revisionism" is the death of the revolution. . . . I have told you that the revolution is also a feeling. If we decide to make of it what the Russians are now doing—a feeling of the past—everything will fall apart. Our revolution cannot be simply the stabilization of a victory.[6]

The many years spent in the wilderness before coming to Yenan, the years in the caves of Yenan, the camaraderie of associates exposed to daily dangers—all these things shaped Mao's thoughts along the lines of austerity and egalitarianism. Obviously, he and his associates accomplished the revolution in a spirit of idealism and self-sacrifice, and these were the virtues he wanted to preserve. He was particularly concerned about the Chinese youth: for a new generation, the struggles and the triumph of the revolution would be ancient history, and they would soon take things for granted. This must be prevented.

A second concern was the possible backsliding of the country—

the possibility of a Mandarin socialism, in which a bureaucracy imbued with the spirit and arrogance of the traditional Chinese bureaucracy would run things. Even in strictly economic terms, the new socialism need not be too different from the mercantilism of traditional China.

Finally, there were the developments in the Soviet Union. Moscow in the time of Stalin was a drab and austere city not very different from Peking. But Moscow was trying to become more glamorous; Soviet youth had forgotten the revolution and was interested in the latest Western fads. One of Marx's basic assumptions was that once abundance had replaced scarcity, there would be an almost automatic transformation of man. No longer having to compete against his fellow men for scarce goods, he would become less selfish, more altruistic, and interested in more lofty concerns. The developments in Moscow led one to wonder whether a long socialist stage, with its emphasis on material incentives, would not lead to the creation of a petty bourgeois mentality—with the result that, with the coming of abundance, competition would be eliminated but petty self-indulgence would take over. If this was to be avoided, the socialist stage would have to be aborted and the country led as quickly as possible into the communist stage. This theory is a variant of Trotsky's idea of permanent revolution and his law of uneven and combined development. Trotsky (who, as we have mentioned, is anathema in China) took the position that Russia did not have to duplicate all the stages of the West—that there was a simultaneous bourgeois and proletarian revolution and that the former could be aborted and transformed into a socialist revolution. In China, it could be said that two revolutions were going on simultaneously, one socialist and the other communist, and that the socialist could be transformed into a communist revolution. Of course, this attitude requires that ideas be divorced from their economic substructure, but Lenin had already done this to a certain degree by working for a socialist revolution in a country that was capitalistically underdeveloped. In Russia, revolutionary rule by an elite was substituted for the ideology that would "naturally" emerge from the economic substructure.

Mao Tse-tung has carried this idea even further: he gives ideas an almost independent character and emphasizes teaching far beyond what Marxists ordinarily would subscribe to.

Men are not the slaves of objective reality. Provided only that men's consciousness be in conformity with the objective laws of the development of things, the subjective activity of the popular masses can manifest itself in full measure, overcome all difficulties, create the necessary conditions, and carry forward the revolution. In this sense, the subjective creates the objective. [*Emphasis added.*] [7]

The Cultural Revolution pitted the party's structure, with its many functionaries, managers, and experts, against Mao Tse-tung and those army leaders for whom the years of civil war and guerrilla exploits represented nostalgic memories. Mao also attracted groups of youngsters through his appeal to their sense of adventure; he organized workers' councils against the party bureaucrats; and at times he used army units both to keep order and to intimidate his opponents.

Mao's Cultural Revolution was undertaken in the name of revolutionary egalitarianism. Mao had fought much earlier for egalitarianism and had achieved notable successes. Even before the upheaval of the Cultural Revolution, every Chinese, however high his position, had to spend one day a week at manual labor. This sometimes led to rather odd situations; for example, a factory manager was once unable to receive a foreign visitor because it was the manager's day for manual work—he was in the kitchen making dumplings. To the managerial mind, such a requirement represented a sheer waste of scarce talent. Egalitarianism is also exemplified in the rule that army personnel do not wear their insignia when off duty, and hence a general is indistinguishable from a private, both wearing nondescript, baggy uniforms.

The extent to which the upheaval of the Cultural Revolution has interfered with the economic progress of the country is unclear. Large areas of the country were very little affected, and the areas that were affected were, perhaps, less disrupted than we would think because the Chinese have developed a great capacity to go on living and working under conditions of chaos. Diligence in attending to work has been greatly internalized by many Chinese. At the same time, Mao is willing to accept temporary setbacks in the economy in the expectation that the new mentality created by the Cultural Revolution will more than compensate for present losses.

How do we measure Mao's success? Certainly Mao is too good a dialectician to assume that he can decisively win all the issues at stake. He views his battle as a 100 percent assault on existing conditions with a 50 percent change as a result. If we visualize the Cultural Revolution as a permanent revolution (though with breathing spells in between), the aggregate of partial successes makes for an ultimate victory.

Mao is convinced that the working classes in the West, including that in the Soviet Union, have ceased to be a revolutionary force. On the contrary, they have become the beneficiaries of imperialism. One indication of this attitude is that the Chinese equate both American and Russian aid given to India as designed to subjugate and exploit India.

It follows from this that the former colonial and semicolonial countries have become the chief (if not the only) revolutionary forces in the world. Foremost among these countries is, of course, the largest and the most powerful: China. This view, however, involves a very interesting reinterpretation of Marxism. Marx saw the struggle for socialism as involving the proletariats of the advanced countries against the bourgeoisie; for Mao the world revolutionary struggle involves bourgeois *nations* versus proletarian *nations* with the historical turning point being the Chinese Revolution. In this scheme, the Chinese Revolution denotes an advance beyond the Bolshevik Revolution, just as the Bolshevik Revolution represented a progression beyond the French Revolution.

Thus, the Marxist theory of revolution has undergone a great change. For Marx, the chief revolutionary force was the working class in the advanced capitalist countries. For Lenin, it was the working class in the least advanced capitalist country, from which the revolution would spread westward, with the colonial and semicolonial countries acting as auxiliaries of the Western proletariat. For Mao, the chief revolutionary force is the formerly colonial and semicolonial countries—the underdeveloped countries—with the advanced detachments of the working class in the West acting (at best) as auxiliaries of these countries. Maoist groups in all Western countries see their role precisely in this light.

NOTES

1. Joseph Stalin, "Political Tasks of the University of the Peoples of the East," in *Marxism and the National and Colonial Question,* ed. A. Fineberg (New York: International Publishers, 1936), p. 215.

2. Joseph Stalin, "The National Question," in *ibid.*, p. 193.
3. Quoted in *The Political Thought of Mao Tse-tung,* ed. and tr. Stuart R. Schram (New York: Praeger, 1963), p. 257.
4. Quoted in *China, the Emerging Red Giant: Communist Foreign Policies,* ed. DeVere E. Pentony (San Francisco: Chandler Publishing, 1962), pp. 166–68.
5. Mao Tse-tung, "On New Democracy," *Selected Works,* Vol. III (London: Lawrence & Wishart, 1954–56), p. 128.
6. Quoted in André Malraux, *Anti-Memoirs,* tr. Terence Kilmartin (New York: Holt, Rinehart and Winston, 1968), pp. 363–75 ff.
7. Quoted in Schram, *op cit.*, p. 80.

PART THREE

CONTEMPORARY REVOLUTIONS

We all are aware that we are living in a revolutionary age; however, being contemporaries, we cannot fully understand its meaning. Not until some time has passed, not until the dust of battle has settled and passions have cooled, will people understand what it was really all about. Yet in spite of these limitations there is a need to come to grips with the events of the age as best we can. In order to live meaningfully, one must try to live with understanding.

On a high level of abstraction, we could certainly say that the contemporary revolution is for equality, and even for brotherhood, but this definition would not be very helpful in the understanding of concrete revolutionary movements. Let us therefore suggest that what we have today are *four* overlapping and interacting revolutions going on simultaneously. These are the revolution against the oppression of poverty, the revolution against authoritarianism, the revolution against alienation, and the revolution against racial discrimination.

The revolution against the oppression of poverty is occurring in the underdeveloped countries. The revolution against authoritarianism is embodied in the changes, or attempted changes, in the Eastern European countries and in the Western communist parties. The revolution against alienation characterizes events in the advanced Western countries. The revolution against racial discrimination is worldwide but at present has special significance for the United States.

This categorization of contemporary revolutions is admittedly somewhat arbitrary. The fight against poverty is not restricted to the underdeveloped countries—it has also its place in the advanced countries. In effect, an element in the alienation of the more "sensitive" youth in the advanced countries is the everyday sight of so much unnecessary poverty. Nor is alienation restricted to the Western countries; it also affects the countries of Eastern Europe. And authoritarianism is not an issue only in the communist countries; it also pervades many institutions of the West. Thus these divisions are less a matter of exclusiveness than of centrality of concern.

CHAPTER ELEVEN

THE REVOLUTION AGAINST POVERTY

The revolution against poverty in the underdeveloped countries is premised on the belief that poverty is not inevitable for a society. This premise distinguishes their revolutions from the economic processes of the West. Furthermore, in the West it was assumed that improvement in the economic lot of society was a natural by-product of technological advances; improvement was not sought in a direct, conscious, or planned fashion. And however great the economic progress, it was also assumed that there would always be poor people. Both religious fatalism and the philosophy of laissez faire contributed to this belief.

It was the prevalence of the laissez-faire philosophy that led the workers to permit the more or less peaceful accumulation of capital largely at their own expense. The legitimacy of a democratic government was not based on its contribution to the public welfare, including economic well-being, but on general and free elections. As we have seen, social affairs were artificially divided into two distinct realms, one economic, the other political; the purview of government was supposed to be limited to the political, while the economy was left to the managers of unequally distributed wealth. The general acceptance of these views permitted a minority to live well amid conditions of general scarcity.

The stability of governments was more or less assured by the fact that the government was not held responsible for economic conditions because economics was outside the realm of politics. When, finally, there was a shift away from laissez faire, enough wealth had been accumulated so that government's assumption of responsibility for economic welfare did not affect the position of those who had been privileged all along. As the division between the economic and the political spheres diminished, economics became the test of politics, with the result that a government that permitted the rise of a severe economic crisis would be defeated at the next election.

In contrast, the peoples of the underdeveloped countries have come to political consciousness in an era when a division between the economic and the political realms is no longer accepted—when the chief function of government is seen to be economic development and equitable distribution of scarce resources. Inasmuch as the government is the chief economic force, the contributions of a few entrepreneurs could not be such that they deserve the good life under conditions of general scarcity.

As formally stated, these ideas can be ascribed only to the intellectual elites, but in some ways the masses have also become imbued with them, and this has affected the relationships between the rulers and the ruled. The test of the legitimacy of a government has become the correspondence of life styles between the rulers and the masses rather than the outcome of general and free elections. The masses readily accept the fact that the issues involved in governing are so far above their heads that they cannot rightly claim to have a part in decision-making processes; but as long as their rulers are austere and modest, they will be considered legitimate rulers. In contrast, politicians who have won their offices in free elections but live in luxury may not be considered legitimate.

The political consciousness of these countries has also been shaped by the fight against imperialism: whether a person in an underdeveloped country is a conservative or a revolutionary, his interpretation of imperialism tends to follow that of Lenin. The Marxist-Leninist influence in underdeveloped countries is considerable, if only in the sense that they have a broad commitment to socialism; and since they have little or no basis for parliamentary institutions, they are not proponents of social democracy.

Whether an underdeveloped country follows authoritarian socialism or communism depends on whether it is allied with the Soviet Union or China and whether it pursues a policy of class struggle. However, the disintegration of international communism and the consequences of revisionism have now made the distinction between authoritarian socialism and communism less clear.

Authoritarian socialism may be expressed in a one-party system or a military dictatorship; an example of the latter was Nasser's Egypt. Socialist military dictatorships, however, are distinct from such old-line military dictatorships as those of Latin America in that the former are made up mostly of young officers who have developed a social conscience and are interested in modernization and some form of social justice. The old-line dictatorships were established by people who used their power to exploit what, in effect, they considered their private possessions. Both forms of authoritarian socialism in underdeveloped countries have to be distinguished from fascism, which is a dictatorship in an advanced country for the purpose of preventing social revolution. Fascism is counterrevolutionary; the socialist dictatorships and one-party systems in the underdeveloped countries are revolutionary. Their goal is to move their societies out of a feudal past.

Since the same organizational forms may operate in different social contexts, they can have different meanings. The one-party system of the Soviet Union operates in an advanced country and is thus a force that stifles energies rather than mobilizes them. In contrast, the one-party systems of the underdeveloped countries are forces for the mobilization of the energies of their peoples.

Of the political systems and their ideologies that at present operate in underdeveloped countries, we will single out two for discussion: African socialism and Castroism. Both are more or less well-developed ideologies whose significance is not limited to the countries of their origin.

AFRICAN SOCIALISM

The characteristics of African socialism are: (1) the absence of class struggle, with the resultant definition of the political public not by particular classes but as the people as a whole; (2) the single-party system; (3) elitist leadership; (4) relative flexibility in the definition of the national sector of the economy vis-à-vis the private sector; and (5) willingness to accept foreign investments within well-defined rules. The absence of the politics of class struggle results from the fact that these societies are emerging from tribalism, and hence are classless to a certain degree. The single party, therefore, expresses not the aspirations or will of a particular revolutionary class but the national will.

Ideologues of this types of party system, such as Julius Nyerere, President of Tanzania, maintain that it represents a democratic form of political management:

Basically, democracy is government by discussion as opposed to government by force, and by discussion between the people or their chosen representatives, as opposed to a hereditary clique. Under the tribal system whether there was a chief or not, African society was a society of equals, and it conducted its business by discussion.

It is true that this "pure" democracy—the totally unorganized "talking until you agree"—can no longer be adequate; it is too clumsy a way of conducting the affairs of a large modern state. But the need to organize the "government by discussion" does not necessarily imply the need to organize an opposition group as part of the system.

I am not arguing that the two-party system is not democratic; I am only saying that it is simply one form which democracy happens to have taken in certain countries, and that it is by no means essential. I am sure that even my friends in the Labour Party or the Conservative Party in Britain would admit that if their party could succeed in winning all seats, they would be perfectly happy to form a one-party government. They—the winning party, that is—would not be likely to suspect themselves of having suddenly turned Britain into a dictatorship! [1]

More cogently, Nyerere points out that governments in newly emerging countries lead a very precarious existence because the aspirations of the masses (who are to a certain extent aware of conditions in advanced countries) are high but the ability of their governments to fulfill them is very limited.

In the past, all that was required of government was merely to maintain law and order within the country and to protect it from external aggression. Today, the responsibilities of governments whether "Communist" or free, are infinitely wide. However nearly its requirements of money and men may be met, no government today finds it easy to fulfill all its responsibilities to the people.

These common problems of a modern state are no less formidable in young and underdeveloped countries. The very success of the nationalist movements in raising the expectations of the people, the modern means of communication which put the American and the British worker in almost daily contact with the African worker, the twentieth-century upsurge of the ordinary man and woman—all these deprive the new African governments of those advantages of time and ignorance which alleviated the growing pains of modern society for the governments of older countries. [*Emphasis added.*] [2]

Nyerere compares the governments in underdeveloped countries to governments in countries that are at war, and believes that in such an emergency situation it would be disruptive and wasteful to have an opposition party. The same thought is expressed by Madeira Keita of Mali:

In the present historical situation in Africa, there is no need to multiply parties. There is no need to indulge in the luxury of a sterile and fratricidal opposition. There is no need to have a ministerial crisis every three months . . . if we wish to realize African unity and raise Africa economically and culturally to the level of other countries and peoples.[3]

When the issue of individual freedom is raised, the ideologues of African socialism point out that the freedom on which all other freedoms depend is freedom from the fear of starvation, and only their type of system can liberate the people from this fear. Thus economic planning, which is most fully achievable in a socialist system, is essential for African governments. As Keita puts it:

As for economic and cultural development, even right-wing economists now admit that the underdeveloped countries can only advance rapidly and develop themselves sufficiently through planning. Even the old industrialized countries now think that they will overcome their backwardness by planning. When a man like Nehru, who seems to me like a good British bourgeois from the City [the financial district of London], *asserts that the underdeveloped countries, which have recently achieved independence after a long period of colonial regime, cannot develop without the methods of socialist planning, I believe that this is a very important indication.*[4]

CUBA AND CASTROISM

After the Spanish-American War, Cuba became a semicolony of the United States, and this status was made official in Article III of the Platt Amendment:

The Government of Cuba consents that the United States may exercise the right to intervene for the preservation of Cuban independence, the maintenance of a government adequate for the protection of life, property, and individual liberty, and for discharging the obligations with respect to Cuba imposed by the Treaty of Paris on the United

States, now to be assumed and undertaken by the Government of Cuba.

Article VII stated:

To enable the United States to maintain the independence of Cuba, and to protect the people thereof, as well as for its own defense, the government of Cuba will sell or lease to the United States lands necessary for the coaling or naval stations at certain specified points to be agreed upon with the President of the United States.

Under this provision, the United States acquired the naval base at Guantanamo.

The United States made frequent use of its right of intervention, and it was only as part of the Good Neighbor Policy of President Franklin D. Roosevelt that, in 1934, the United States abrogated the Platt Amendment—without, however, giving up Guantanamo.

But up to the time of Castro, Cuba could still be considered a semicolony of the United States in an economic sense. American interests owned 40 percent of the sugar land, including seven of the ten largest plantations. (Much of this land was acquired after the Spanish-American War.) American interests also owned 54 percent of the sugar mills. According to the U.S. Department of Commerce, American ownership exceeded 90 percent in the telephone companies, electric power supply, and railways.[5]

Within Cuba the most depressed group was the peasantry, or the agricultural workers. In 1946, 8 percent of the farmers owned 71.1 percent of the land held by Cubans, while 39 percent owned only 3.3 percent. The typical Cuban agriculturist was not really a peasant but a landless agricultural worker who worked for wages in gangs under the supervision of bosses. He was employed only a few months of the year, and could barely eke out an existence for the remainder of the year.

There was also a stark contrast between the style of life in Havana, which was a cosmopolitan city (with the usual slums, of course), and that in the rest of the country. For example, in Havana 87 percent of the dwelling units had electricity, while in rural areas only 7 percent of the dwellings were so equipped. One explanation, of course, is that it did not pay for the private utilities to make investments for rural electrification. (A comparable situation also existed in the United States before the New Deal, but was remedied by the establishment of the Rural Electrification Administration.)

Cuba has often experienced the instability and violence that are part of the Latin American tradition. Spurious revolutions, or rather *coups d'état* and dictatorships, have been part and parcel of Latin American politics. They have traditionally involved only transfers of power within the ruling class—the landed gentry and its military allies—although they have occasionally made it possible for people of humble origin to acquire economic power through the acquisition of political power.

Instability, whether provoked by political ambition or the quest for economic power, is complemented by the authoritarian heritage that Latin America received from the Spanish Empire. The strong, centralized, divine-right monarchy of Spain exercised its influence even after the countries of Latin America had achieved their independence. Simón Bolívar, the liberator of Latin America, had this to say:

The President of the Republic becomes in our Constitution the sun, which, firm in the center, gives life to the universe. I have never been an enemy of monarchy, as far as general principles are concerned; on the contrary, I consider monarchies essential for the respectability and well-being of new nations. . . . The new states of America . . . need kings with the name of presidents.[6]

This attitude has led to reverence for the strong man, the *caudillo.*

Men have therefore played a greater role in Latin America than parties. More often than not, political parties are cliques of people surrounding a strong man, and politics is personalized. The qualities that are most appreciated are flamboyance and bravado—a leader must provide drama. The romantic character of Latin American politics (like that in Spain and Portugal) prevents these countries from extricating themselves from the culture of European feudalism.

Thus instability and dictatorship are part and parcel of Latin American politics; but the more things changed the more they remained the same.

The Mexican Revolution

Prior to the Cuban Revolution, there had been only one genuine social revolution in Latin America: the revolution in Mexico that started in 1911 and, over a period of twenty years, led to substantial reforms, including land redistribution, the expropriation of American oil companies, and the strict regimentation of foreign investments according to which some businesses and enterprises were closed to foreign investments, others were open on a limited basis, and still others were free from limitations. The expropriation of American oil holdings and Mexico's restricted investment policies created an antagonism on the part of the United States toward Mexico that was not very different from the attitude displayed toward Cuba today. Subsequently Mexican society became fairly conservative, and American-Mexican relations are now cordial.

Castro

In 1953, when Fidel Castro (1926–   ) initiated the revolution that was to bring him to power, Cuba was ruled by a dictator, Fulgencio Batista, an ex-sergeant who had been president between 1940 and 1944 and who had regained power in 1952 through a *coup d'état.* Castro, who came from a well-to-do family, seemed to have been imbued with a deep sense of justice early in his life. At the age of thirteen he encouraged his father's employees to protest their wages and working conditions. Later, he attended the University of Havana, which was a hotbed of nationalism and antiimperialism, and became part of a bizarre enterprise to overthrow Rafael Trujillo of the Dominican Republic. This attempt was a failure, and Castro ended up swimming back to Cuba across the shark-infested Nipe Bay. At the university, Castro was also drawn into innumerable political and ideological squabbles. Some of the students had embraced communism; others were ardent nationalists with some communist leanings. Castro at that time belonged to the latter group, and it can be assumed that the discipline of being a communist did not appeal to a person of his temperament. It was less his politics than his personality that made him outstanding at the university; he showed qualities of leadership and possessed a great gift of oratory. In 1948 he was made president of the law school student body.

On graduation, he took up the practice of law, and was more concerned with helping poor people gain justice than with the remuneration he would receive. Living on a small allowance from his father, he dabbled in politics, but emerged as a prominent political figure when Batista carried out his *coup.*

Incensed at Batista's action, Castro prepared a legal brief accusing him of a breach of the constitution and the usurpation of power. When he saw that legal action was of no avail, he organized an attack on Ft. Moncada and an army depot at Bayamo. The idea was to attack the fort at dawn, taking the 10,000 soldiers by surprise, and to seize the radio station in order to call the people to support the revolutionary movement against Batista's dictatorship. On July 26, 1953 (which the Castroites consider to be the starting date of the Cuban Revolution), he led a group of 165 people against the fort. A dozen students were killed in the attack and a number were killed after their capture. Castro was among those captured. He was brought to trial on October 16, 1953, and used the trial as a forum to lash out against Batista. He and his brother Raoul were each sentenced to fifteen years in prison, but were amnestied in 1955.

After a trip to New York, Castro went to Mexico, where he established a headquarters for recruiting an expeditionary corps to invida Cuba. While in Mexico, he met Ernesto ("Che") Guevara (1928–67), who came from a prosperous Argentinian family and who had received a medical degree in 1953. Che at first decided to work among the Latin American Indians in Mexico, whose misery he had taken to heart, but seems to have been too restless to make medicine his career. In 1953 he went to Guatemala, and later back to Mexico, where he met Castro for the first time in July or August, 1955.

The invasion of Cuba in 1956, led by the two Castro brothers and Che Guevara, was unsuccessful. Most of the invaders were killed by strafing airplanes; but the two Castros, Guevara, and a few others survived and took refuge in the Sierra Maestra Mountains. Castro and his associates raised guerrilla forces among the peasants of the area and established links with middle-class supporters in the cities whose aim was the overthrow of the Batista regime and the establishment of constitutional government. The Communist Party did not support Castro at that time. It had cooperated with Batista all along, and had denounced Castro's attack on the military camps in 1953:

We repudiate the putschist method, peculiar to bourgeois political factions, of the action in Santiage de Cuba and Bayamo, which was an adventuristic attempt to take both military headquarters. The heroism displayed by the participants in the action is false and sterile, as it is guided by mistaken bourgeois conceptions.[7]

The relationship between Castro and the workers of Havana was rather tenuous; they were by and large indifferent to his movement.

(As late as April, 1958, when Castro issued a call for a general strike, there was little response and the strike proved to be a fiasco.) The cool attitude of the workers during his years in the Sierra Maestra caused Castro to revise his thinking. He had previously assumed that the decisive blows would come from the workers, but he had to revise his strategy and give the central place to guerrilla warfare.

In the end it was the disintegration of the Batista regime which enabled Castro to take Havana in December, 1958. Army commanders and officers had begun to desert Batista during the final months of 1958, and this led Batista to the decision to quit. He left Cuba with a small group of his top lieutenants for a pleasant retirement in Portugal, abandoning the smaller fry to face Castro's firing squads.

Castroism

Castro the flamboyant, romantic hero is central to Castroism. He captured the imagination of many Cubans who by and large were not quite sure of what he stood for programatically. Indeed, all the evidence indicates that even Castro himself was not sure of what course he would pursue once he gained power. In December, 1961, he declared himself a "Marxist-Leninist," which led some to think that that had been his position all along but that he had, for tactical reasons, covered it up. But his past statements concerning communism show otherwise. In April, 1959, Castro lumped fascism, Peronism, and communism together as different forms of totalitarianism. In May, 1959, he referred to communism as a system "which solves the economic problem, but which suppresses liberties, liberties which are so dear to man and which I know the Cuban people feel." [8]

His testimony at his trial in 1953, that after being edited and reworked during his imprisonment was published as *History Will Absolve Me,* contains a program to which every liberal in Cuba could have subscribed. Similarly, his manifesto and the program of the 26th of July Movement, issued in 1957, while more radical than *History Will Absolve Me,* could find ready acceptance by any noncommunist radical. "The Declaration of the Sierra Maestra" stated that the 26th of July Movement was "fighting for the beautiful idea of a Free Cuba, democratic and just," basing itself on the constitution of 1940, and having a leadership that has emerged from genuinely free elections. The declaration went on to call for the unity of all groups opposed to Batista. It advocated land reform, a planned economy, and in a veiled form the government control of all natural resources, credit facilities, and means of transportation.[9]

This program clearly explains why Castro found such broad support and, at the same time, why the Cuban communists were not particularly enthusiastic about Castro. His program appeared to them bourgeois and his tactics romantic. In the summer of 1958 they sent a few of their followers to join him in the mountains, but it was not until after his victory that Castro decreed a fusion between the communists and his own movement, which contained both procommunists (of whom the most outstanding was Che Guevara) and democratic revolutionaries. At some point, he had to make a choice between communism and a noncommunist radicalism. In late October, 1959, quite some time after he had emerged as the leader of Cuba, Castro decided to take the procommunist road. Once Castro declared himself a Marxist-Leninist, his program for Cuba was no longer in doubt; it would encompass the usual collectivization of land, nationalization of industry, and economic planning, all imposed from above by a self-appointed leadership.

But the real significance of Castroism lies not in the social and economic reforms but in his tactics, and in the extent to which they lend themselves to a more generalized application for other areas. Castro's tactics, as they ultimately evolved, rested on guerrilla warfare as the catalyst of revolution. It was Che Guevara, however, who, drawing on his observations of Castro's genius, synthesized these tactics into a theory.

Che Guevara on Guerrilla Warfare

Guevara's espousal of guerrilla warfare implied more than a tactic; it contained a revolutionary theory. In *Guerrilla Warfare* he wrote:

The armed victory of the Cuban People has been a modifier of old dogmas about the conduct of the popular masses of Latin America, and has clearly demonstrated the capacity of people to free themselves by means of guerrilla warfare from a government that oppresses them.

We consider that these are the three fundamental contributions which the Cuban Revolution has made to the conduct of the revolutionary movements in America.

(1) Popular forces can win a war against the army.

(2) It is not always necessary to wait for all the conditions for a

revolution to exist; the insurrectional focal point can create them.

(3) *In underdeveloped America, the countryside must be fundamentally the locale of the armed struggle.*[10]

Points 1 and 3 are hardly original; they are part of Mao Tse-tung's theory (though Guevara maintained that the Cuban revolutionaries pursued their course without knowledge of or reference to Mao). Point 2 is crucial because Guevara is saying that one creates a revolutionary situation simply by engaging in revolution. In his address to the Tri-Continental Conference in January, 1966, Castro put it this way: "The duty of every revolutionary is to effect the revolution, and effect it in deed, not in word."

As Theodore Draper has pointed out, Guevara did not derive guerrilla warfare from the nature of an agrarian revolution. His central concept was guerrilla warfare, and the role of the peasantry follows from it for technical or pragmatic reasons.[11] Thus it is the revolutionary will that counts; analyzing a situation in terms of objective conditions is a form of escapism. Revolutionary action in Latin America means forming guerrilla bands, and very few are needed to undermine a government. Of course, there is no guarantee of success; whether one will be successful or not can be known only after one has tried.

These thoughts on guerrilla warfare were aptly summarized by Castro in his introduction to the published version of Guevara's diary: *

From Che's diary it is possible to gather how real the possibilities of success were and how extraordinary the catalyzing power of the guerrilla was. On a certain occasion, in the light of the weakening and rapid deterioration of the Bolivian regime, he said, "The government is disintegrating rapidly; it is a pity we don't have 100 more men right now."

Che knew from his experience in Cuba how often our small guerrilla detachment was on the verge of being extinguished. This could have occurred because of the likelihood of the hazards and imponderabilities of war, but, if we had indeed been extinguished, would it have given the right to anybody to consider our line erroneous or to

* Che left Cuba in the spring of 1965 to organize a guerrilla movement in Bolivia for the overthrow of the Bolivian regime; he was captured and killed in October, 1967.

use this as an example to discourage the revolution and to instill impotency in the people? Many times in history the revolutionary processes have been preceded by adverse episodes! . . .

In all ages and under all circumstances there will always exist abundant reasons not to fight, but that will be the only way not to obtain liberty. Che did not outlive his ideas, but he fecundated them with his own blood. With all certainty the pseudorevolutionary critics with their political cowardice and their eternal lack of action will survive to evidence their own stupidity.[12]

The pseudorevolutionaries of whom Castro speaks are none other than the regular communist parties of Latin America. These parties, which are dominated by Moscow, have always condemned adventurism and reliance on guerrillas and the peasantry as the initial and main revolutionary force. According to them,

Latin America is in the throes of a "democratic revolution" led by the progressive bourgeoisie and its parties against U.S. imperialism and the "feudal" landowners. This "national democratic" revolution is in the first of two stages, to be followed at some undisclosed date by the "socialist" revolution. The immediate task is the formation of of middle class–led popular front governments. In practical terms, this means to support the electoral aspirations of middle class parties.[13]

Whatever merits (from the standpoint of drastic change) the policies of these communist parties may have, none of their leaders has been able to capture the imagination of the people of Latin America in the same way as Castro and Guevara have. Indeed, Guevara has become a legend. Romantic though he was, he was at the same time capable of detachment and introspection, as these words written in a letter to his parents testify:

Nothing has changed in essence, except that I am much more aware, my Marxism has taken root and become purified. I believe in the armed struggle as the only solution for those peoples who fight to free themselves, and I am consistent with my beliefs. Many will call me an adventurer—and that I am, only, one of a different sort—one of those who risks his skin to prove his platitudes.[14]

Castroism Within the Communist Movement

Castro came into the communist movement from "the outside" and was never subject to its discipline; even fusion of his movement with the Cuban Communist Party was effected on his terms. Nothing in his personality or actions indicates that Castro can be expected to toe anybody's line. However, he was convinced that once he declared himself a Marxist-Leninist he had the prestige and support of the Soviet Union committed under all circumstances. The withdrawal of the Soviet missiles in 1962 without his consent was a hard blow to this assumption, and even more so to his ego. Castro saw this as typical behavior of a great power. He was also annoyed that the Soviet Union continued to support what he considered to be conservative communist parties (especially in Latin America) and to make economic agreements with the very same Latin American governments to whose overthrow he was committed. And though his tactical commitment might have drawn him closer to China, he also came to see Chinese behavior as another form of great power chauvinism.

To Castro's mind, the very existence of powerful and weak communist countries was bound to lead to a situation where the weak would become mere instruments for achieving the purposes of the strong. To meet this danger, he proposed an international organization of small communist countries, including nonruling communist parties and other radical groupings in the underdeveloped world, that would be committed to his strategy of armed struggle against imperialism. This struggle, to be directed primarily against the United States, would have to be waged in a number of countries, and it should not be hampered by conflicts with the interests of either the Soviet Union or China. In January, 1966, Castro convened the Tri-Continental Peoples' Solidarity Conference at Havana, which was attended by governmental delegations from communist countries and a number of African countries, by delegations from many nonruling communist parties, and by radical groups of a wide variety. The conference pointedly refused to be drawn into the Sino-Soviet conflict, which was made to appear as completely irrelevant to its concerns. It adopted a program of armed struggle against imperialism, linked social revolution with national liberation, and expressed its support of wars of national liberation.

As of late Castro has played down the issue of guerrilla warfare in Latin America. Whether this is only a temporary position or represents a definite trend toward moderation is as yet difficult to say.

NOTES

1. Julius Nyerere, "One-Party Rule," in *The Ideologies of Developing Nations,* ed. Paul E. Sigmund, Jr. (New York: Praeger, 1963), pp. 197–98.

2. *Ibid.,* p. 200.

3. Madeira Keita, "Le Parti Unique en Afrique," in *ibid.,* pp. 178–79.

4. *Ibid.,* p. 180.

5. U.S. Department of Commerce, *Investment in Cuba: Basic Information for United States Businessmen* (Washington, D.C.: Government Printing Office, 1956), p. 21.

6. Quoted in *The Revolution in World Politics,* ed. Morton A. Kaplan (New York: Wiley, 1962), p. 116.

7. Quoted in Robert Scheer and Maurice Zeitlin, *Cuba: Tragedy in Our Hemisphere* (New York: Grove Press, 1963), p. 126.

8. Quoted in Theodore Draper, *Castroism: Theory and Practice* (New York: Praeger, 1965), p. 37.

9. See Loree Wilkerson, *Fidel Castro's Political Programs from Reformism to "Marxism Leninism,"* Latin American Monographs, Second Series (Gainesville, Fla.: University of Florida Press, 1965), pp. 38–42.

10. Ernesto ("Che") Guevara, *Guerrilla Warfare,* tr. J. P. Morray (New York: Monthly Review Press, 1961).

11. Draper, *op cit.,* p. 67.

12. Fidel Castro, "A Necessary Introduction," *Ramparts* (July 27, 1968), pp. 5–6.

13. James Petras, "Guerrilla Movements in Latin America," *New Politics,* Vol. VI, No. 2 (Spring 1967), p. 64.

14. Ernesto ("Che") Guevara, *Reminiscences of the Cuban Revolutionary War,* tr. Victoria Ortiz (New York: Monthly Review Press, 1968), p. 286.

CHAPTER TWELVE

THE REVOLUTION AGAINST AUTHORITARIANISM

REVISIONISM IN THE SOVIET UNION

Revisionism can mean three different things: (1) de-Stalinization and constitutionalization within an established communist one-party system; (2) a critique of such a system, with either the implicit or explicit intention of changing it; or (3) rethinking of the whole meaning of communism, particularly as it bears on the role of the individual (Neo-Marxism). This division follows the lines of actual developments in the Eastern European countries and the Western European communist parties. Philosophically, of course, there is an interrelationship among the three, chiefly between (2) and (3).

In line with our concern to examine ideological forces within their specific settings, we will discuss de-Stalinization and its practical ramifications in the Soviet Union, and then we will treat revisionism outside the Soviet Union—again in relationship to its political contexts. Neo-Marxism, however, will be discussed in the next chapter, since the issues it raises go beyond the others involved in revisionism.

De-Stalinization

De-Stalinization in the Soviet Union was a result of the need for change within Soviet society, various international developments, and the personal experiences of Stalin's associates. Even aside from humanitarian considerations, Stalin's methods, once the development of the Soviet Union had reached a certain level, became completely counterproductive. Terror may work as an incentive where social tasks are simple, but not when advances depend on the release of creative energies. Centralization of the economy may make sense when talent is scarce, but it hinders further development unless there is scope for creative decision-making on lower levels. Also, the development of atomic weapons made it clear that certain doctrinal positions would have to be redefined; other developments in the international field also called for new ideological interpretations. Finally, the widespread terror experienced even by Stalin's close associates must have created an urgent demand for introducing some constitutionalism into the Soviet system—at least to the degree that a person who lost his political power would not also lose his head.

De-Stalinization was introduced by Nikita S. Khrushchev (1894–1971) at the Twentieth Party Congress (1956) in his "secret" speech that detailed the crimes of Stalin, and was expressed in the program he submitted to the congress. In essence, these are the main points Khrushchev made: (1) war between capitalism and communism is no longer inevitable, and therefore international relations should be based on peaceful coexistence; (2) there are different roads toward socialism, but it is necessary to have a center for the international movement; (3) national liberation movements in the colonial and semicolonial countries should be supported by the Soviet Union even though they are not under communist control; (4) communism will triumph over capitalism as the result of communism's winning the economic competition.

More specifically, on the problem of war between capitalist and communist countries, Khrushchev said,

There is, of course, a Marxist-Leninist precept that wars are inevitable as long as imperialism exists. This precept was evolved at a time when 1) imperialism was an all-embracing world system, and 2) the social and political forces which did not want war were weak, poorly organized, and hence unable to compel the imperialists to renounce war.

People usually take only one aspect of the question and examine only the economic basis of wars under imperialism. This is not enough. War is not only an economic phenomenon. Whether there is to be a war or not depends in large measure on the correlation of class, political forces, the degree of organization and the awareness and resolve of the people.[1]

Nevertheless, the policy of peaceful coexistence does not apply in the ideological sphere:

We cannot pass by the fact that some people are trying to apply the absolutely correct thesis of the possibility of peaceful co-existence of countries with different social and political systems to the ideological sphere. . . . It does not at all follow from the fact that we stand for peaceful co-existence and economic competition with capitalism, that the struggle against bourgeois ideology, against the survivals of capitalism in the minds of men, can be relaxed.[2]

The ideologists of the bourgeoisie distort the facts and deliberately confuse questions of ideological struggle with questions of relations between states in order to make the Communists of the Soviet Union look like advocates of aggression.[3]

It is untrue, Khrushchev asserted, that the communist road to victory leads through violence and civil war. It is possible for the working class in a number of capitalist countries to get the overwhelming majority of people behind it, to capture stable majorities in parliaments, and to transform the latter from organs of class into instruments of the popular will. In these efforts, communists should seek the cooperation of social democrats. But if peaceful roads should be precluded, violence continues to be legitimate.

Khrushchev also proposed to extend support to national liberation movements in the form of economic assistance:

These countries, although they do not belong to the socialist world system, can draw on its achievements to build up an independent national economy and to raise the living standards of their peoples. Today they need not go begging for up-to-date equipment to their former oppressors. They can get it in the socialist countries, without assuming any political or military commitments.[4]

While on the surface the support to be given these countries seemed to be the result of socialist-humanitarian considerations, the real motivation was the extension of Soviet influence and the undermining of the economy of the West by contracting its scope and opportunities. The neat Stalinist division of the world along the line of "who is not for us is against us" was abandoned by Khrushchev. (China, in contrast, contended that giving aid to nonsocialist regimes would only strengthen capitalism.) Khrushchev saw the victory of communism as resulting from the Soviet Union's overtaking the United States in economic competition. In his speech before the Twenty-first Party Congress in 1959, he reckoned that by 1972 the Soviet Union would have overtaken the United States in per capita production of industrial commodities. In the last few years, however, nothing has been heard of this boast.

But one difficult problem remained. If communists were to accept the thesis that there are different roads toward socialism, how could the world communist movement be unified or coordinated?

And what authority should the Soviet Union exert in international communism? These questions became acute after the revelations made at the Twentieth Party Congress resulted in a great ferment that culminated in the Polish and Hungarian uprisings in the fall of 1956.

A meeting of twelve ruling communist parties was convened in 1957 and addressed itself to these issues. The declaration adopted at the meeting spoke of a "socialist commonwealth of nations." It accepted the sovereignty of socialist nations but emphasized that their relationship also involves special obligations. The Soviet Union was recognized as heading the communist camp. Thus, Khrushchev was willing to let each communist party have sufficient flexibility to be optimally successful within its own setting, but at the same time he maintained the Soviet Union's preeminent position for purposes of coordination. In a way, this would have meant the internationalization of communism—that is, communism abroad would cease to be a mere extension of Soviet foreign policy. We will discuss the outcome of this approach in a different context later on in this chapter.

The Political Aspects of De-Stalinization

One of the earliest effects of de-Stalinization on the party was a devolution of power. As we observed earlier, the rise of Stalin had involved a number of substitutions (the proletariat for the people, the party for the proletariat, the Central Committee for the party, the Politburo for the Central Committee, and finally Stalin for the Politburo), but the devolution from single-person rule to a collegial rule was incomplete while Khrushchev was still in power. Combining the positions of first secretary of the Central Committee and chairman of the Council of Ministers, together with his unique personality, Khrushchev was able to dominate the entire Soviet apparatus. It was only with his displacement in 1964 that collegial rule within the party seems to have emerged. The Politburo now seems to be the real policy-making body, and the Central Committee has become something more than a rubber stamp.

An attempt to democratize the party was made at the Twenty-second Party Congress in 1961, which adopted new party statutes that provided for a membership turnover in all party bodies according to a rigid formula. These specific statutes were abolished at the Twenty-third Party Congress (1966), but the turnover principle was retained.

In the political decision-making process, the government hierarchy has assumed greater significance. While top policy decisions continue to be made by the party (and there is still a link at the top between government and party in that Kosygin is both Prime Minister and a member of the Politburo) the implementation of decisions is increasingly left to the government agencies, which in essence means an accretion of power to the experts. If constitutionalization involves a dispersal of power, the increased role of the government agencies must be viewed as significant.

A new theory of government is also important for the process of constitutionalization. Instead of being defined as a dictatorship of the proletariat, the government of the Soviet Union is now defined as the government of the whole people. Thus to the extent that socio-economic classes disappear and socialism makes progress, the co-ercive aspects of the state can be lessened and its educative aspects can assume greater significance. In contrast, Stalin contended that the bourgeois remnants within Soviet society, powerfully supported by subversion from abroad, become more desperate as socialism pro-gresses, and hence the coercive character of the state has to increase. This theory, of course, was used to support Stalin's use of terror.

At present, there is no evidence or contention that the state is withering away, but in the long run, when Soviet society moves into the stage of communism, the role of the state vis-à-vis the party is supposed to decline. When the stage of communism has been reached and all of the socialist values will have been fully internalized, the spirit of fraternity—as represented by the party—will guide the people's further destinies. In asserting the permanence of the party, the Soviet party leadership can also continue to assert its own pre-eminence.

The Party is the brain, the honor and the conscience of our epoch. . . .

The period of full-scale communist construction is characterized by a further enhancement of the role and importance of the Communist Party *as the leading and guiding force of Soviet society.*[5]

Public functions similar to those performed by the state today . . . will be preserved under communism. . . . But the character of the functions and the ways in which they are carried out will be different from those under socialism. The bodies in charge of planning, ac-counting, economic management, and cultural advancement, now government bodies, will lose their political character and will become organs of public self-government.[6]

"Socialist Legality"

The post-Stalin period saw the restoration of "socialist legality," which is something akin to due process. As the massive and arbitrary terror of Stalin's time disappeared, the power of the secret police to "try" people and send them to labor camps was eliminated; these prisoners were released and the special labor camps abolished. Criminal procedure is now based on establishing objective truth (as opposed to the earlier principle of "maximum probability"), the presumption of innocence until one is proved guilty, the abolition of the principle of "crime by analogy" (by which a person could be condemned even though his action was not covered by a specific statute), the limited character of confession as evidence,* the acceptance of the role of defense counsels as responsible to defendants (rather than as "aides" to the court), and the limitation of detention before trial.

Although the existence of these legal safeguards does not mean that they are necessarily observed in practice, they provide a basis for appeal in cases in which they are ignored. When these principles were violated during the trials of a number of writers and intellectuals between 1966 and 1968, widespread criticism of the procedures was made in the Soviet Union and protesting letters and petitions were sent to the authorities. In addition to complaints about the violation of procedural safeguards, there have also been complaints about parts of the Criminal Code that still greatly limit the freedom of citizens.

Thus the Soviet Union of 1971 is not the Soviet Union of 1937, when the great purges and show trials took place and arbitrary terror was the order of the day. The country is still far removed from constitutionalism, however.

Economic Reforms

Industry Economic reforms in the industrial sector were promulgated in 1965 as a result of suggestions by a number of Soviet econ-

* "Confession is one form of evidence, which like any other form is subject to the most painstaking verification by means of a thorough investigation of all the rest. The confession of the defendant cannot, therefore, be taken as conclusive proof for handing down a verdict of guilty" (Soviet source quoted in Stephen Weiner, "Socialist Legality on Trial," *Problems of Communism,* Vol. XVII [July–August 1968], p. 11).

omists (among whom a Kharkov professor of economics, Y. G. Liberman, became most prominent). The essence of these reforms is the switch from a "command" economy to what is called a socialist market economy, which involves a less rigid type of central planning and a shift in emphasis from exceeding quotas to profitability. (The deemphasis on quantity is a result of the fact that the Soviet economy has reached a level of production where its main emphasis can be on efficiency. Up to now, it operated as a "crisis" or "siege" economy.)

The new system also makes it necessary for enterprises to satisfy their customers. Under the old system, whatever was produced was "sold": if items were not sold by the state stores, the state purchasing organization "purchased" them as a matter of course, even if the commodities rotted in its warehouses. The new arrangement orients production toward quality, particularly in the consumer field.

The old emphasis on quantity not only led to the production of shoddy goods, but also created an uneconomical incentive system. Since bonuses were based on exceeding production assignments, managers tried to get low assignments, used excess labor, and squandered raw material. With the shift to an emphasis on profitability, these abuses are bound to disappear. The new profit incentive derives from the fact that all the above-plan profit can be retained by the individual enterprises for use in expansion, bonuses for workers and employees, and general improvements in their social and cultural facilities. Accompanying this shift in emphasis has been the cost-accounting of capital. Under the old system, capital was more or less arbitrarily allotted to enterprises by the ministries, with the result that enterprises hoarded machines that would not be used or were underused, and concerned themselves little about their upkeep. Under the new system enterprises have to pay interest for the capital goods they receive.

Under the new system, the power of management has also increased, so that, within the broad targets set by the planners, it can make all the necessary production decisions. For example, it has complete freedom in determining the assortment of goods produced. The Soviet system maintains the one-man responsibility of the manager. He is supposed to consult the trade union representatives at the plant, but there are no workers' councils.

Agriculture Economic reform also extended to agriculture. The income of collectives has been increased because the state now pays higher prices for their commodities. The same social services that are provided for industrial workers are now available to collective farmers. Peasants on the collective farms now receive minimum monthly wages each month and if the year-end receipts from the sale of produce do not cover the outlay in wages, a collective can borrow money from the banks to make up the deficit. Collective farms also have greater latitude in determining what they will plant. Furthermore, the private plots have been enlarged in size, and, under a new arrangement, small groups of peasants are given a tract of land, told what to sow, and then left to their own devices in maximizing production.

Finally, the state farms have been brought under a profit scheme that is similar to industry's. Previously, the *sovkhoz* was indifferent to whether it made a profit or had a loss: profits were taken by the state and losses were made up by a state subsidy. Now, however, their workers do not get bonuses and the farms do not get investment funds if they fail to make a profit.

Sources of Change in Soviet Society

Change in Soviet society is a result of three separate forces: the decentralization of the economy, the Soviet intelligentsia, and Soviet youth. The command economy had viewed Soviet society as a unit; there was no scope for particular purposes, and a complete identity of interests on all levels of society was assumed. The decentralization of the economy, in contrast, has introduced clusters of particular interests, and the role of the government is to harmonize these interests in some form or other. In short, economic decentralization has given rise to something akin to pluralism.

The role of the Soviet intelligentsia has become very similar to that of the Russian intelligentsia in the nineteenth century; in both cases the fight has been against a narrow-minded autocratic system. The tug-of-war that has been waged between the party and the intelligentsia for a number of years has had its ups and downs, but over a long period of time there is no doubt that the system has yielded on many important points, also in large part because of the attitudes of a number of communist intellectuals in the Western countries.

Criticism of the Soviet system is now possible if it takes the form of an attack on Stalinism and if its spirit is "positive" and "constructive." Obviously, these limits are rather flexible, so that a writer may nevertheless run afoul of the system, be unable to have his work published, or be reprimanded; but as long as he operates aboveboard he will not be criminally prosecuted. If, however, a writer circulates a manuscript secretly, uses a pseudonym, or has his work smuggled to the West and printed by a "bourgeois" publisher, he is liable to prosecution. A gray area surrounds a writer whose work is refused publication in the Soviet Union but is published abroad by a communist publishing house; the chances are, however, that he will not be held criminally responsible.

The third force for change is Soviet youth. Though the party vehemently denies that there is a generation gap, there is no doubt that Soviet youth is rather uninterested in ideology (though this does not mean that they are not believers in communism or that they are not proud Soviet citizens). The Soviet young person is interested both in a career and in the special interests of the educated, such as art, literature, and music. Soviet youths also have a greater *joie de vivre* than their elders, and Western fads and styles have made inroads among them. After many years of austerity, there is a desire not only among youth but also among the older generation for beauty, modern conveniences, and cars. These are some of the sources of "embourgeoisement" that visitors to the Soviet Union must readily notice.

REVISIONISM OUTSIDE THE SOVIET UNION

Yugoslavia

The Soviet-Yugoslav break in 1948 planted the seeds of revisionism in Eastern Europe, although the doctrinal differences that were advanced to rationalize Yugoslav policies were not developed until after the break had occurred. However, the Yugoslav leaders seem to have persuaded themselves that ideological differences were the cause of their conflict with the Soviet Union. Obviously, people do not like to think that their ideological originality was the result of political necessity and a combination of circumstances.

The Yugoslav communists, having made their own revolution, saw no reason why they should be treated, as Stalin intended, as a satellite country whose communist regime had been imposed by the Soviet army. Furthermore, Marshal Tito (1892–) was a strong-willed, independent leader who refused to take orders from Stalin. But the evolution of Yugoslav communism was a tortuous process, and if the break with the Soviet Union was to be doctrinally legitimized, the first step was to redefine the relationship between communist parties and the Soviet Union.

It was maintained that so long as the Soviet Union had been the only communist state, outside communist parties had to subordinate themselves to the needs of the Soviet Union; but the moment a number of other communist states arose, the relationship with the Soviet Union had to be one of equality and independence. Individual communist states had to guard their independence carefully even in relationship to fellow communist states, for the strong ones might be tempted to assert hegemonic claims. But the Yugoslavs ascribed the Soviet Union's unjust actions vis-à-vis Yugoslavia to a deeper flaw —to a fundamental perversion: the Soviet system had ceased to be socialist and had become "state capitalist." The party and the bureaucracy had set themselves up as overlords over the people.

After a revolution, they conceded, there is need for a strong state apparatus to guard against counterrevolution and to reorganize society and the economy; but once these tasks have been fulfilled the state apparatus should become increasingly responsive to the people, and in the end must belong to the people and not be its master. In the Soviet Union, the very opposite had happened; the party and the bureaucracy became independent of the people—independent social forces following their own laws of social development. At one point the Yugoslavs even compared communism to fascism. It was said that fascism emerges when the bourgeoisie is no longer strong enough to hold power and the working class is still too weak to gain it; the fascist dictator then emerges as a savior and, in the name of national unity, oppresses the people. In the Soviet form of communism, the proletariat is too weak and backward to hold the power it has gained; the party and the bureaucracy theoretically rule on behalf of the proletariat, but in reality place themselves above it. The cult of the personality is an inevitable result of such a development. The state, and even the Communist Party, must be allowed to wither away, according to the Yugoslavs, if the danger of centralist bureaucracy is to be avoided.

The Yugoslavs also asserted that communist parties have no monopoly on the building of socialism. They saw no reason for maintaining a rigid division between the capitalist and the noncapitalist worlds with the attendant tensions of competing power blocs. They saw the tendency toward state capitalism in capitalist states as proof that mankind is moving inevitably into the era of socialism.

All these points were summarized and authoritatively stated early in 1958 in the program of the League of Yugoslav Communists, which drew the ideological battle line between the Soviet Union and

Yugoslavia. In April, 1958, in answer to the program, the Soviet theoretical magazine *Kommunist* charged that international tensions are not the result of competing power blocs but are due exclusively to the existence of imperialism and imperialist countries. Furthermore, it is impossible for state capitalism to transform itself into socialism, and it is false to say that a state apparatus can rise above class interests. Bureaucracy is therefore a false issue. The dominant concern of socialists must be the overthrow of capitalism, and the transition to socialism must be revolutionary, though not necessarily violent. Nor is the withering away of the state an immediate or realistic issue, since it presupposes the disappearance of classes on a worldwide basis and the merger of nations. The Yugoslavs' position was incongruous because they advocated the withering away of the state but, in the same breath, insisted on the need for autonomy in the relationship among socialist states, which presupposes the existence of states.

Kommunist went on to assert that, by definition, it is impossible for one communist state to exploit another. Under certain circumstances, however, the interests of the proletarian struggle in one country may have to be subordinated to such interests on a worldwide scale. Thus the leading role of the Soviet Communist Party is not the result of subjective desire but objective conditions. It was history that made the Soviet Union the first socialist country.

The ideological battle between the Soviet Union and Yugoslavia has not been characterized by constant warfare; periods of cold war have been followed by spells of warm relations. Depending on the state of Soviet-Yugoslav relations, ideological differences are either emphasized or toned down, points that are particularly obnoxious to either country are either stressed or passed over in silence. But the end result has been two forms of communism that are far removed from each other.

Yugoslavia's Economic Reforms Yugoslavia's economic organization, in line with Yugoslavia's divergences from the Soviet line, is based on the self-management of individual enterprises, the curtailment of government investment in setting up new plants, the elimination of nonprofitable businesses, and the influencing of the economy by the government through credit policies rather than through strict planning. Each enterprise has a juridical personality similar to that of corporations in the West, and is run by a workers' council that appoints all members of management—but to what degree this model is followed in practice is difficult to say. To what extent management, once in office, develops a staying power all its own (similar to corporate managements in the West) is also an interesting question.

Enterprises deal with each other strictly on a market basis. The sources for financing operations and expansion are profits, bank loans, and (mostly recently) bond isues. A recent innovation permits partnerships with foreign businesses, which are run by joint boards of directors.

The influence of the government, as we have indicated, is exercised through credit policies; the government may instruct the state bank to facilitate loans to industries whose expansion is considered in the national interest and to restrict loans to other industries that are less important. The most prevalent mechanism of effecting these policies is differential interest rates.

The workers' councils decide what compensation will accrue to workers on the basis of profit and the desired allocation between wages and investments. However, great differences in profitability in different factories and the limited labor mobility lead to great differences in wages among people doing the same kind of job. And rather than hire new people for expanding production, the workers' councils too often let the regulars work overtime.

Perhaps the chief problem in the economic decentralization of Yugoslavia is the uneven economic levels of different parts of the country. Since direct investment by the government has been greatly curtailed, the only way to develop the underdeveloped regions is to entice successful enterprises to invest in underdeveloped sections by granting incentives. However, it is questionable, from the standpoint of purely economic rationality, whether such investments are truly attractive.

Liberalization, economic decentralization, and the introduction of a market economy have also oriented the Yugoslavs toward concentration on consumer goods. They have a wide range of choice of consumer items, and there are no limitations on what a person can buy with his own money. Obviously, this development entails a shift from social concerns to individual satisfaction.

Party and State The most interesting characteristic of the Yugoslav Communist Party is its national decentralization, especially since Yugoslavia is composed of six republics reflecting its major nationalities. Their relationships have always been far from harmonious. The national party is at present only a confederation of the parties of the six republics, and thus it has relinquished one of the most important functions of a communist party in a multinational state: being a force for unity through its monolithic structure.

The whole meaning of the party has come under increasing scrutiny in Yugoslavia. In 1954 the maverick Milovan Djilas (1911–), at that time a Vice President of Yugoslavia, ran afoul of his colleagues for advocating the withering away of the Communist Party. He was subsequently tried and sent to prison, was amnestied, but again incurred the wrath of Tito, and was once more imprisoned until late 1966. His special target was the new class of communist functionaries, whom he criticized in his famous book *The New Class*. Djilas's thoughts are now widely discussed in Yugoslavia, and there is a tendency to shift more and more power from the Communist Party to the governmental organs. At the same time, there is a tendency to separate leadership of the party from leadership in government.

The electoral policies allow citizens to sponsor candidates for the various legislative bodies at local citizen meetings and the ballots carry more than one name for each post that is open. Whatever influence the party exerts in the choice of candidates is subtle and is designed to reflect the sentiments of the citizenry. The best illustration of change in Yugoslavia's political system was the resignation of the Prime Minister of Slovenia after a measure he had introduced in parliament received an adverse vote. This was the first time in the history of a communist country that a leader lost power as a direct result of the workings of a parliamentary system.

The most important current debate relates to internal party democracy; some members even go so far as to advocate the formation of factions within the party. Others question whether the Leninist conception of the party can have relevance once a socialist state has been established. Lenin's elitist party is needed during the time of class struggle, but later the party should become a party of the people, encompassing all strata of the population. Thus there is a tendency to juxtapose Lenin's conception of a cadre party and Marx's notion of a mass party.

Revisionism in Eastern Europe

Other developments in Eastern Europe after Stalin represent an interaction between the particular conditions and needs of individual countries and the power shifts in the Soviet Union. Change has not been continuous and regular; some countries have suddenly burst forth with reforms that surpassed those that other communist countries had inaugurated earlier. Different countries have also given different stress to particular aspects of development.

Liberalization occurred first in Poland, when a shift in power from the Stalinist wing to the Gomulka wing of the Communist Party took place. A plateau was soon reached, and today Poland is more or less in the backwaters of liberalization. Whether the fall of Wladyslaw Gomulka (1905–) in December, 1970, will bring substantial changes in this respect is still an open question.

While the 1956 upheaval in Poland involved only the transfer of power from one wing of the Communist Party to another, the Hungarian revolution in the same year involved a shift in power from communists to noncommunists, and eventually would have moved Hungary out of the Soviet orbit. The Hungarian revolution was crushed by Soviet tanks, and there was a period of repression, but ultimately Hungary was able to settle on a course of mild liberalization. The Hungarian parliament has ceased to be an abject rubber stamp. Ministers have to answer questions in parliament, and occasionally a minister's reply is rejected by the house.

Bulgaria's relations with the Soviet Union are the closest of all the communist countries for reasons that antedate the Bolshevik Revolution. Bulgarians have always had a feeling of kinship with the Russians, and it was Russian influence that liberated the Bulgars from the Turks in 1870. Reforms in Bulgaria have closely followed those in the Soviet Union.

Rumania is the maverick among the East European communist countries; its leadership is doctrinaire but it has pursued the most independent course vis-à-vis the Soviet Union of all the East European countries. A source of friction with the Soviet Union has been the unwillingness of Rumanian leaders to integrate their country in the economic system of East European communist countries. The Soviet Union has established a union similar to the European Economic Community, called the Council for Mutual Economic Cooperation (COMENCON), in order to coordinate planning in all East European countries and to devise programs of national specialization. Because only the Soviet Union would have continued to develop an all-around economy under this scheme, Rumania, though a member of COMENCON, has often challenged policies advocated by the Soviet Union. Next to Yugoslavia, Rumania has most strongly insisted on the sovereignty of communist countries. She has refused to condemn Red China and has constantly made difficulties when international communist conferences have tried to formulate guidelines for communist states.

Since East Germany is a creation of the Soviet Union, the close relationship of its leaders with the Soviet Union is axiomatic. In spirit, East Germany is the most communist country. Orthodoxy, discipline, and hard work are its hallmarks. East Germany has been most successful in its post-Stalinist economic reforms. With a population of only 18 million, it is the ninth-ranking industrial country in the world.

One of the most dramatic events in the liberalization movement in Eastern Europe was the Czech-Soviet confrontation in the summer of 1968, which represented the culmination of an intellectual and political fermentation that had gone on for several years. In cinematographic art, for example, Czechoslovakia had become avant garde; closer cultural relations had been established with the West; prewar cultural figures were restored to their former status; and Thomas Masaryk (1850–1937), the founder of the Czechoslovak state (who earlier had been vilified), was again given a hero's place of honor.

As part of the same process of fermentation, many Czechs advocated a more flexible interpretation of communist commitments. Greater emphasis was placed on the independence of the individual communist countries, and their need to define socialism in line with the conditions of their societies. The meaning of peaceful coexistence and the exact nature of the relationship between the socialist and the capitalist worlds were reconsidered. There was also greater questioning of the stereotypes of Western capitalism. Writers discussed the economic and technological successes of Western capitalist countries, and even went so far as to maintain that Marxist analysis was inadequate for understanding what was going on in the world. Spokesmen for the restoration of private enterprise ventured to the fore and made a case for privately owned service industries (especially restaurants and places of amusement). Some of them also advocated a return to private farming. Economic ties with the West, including West Germany, became stronger.

This groundswell in favor of change found political expression in a shake-up of the communist leadership. The liberal wing of the party, led by Alexander Dubcek, came into power. Dubcek was committed to a "communism with a human face," but he did not favor a break with the Soviet Union. Other forces, however, wanted to go the whole way.

By the spring of 1968, the demand for complete freedom of expression, the right of assembly, and independence from the Soviet Union was loud and clear. In July, a "Two-thousand-word Manifesto" was issued by a number of intellectuals, blaming the Communist Party of Czechoslovakia for all the ills that had befallen the country, but granting party leaders a period of grace to remedy the situation. The manifesto openly stated that it was not love for the party that made these intellectuals call on it for action but the absence of any other group that had the necessary organizational apparatus.

Alarmed by these developments, the Soviet leaders held meetings with the Czech leaders in attempting to stabilize the situation, but subsequent events did not satisfy the Soviets, and military intervention followed. The Soviet leadership was particularly concerned over the prospect of increased West German influence in Czechoslovakia, with its adverse effects on the stability of the East German regime and its repercussions in the rest of Eastern Europe.

If Czechoslovakia had been allowed to develop without intervention, the new trends would probably have led in internal affairs to the establishment of a multiparty system and a mixed economy, with the basic industries most probably remaining in the public sector.

Revisionism in the Western Communist Parties

During Stalin's lifetime the Italian and the French communist parties had followed the Moscow line (the French wholeheartedly, the Italians less so), but with the demise of Stalin the two parties pursued policies that were more meaningful within the context of their respective countries. The initiative was taken by the Italian Communist Party, under its leader Palmiro Togliatti (1893–1964).

After the Twentieth Party Congress, Togliatti took a middle course between those who maintained that Stalinism represented the aberration of an individual and those who blamed the structure of the Soviet Communist Party itself. Togliatti declared that the party structure was sound, but Stalin's aberration represented a flaw in leadership. It was from the top leadership, he contended, that the tendency arose

to restrict democratic life, initiative, and dynamic thought and action in numerous fields (technical and economic development, cultural ac-

tivity, literature, art, etc.), but it cannot be stated categorically that there has arisen from this the destruction of those fundamental features of Soviet society from which it derives its democratic and socialist character. . . .

I do not mean to say by this that the consequences of Stalin's errors were not extremely serious. They were very serious; they touched many fields, and I do not think it will be easy to overcome them, nor to do so quickly. In substance, it may be said that a large part of the leading cadres of Soviet society (Party, state, economy, culture, etc.) had become torpid in the cult of Stalin, losing or lessening its critical and creative ability in thought and action.[7]

Togliatti, surprisingly, was quite frank in accepting co-responsibility for what had happened in the Soviet Union.

As regards our "co-responsibility," of which so much is being said today by our adversaries . . . it has a political substance. It exists because we have accepted, without criticism, a fundamentally false position in regard to the inevitable exacerbation of the class struggle along with the progress of socialist society, a theory which was enunciated by Stalin and from which stemmed terrible violations of socialist legality. We also have a responsibility for having accepted, and for introducing into our propaganda, the cult of the person of Stalin. . . .[8]

In regard to the question of a single-party versus a multiparty system, Togliatti took the position that one or the other was not, by itself, a distinguishing element between bourgeois and socialist societies. While it was true that there was no reason to have a multiparty system in the Soviet Union, the situation in Italy was different, and the Italian Communist Party was fully prepared to operate within the Italian system and use only parliamentary means to exercise power. He also rejected the accusation that this commitment to democratic means was made in bad faith.

The most serious of . . . misunderstandings and reservations, in my opinion, was that which consisted . . . in considering that our affirmation of the democratic nature of our struggle for the alteration of Italian society was a sort of trick, something which we made use of in order to deceive the enemy or to overcome difficulties. . . .[9]

Of far-reaching consequences was Togliatti's restatement of the relationship between the Soviet Communist parties and the other parties, and his term *polycentrism* entered the vocabulary of communism and received almost universal currency. There was a time, Togliatti said, when the Soviet Communist Party had to make decisions that were valid for all communist parties, but this time was long past. Certainly the experiences of the Soviet Union are instructive, but they

cannot contain instructions for resolving all the questions which may present themselves today to us and to the Communists of other countries, whether in power or not. . . .

Thus various points or centers of development and orientation are established. There is established . . . a polycentric system, corresponding to the new situation, to the alteration in the world make-up and in the very structure of the workers' movements, and to this system correspond also new types of relations among the Communist parties themselves. The solution which today probably most nearly corresponds to this new situation may be that of the full autonomy of the individual Communist parties and of bilateral relations between them. . . .[10]

In achieving socialism in Italy, the Communist Party visualizes broad popular fronts composed of all progressive forces.

In countries with highly advanced capitalism . . . it may happen that the majority of the working class follows a non-Communist party, and we cannot rule out that even in these countries, parties which are not Communist but are founded in the working class can express the drive provided by the working class in the march to socialism. . . . The effort to carry out radical economic changes in the capitalist system, along lines which in general are those of socialism, can also originate, lastly, from movements which are not considered socialist.[11]

In the following years even more revisionist ideas were put forth. The party abrogated its atheistic commitment and took the position that there is no reason why communists and Catholics cannot cooperate.

At the Tenth Italian Party Congress in 1962, it had been suggested that a person no longer need be a Marxist to become a member of the party. At the same time, it was decided to democratize decision-making within the party by permitting free debate and dissent. In fact, the party has abandoned the principle of democratic centralism. Moreover, the Italian Communist Party expressed its opposition to the Soviet interventions in Hungary in 1956 and in Czechoslovakia in 1968. In summary, the Italian Communist Party has for all practical purposes ceased to be a communist party (as this term is strictly understood) and has become a left-wing socialist party.

Revisionism in the French Communist Party has been less clear cut than in the Italian party. At the time of Stalin's death in 1953, the French party was dominated by an old Stalinist, Maurice Thorez (1900–64), who refused to join in the anti-Stalinist outpourings of the Italian party. The political bureau of the French Communist Party put out the following statement on June 19, 1956:

Stalin played a positive role in a whole historic period. With other leaders of the Party, he took an active part in the October Socialist Revolution, then in the victorious struggle against foreign intervention and counterrevolution. After the death of Lenin, he fought against the adversaries of Marxism-Leninism and for the application of the Leninist plan for the construction of socialism. He contributed in great measure to the formation of all Communist Parties.

Stalin acquired a deserved prestige, which he allowed to be transformed into a cult of the individual. The development of this cult was facilitated by the position of the Soviet Union, for a long time exposed alone to the undertakings of a world of enemies. This necessitated an extreme test of the people's strength, an iron discipline, and strict centralization of power of the proletarian state. These circumstances help to explain the enormous difficulties the Soviet Union had to face, without justifying Stalin's activities, however.[12]

The French Communist Party had followed all the zig-zag changes of Soviet policy. Having denounced Tito in 1948, it hailed the mending of the Soviet-Yugoslav rift in 1956. Thorez also supported the Soviet intervention in Hungary in 1956, calling the Hungarian leader Imre Nagy a revisionist traitor. However, the party's rank and file did not support the intervention, many intellectuals left the party, and others who stayed began to publicly criticize the French leadership's slavish following of the Soviet line. Subsequently, the new climate forced Thorez to make some concessions. The French party even decided to reject the so-called Illechev thesis that made it mandatory for a communist to disavow religion.

After the death of Thorez in 1964, there was more give-and-take within the party. In the last few elections, the French Communist Party has been a strong advocate of a broad "front of the left." For the 1973 elections to the National Assembly the communists joined the socialists in the formulation of a common program and in the establishment of electoral alliances.

NOTES

1. Nikita S. Khrushchev, *Report of the Central Committee of the Communist Party of the Soviet Union to the 20th Party Congress, February 14, 1956* (Moscow: Foreign Languages Publishing House, 1956), p. 41.

2. *Ibid.*, p. 140.

3. *Ibid.*, pp. 39–40.

4. *Ibid.*, p. 27.

5. *Program of the Communist Party of the Soviet Union,* adopted by the 22nd Congress of the C.P.S.U., October 31, 1961 (New York: Crosscurrents Press, 1961), p. 137.

6. *Ibid.*

7. Palmiro Togliatti, "9 Domande sullo Stalismo," in *The Anti-Stalin Campaign and International Communism,* ed. The Russian Institute, Columbia University (New York: Columbia University Press, 1956), pp. 103–04.

8. Palmiro Togliatti, "Report to the Central Committee of the Italian Communist Party, June 24, 1956," in *ibid.*, p. 230.

9. *Ibid.*, p. 242.

10. *Ibid.*, p. 215.

11. *Ibid.*, p. 213.

12. "Statement of the Political Bureau of the French Communist Party," in *The Anti-Stalin Campaign and International Communism,* pp. 169–70.

CHAPTER THIRTEEN

THE REVOLUTION AGAINST ALIENATION

NEO-MARXISM

After de-Stalinization, a number of issues confronted thoughtful communists. For East European communists the issues were how to prevent communism from settling into a new rigidity and how to rehabilitate Marxism (to which they were committed) after its long identification with Stalinism. The solution was found in emphasizing the humanism of Marxism. By equating the process of humanization with the building of socialism, and by connecting this humanism with Marx, they could differentiate Marxism from Stalinism and make it serve a new order.

For West European communists an additional problem arose: how to build a new base for the transformation of capitalism given the fact that the West European working class had become conservative. In the Stalinist period, communists dogmatically asserted that the working class was a revolutionary force; but now they were free to view things more realistically. Committed to the notion that capitalism could not represent the ultimate in human development, they had to find a force other than the proletariat for bringing about the demise of capitalism.

Concern with the future of capitalism was not restricted, however, to communists; many socialists, and particularly left-wing socialists who had never yielded Marxism to the communists, looked to Marx for clues to the solution of problems they felt the capitalist welfare state was unable to cope with. In its most elementary form, the question was this: What accounts for the fact that man has become the mere object of forces beyond his control, and what is to be done to overcome this situation?

The search for an answer to this question among all these people—East European communists, West European communists, left-wing socialists—led to the movement that places Marx's humanism at the center of his thought and that has become known as *neo-Marxism*. The term is used to point up the shift in concern from

SHIFT FROM MARXISTS DIALECT MATERIALISM

Marxism's traditional emphasis, which has centered on Marx's dialectic materialism. Traditional Marxism had emphasized history as the gradual unfolding of higher forms of production relationships, higher cultural attainments as automatic concomitants of economic advances, and the proletariat as the carrier of progress. In other words, the downfall of capitalism would not result from spiritual problems to which it had given rise; its irrational economic contradictions would lead to its downfall.

Many of the concerns of neo-Marxism are shared by the New Left; but while the neo-Marxists connect themselves with Marx, the New Left is under so such obligation. The two movements are divided, however, by much more than this formal difference. If nothing else, Marxism imposes an intellectual discipline that the free-floating spirit of the New Left lacks.

Marx and Alienation

The neo-Marxists rely on the "young Marx," who at the age of twenty-six wrote a set of essays that have become known as the *Economic and Philosophical Manuscripts* (1844).* His major concern in the *Manuscripts* was man's alienation, which he viewed as the result of both the division of labor and private property. According to Marx, man is alienated (1) from his work, (2) from his productivity, and (3) from the capital he produces for somebody else.

> *The worker is related to the* product of his labour *as to an* alien *object. For it is clear on this presupposition that the more the worker expends himself in work the more powerful becomes the world of objects which he creates in face of himself, the poorer he becomes in his inner life, and the less he belongs to himself. . . . The* alienation *of the worker in his product means not only that his labour becomes an object, assumes an* external *existence, but that it exists independently,* outside himself, *and alien to him and that it stands opposed*

* There is a scholarly dispute whether the "older" Marx, concerned with capitalist economics, had in fact repudiated the "young" Marx, concerned with humanist moralism, or whether the "older" Marx the economist merely provided the logical assurance that those things must happen that the "young" Marx the moralist had said ought to happen. However, we need not be concerned with these arguments because we are dealing with ideological questions as they influence people's behavior and not with scholarly analyses of the evolution of Marx's thought.

to him as an autonomous power. The life which he has given to the object sets itself against him as an alien and hostile force. . . .

. . . Alienation appears not merely in the result but also in the process of production, *within* productive activity *itself. How could the worker stand in an alien relationship to the product of his activity if he did not alienate himself in the act of production itself? . . .*

What constitutes the alienation of labour? First, that the work is external *to the worker; that it is not part of his nature; and that consequently he does not fulfill himself in his work but denies himself, has a feeling of misery rather than well-being, does not develop freely his mental and physical energies but is physically exhausted and mentally debased. The worker, therefore, feels himself at home only during his leisure time, whereas at work he feels homeless. His work is not voluntary but imposed,* forced labour.[1]

Thus far Marx has dealt with alienation as representing the drudgery of routinized work and as reification (as making a fetish of *things*); realistically, these forms of alienation are not necessarily tied to a capitalist system. But the third form of alienation rests on the fact that alienated labor belongs to someone else:

If the product of labour does not belong to the worker, but confronts him as an alien power, this can only be because it belongs to a man other than the worker. *If his activity is a torment to him it must be a source of* enjoyment *and pleasure to another.*[2]

The labor of the worker creates capital for the capitalist; the worker is also alienated from the capital he produces:

Thus, through alienated labour the worker creates the relation of another man, who does not work and is outside the work process, to this labour. The relation of the worker to work produces the relation of the capitalist (or whatever one likes to call the lord of labour) to work.[3]

Writing of the man who is no longer alienated, Marx made the following points in a notebook in 1844.

Supposing that we had produced in a human manner; each of us would in his production have doubly affirmed himself and his fellow man. I would have (1) objectified in my production my individuality and its peculiarity and thus both in my activity enjoyed an individual expression of my life and also in looking at the object have had the individual pleasure of realizing that my personality was objective, visible to the senses and thus a power raised beyond all doubt. (2) In your enjoyment or use of my product, I would have had the pure enjoyment of realizing that I had both satisfied a human need by my work and also objectified the human essence and therefore fashioned for another human being the object that had met his need. (3) I would have been for you the mediator between you and the species and thus been acknowledged and felt by you as a completion of your own essence and a necessary part of yourself, and have thus realized that I am confirmed both in your thought and in your love. (4) In my expression of my life I would have fashioned your expression of your life, and thus in my own activity have realized my own essence, my human, my communal essence. In that case our products would be like so many mirrors, out of which our essence shone.[4]

Alienation in Neo-Marxism

Revisionist Marxists in Eastern Europe have broadened Marx's concept of alienation into a rationale for keeping socialist regimes on a progressive course by suggesting that alienation is inescapable. As Predrag Vranicki states,

While all of human history and all historical creations (the state, culture, religion, etc.) are man's work and the expression of man's own potentialities and powers, man has been capable of existing only by separating these powers from himself, and by finding these same powers counterposed to himself as specific material, social or ideological forces.

So long as man's work continues to exist as something external to him (the political sphere, religion, the market, money, etc.) and to oppose itself to him in the form of a superior authority, we will encounter the phenomenon of alienation. Man's world up to now has always been a world divided against itself—a world in which man, the creator of history, has been largely powerless, disfranchised, and debased in historical terms. History is a constant tyranny over man to this day.[5]

Though alienation is thus part and parcel of life, Vranicki maintains that it can take different forms and have different consequences. A particular form of alienation becomes intolerable if the means for overcoming it are already at hand. Bourgeois society has many accomplishments to its credit, but it has reached a stage where the alienation that is based on the fetishism of commodities has become stifling. "Man comes to believe that the possession of certain commodities alters his qualities as a man and that wealth in commodities can be identified with enrichment as a human being. Man becomes wholly oriented in the direction of this externality, and thus impoverishes himself." [6]

Socialism, it is held, can overcome this fetishism and its concomitant alienation (although there is an incongruity between the philosophical position of revisionist communism on the one hand and its practical concern with producing consumer goods and improving the material aspects of life on the other). But socialism has its own form of alienation that arises from the opposition between people and authority; Stalinism represents the extreme form of this opposition. Instead of reducing the impact of authority once the revolution was successful, Stalin had strengthened it. Under Stalin's rule, the worker was not less alienated from his work than under monopoly capitalism; since he had no say in planning, he had become little more than part of the plan. Only if the worker becomes a participant in the overall decision-making process can this form of alienation be eliminated. Thus the constant danger of socialism is bureaucracy; in order to overcome alienation bureaucracy must be constantly and successfully challenged in the name of self-management (the linear relationship between substructure and superstructure is therefore abolished by the revisionists). The more orthodox Marxists find fault with such a broad interpretation of alienation because it precludes the opportunity of a wholesale attack on capitalism.

Whereas in Eastern Europe the concept of alienation has been used to further de-Stalinization, in Western Europe the notion of alienation is employed in the war against capitalism. The difficulty confronting Western Marxists is that the critique of capitalism can no longer rest on the thesis of the workers' impoverishment and exploitation (at least such allegations would be very tenuous); hence capitalism is now criticized for its inability to create a sense of community and its tendency to manipulate people for commercial ends.

One consequence of this view is that the workers are no longer the sole victims of the bourgeois order; many other groups are also victims, primarily the intellectuals, who perhaps, given their greater sensitivity, are greater victims than the workers. A second consequence is that radical social change is not the result of a proletarian revolution, inasmuch as workers cannot be expected to revolt for reasons of alienation. This, in turn, means that the superstructure of capitalism, despite its flaws, cannot be expected to change as a result of change in the substructure. It follows, therefore, that socialists must try to influence people on the level of the superstructure—that is, in their thinking about social, political, and artistic matters.

Intellectually, Marxists had to cope not only with the issues that arose from de-Stalinization in the East and from the deradicalization of the working class in the West, they also had to meet challenges on purely philosophical grounds, such as from Sartre's existentialism. They even found themselves engaged in a dialog with concerned Christians.

The Marxist-Existentialist Dialog

The questions raised by Jean Paul Sartre centered on man as a free individual versus man as a product of his environment, man as a maker of history versus man as an object of history. (These questions were elucidated most incisively in a debate between Sartre and Adam Schaff of Poland.) Stated in its simplest terms, existentialism holds that existence precedes essence; man is what he *does,* and since doing means choosing, man is determined by his free or voluntary choices. Sartre, however, is basically sympathetic to Marxism and close to the Communist Party (without forgoing the right to criticize it), and the purpose of his challenge was to improve Marxism, not to reject it.

While Sartre admits to a dialectical relationship between the individual and society, he nevertheless insists that man's consciousness is not wholly determined by social conditions and that there is a "realm of freedom"—choice—that is not determined by society. Sartre holds that freedom is within man, not outside him, and thus denies historic determinism. In the extreme, freedom is the ability to say no to a hostile environment. The greater the threat, the greater the freedom the individual experiences in saying no.

We were never more free than during the German occupation. We had lost all our rights, beginning with the right to talk. Every day we were insulted to our faces and had to take it in silence. Under one pretext or another, as workers, Jews, or political prisoners, we were deported en-masse. *Everywhere, on billboards, in the newspapers, on the screen, we encountered the revolting and insipid picture of ourselves that our oppressors wanted us to accept. And, because of all this, we were free.*[7]

To Marxists, this conception of freedom appears absurd as it cannot be connected with meaningful social action. Freedom as Sartre defines it can merely preserve the integrity of an individual within an environment that wants to destroy him morally or psychologically.

Adam Schaff, in contrast, insists that freedom lies in understanding the laws of nature and society and using them for constructive human ends. However, Schaff admits that existentialism, by raising the issue of the autonomy of the individual in an extreme form, has made Marxists much more concerned about the individual than they previously had been.

The problem of the individual was overlooked in the later phase of Marxism for two reasons. The first is of an objective nature and is connected with the concentration of forces—poor as they were in comparison with the opponent's power—on what was the most important thing at that time—the struggle of the masses. The other reason is of a subjective character and was connected, particularly during the rapid growth of the movement and in view of the long struggle facing it, with the fact that many of those taking part in the movement began to forget about the difference between the actual aim of the struggle and the ways and means leading to this end. . . .

The reversion of Marxists today to the problems of the philosophy of man is due to at least three concurrent factors.

First, there are the objective requirements of the movement that —after seizing power in a number of countries—is now not only confronted with tasks connected with the struggle against the old system, but, primarily, with the task of creating new ways of life.[8]

Schaff goes on to say that these objective conditions also create new ideas in theory and, finally, that a Marxist philosophy of man is necessary for the ideological competition with the West.

The Marxist-Christian Dialog

Of more far-reaching significance than the Marxist-existentialist dialog has been the Christian-Marxist dialog, which was initiated in 1965. It is based on a number of common assumptions. In an ever-shrinking world, people must find a universally common ground; in order to do this they must reexamine past attitudes with an open mind and a willingness to engage in doctrinal give-and-take. And given the great dangers besetting the world, the two great mass movements of our times, Christianity and Marxism, have a special obligation to try to establish some form of cooperation. The reforms made in the Catholic church by Pope John XXIII, along with his invitation to nonbelievers to engage in a dialog with the church and developments in communism since the Twentieth Party Congress, provided propitious circumstances for Christians and Marxists to meet face to face.

The most active organization in sponsoring the dialog was the Catholic Paulusgesellschaft, whose first congress convened in Salzburg in 1965. It discussed the topic "Christianity and Marxism Today." In 1966 it met in Bavaria on the topic "Christian Humanity and Marxist Humanism." The third congress, held in Czechoslovakia in 1967, discussed "Creativity and Freedom." In these meetings, communists from Western and Eastern European countries (except the Soviet Union) and Catholics and Protestants, both theologians and scholars, took part.

The communists acknowledged the new, revolutionary spirit that had gained ground among Christians, and took the position that once religion ceased to be a bulwark of the establishment, Marx's position on religion would cease to be justified. A few communists even declared that Marxism had not yet answered the question of the meaning of life and that, consequently, a metaphysical approach to this question should be taken seriously. According to Roger Garaudy, the new attitude of the church

> *renders possible a deep encounter with the Marxists on the basis of humanism,* i.e., *the reinforcement of the autonomy of man so strongly emphasized both by* Gaudium et Spes *and* Populorum Progressio [*two papal encyclicals*]. . . . *The very last contested problem between us is to know which one of the two world concepts will more concretely recognize man's responsibility toward history, and which one will give him the methodology to create his own history most effectively.*[9]

The Christians, while they emphasized their conviction that a true humanism must have a foundation in religion, readily admitted that the church has for too long in its history been a bulwark of conservatism, and even reaction, and that her metaphysical concerns had not infrequently been a way of avoiding coming to grips with the evils of this world.

Vincenzo Miano, the representative of the Vatican's Secretariat for Non-Believers, had this to say:

We believers are, no doubt, convinced that a humanism isolated from spiritual values and from their source (which is God) can, after all, organize the world only against the people. This conviction, however, does not prevent us from recognizing the many human values contained in the humanism of nonbelievers, and what possibilities present themselves for cooperation we consider good.[10]

And Jerzy Turowicz, a prominent Polish Catholic, commenting on the new social role of the church, added:

Under the powerful impact of the [*Vatican*] *Council the Catholic idea revises the attitude toward the world, man and history; it proclaims Christianity's independence of all cultures and all political, social and economic systems. This independence allows a far-reaching revision of the traditional "social doctrine" of the Church.*[11]

THE NEW LEFT

Even more than other revolutionary movements, the New Left is difficult to analyze because it is so amorphous, so elusive, and its various manifestations so fleeting. The general problem in the analysis of any revolutionary movement is to disentangle the underlying rationale from the excrescences. (Every revolutionary movement has an emotional, spasmodic character, and the surest way of misunderstanding a movement is by applying the yardsticks of neatness and rationality that characterize evolutionary politics.) The matter is further complicated by the need to separate those members who are seriously committed to the movement from those who attach themselves for psychological reasons or from sheer ennui. In short, the analyst must discern the authentic voices.

There are, however, a few stable characteristics of the New Left, such as the age and occupations of its adherents and the places where it has taken hold. The New Left is made up of students and young intellectuals, and in some countries of youth in general, whose importance derives from the fact that the world's population is getting ever younger. The New Left is also a phenomenon of the more advanced countries and the post-scarcity stage. (In countries where the bulk of people is still concerned with keeping body and soul together, there is hardly any trace of the movement.)

The New Left emerged as a result of various widespread grievances in the advanced countries. Although these grievances may have different priorities or emphases in different countries, a catalog of them includes the hypocrisy of the adult world, which preaches one thing and does another; the waging of war and preparations for war; the exclusion of the young from political influence; the plight of the poor, the oppressed, and those who are discriminated against; bureaucratization; the individual's powerlessness in a highly technological society; materialism; the ruthless, unending cycle of competition; the remoteness of decision-making from the level of those whom it affects; and, finally, the role and organization of the university.

Undeniably, there is a basis for at least some of these grievances, which are but a part of a general malaise that afflicts large parts of the world. This malaise, with which "more mature" people are willing to live, suffering in silence, signifies the decline of values that have long been dominant, especially the importance of power, which is the central value under challenge by the New Left. Power as the paramount factor in life has dominated the world since the Renaissance, so that the model of competitive man and the competitive nation in quest of power and wealth has been the paradigm for Western man. But today, in a shrinking, interdependent, and overpopulated world frightened by the prospect of universal destruction, this model is being challenged. Cooperation not competition, understanding not hostility, are required.

Today, in many places in the world, we see revulsion against the exercise of physical power in international relations, and this revulsion is accompanied by a loss of awe toward power, especially on the part of the weak. No longer is the tradition of the strong inevitably imposing their will on the weak acceptable. We should not be deceived by the fact that, at the very time we say power politics is on the way out, it seems to have reached an apogee in some places. Developments are not always what they seem; furthermore, before expiring historical forces spend themselves, they usually try to assert themselves with a vengeance.

There is not only a decline in obeisance before raw power, there is also a decline in respect for authority, which is constantly called on to justify itself. Paradoxically, the attack on power and authority is often accompanied by violence. The justification offered for this is that violence has always been the rock-bottom foundation for authority (such as policemen and soldiers), so that the use of counterviolence confounds the guardians of the established order and puts them psychologically on the defensive.

The attack on power goes hand in hand with the quest for equality, for as long as some people are more powerful than others, equality remains an abstraction. But in a wider sense, the oppression of the individual is not merely a matter of his relationship to government, or even a matter of governmental action; it is a result of our technological society.

The most remarkable fact about the New Left is that its critique of American society is far removed from the struggles and great debates of the 1930's; its members see this as ancient history with no relevance for the present. If some of the New Left are Marxist, they are Marxist in only a very general way. While economics is of concern, given their commitment to improving the lot of the poor, it is not considered the end-all; the New Left represents posteconomic radicalism. New Leftists attack the bureaucratization of modern industrial society, whether capitalist or communist. They have very little interest in the Soviet Union or China. They have sympathy for communism only in underdeveloped countries that want to chart their own courses independently of the Soviet Union and China. Mao Tse-tung is a hero to them only as a symbol of defiance of both the West and the Soviet Union. For similar reasons, they lionize Ho Chi Minh and Fidel Castro. Castro is a hero because he defied the United States and criticizes both the Soviet Union and China. His guerrilla warfare is not viewed primarily as a revolutionary technique but as representing the grass-roots camaraderie forged by a common danger and against overwhelming odds.

Of special import is the fact that the radicalism of the New Left, unlike communism earlier, is not subversive in the ultimate sense. It does not involve transferring one's loyalty to another powerful country; rather it is interested in the radical change of the socioeconomic system within the given country.

If the New Left subjects the American system to especially harsh criticism while exempting Soviet communism, it is not because it is partisan to the Soviet Union but because it considers Soviet communism irrelevant. The New Left particularly criticizes the close relationship of American capitalism with armaments. It views America as a warfare state, and maintains that its economy is greatly dependent on a continuous buildup of arms.

The posteconomic orientation of the New Left is manifested in the contempt of many New Leftists for material comforts; for example, many prefer apartments in the slums to the suburban homes of their parents. The New Left also opposes the artificially created "needs" of the economy; it believes the economy would collapse if it did not constantly whet the people's appetities for more and more consumer goods. In place of such an economy, the New Left advocates an economy based on social needs, which would include intellectual and cultural needs.

Observing the establishment-linked trade unions and the conservatism of the working class, many New Leftists in America have written off the usefulness of the workers as a progressive force. (New Leftists in France, however, take a more hopeful view of the working class, particularly the young workers.) In theory, blacks are substituted in place of the worker as the agents of radical social change. In practice, however, the New Left seems to assign the role of the social force that will bring about the transformation of society to the intellectual and the student.

The contempt the New Leftist has for the "establishment liberal" is primarily due to what he considers hypocrisy. Though the liberal's heart bleeds for the people of the inner city, he lives in the suburbs and sends his children to private schools. Though he parades his commitment to social change, at the same time he admires the giant corporations and voices the belief that they are indispensable for the solution of the social problems of society.

The special target of the New Left, both in the United States and all over the world, is the university. It condemns the aloofness of professors vis-à-vis their students in mass production universities, the priority of research over teaching and the involvement of universities in war-applicable research, and the availability of university premises to recruiters from the armed services and defense-related industries. A particular complaint of students is that they are treated as automatons in an educational enterprise and that they have had no say in the content of their courses, the assignment of teaching personnel, and in the determination of educational policy. But an even more fundamental charge against the university is that, under the guise of objectivity and detachment, it is an upholder of the status quo and accepts the definitions of social problems as they have been laid down by those in power. The social sciences ignore radical social criticism and are engaged in work that is considered irrelevant for our times.

Finally, the university is criticized not only for its scholarly conservatism, but also for failing to be an agency for social change. Obviously, the latter criticism overlooks the fact that the university is not central to the power structure; the university can reform itself, but this is not tantamount to reforming society. Some of the tactics of the New Left in regard to the university are of dubious worth; one cannot help observing that the university is a rather delicate institution that can stand only a small amount of disruption before it suffers serious damage.

The disruptive tactics of the New Left have aroused the severest criticism of the movement and have raised not only the question of propriety but—in view of serious campus disturbances—the issue of the right of a minority to dictate to the majority. A philosophical defense of its tactics would have to resort to Rousseau's concept of the "general will," which the New Left would have to maintain it represents; how convincing this hypothetical defense would be is open to serious question.

Another criticism of the New Left is that it lacks a program of positive social change—it does not offer a recognizable image of a new society. There is, in its wholesale attack on the existing order, a strong streak of anarchism. The New Left seems to reject organization in any form without any suggestion of how the complex affairs of a modern society could be conducted without such organization.

Some New Leftists imply that before any new social program can be developed, one has to "clear the rubble away," but this attitude is merely reminiscent of the romantic view of the Russian nihilists of the late nineteenth century. More generally, the New Left believes that ideas about a new society are born in the process of making a revolution. Ideology, then, does not precede the revolution but results from it. The following paraphrased testimony of one of the French New Leftists is also characteristic of New Leftists in the U.S.:

To launch the revolutionary process only one thing is needed: "to will the revolution." Organization is unnecessary; in fact it is a danger and a handicap. Ideology is irrelevant. Get the revolutionaries acting together and they feel together, even if they do not think together; barricades before dialectics. Physical destruction of the enemy is not essential; it is enough to destroy him symbolically, to shatter his morale by spectacular acts of resistance and defiance, "to do some-

thing striking and forbidden"—e.g., *in a university to occupy the administrative offices as the seat of "institutional repression."* [12]

Perhaps the only valid ideological contribution the New Left has made thus far is the emphasis on "participatory democracy," which has almost become a mystique. The assumption is that if decision-making takes place at a grass-roots level the decisions made will be most ideally suited to the people they affect. Despite the dubious optimism about the relationship between process and output, the idea that the decisions should be made on the level of those who will be affected by them has much to commend it. But, realistically, a highly technological society (which the New Left cannot rescind), with its intricate interdependencies, requires the coordination that only a very high level of decision-making can achieve. Thus, in practical application, the ideal of participatory democracy must be viewed as an inherently valuable questioning process: what level of decision-making is really necessary, and to what extent the people who will be affected by the decisions can be involved in making them. In short, it can be a guiding principle but not an all-sufficient process.

The reaction of the Soviet Union and communist parties in general to the New Left has been utterly negative; they have denounced the movement as representing petty bourgeois romanticism. (Their special target has been Herbert Marcuse, the philosopher of the New Left, whose insistence that society must move beyond Marx has only provoked the ire of communist ideologues.)

The relationship between a Communist Party and the New Left was best illustrated by the events of May, 1968, in France. These disturbances, which originated in the universities but later spread to large portions of the working class, were at first ignored by the French communists. Only when the Communist Party became afraid that it would be outflanked on the left did it support the movement, though without great enthusiasm. The reason for its reluctance (at least in part) was that the party was eager to show its respectability in order to be eligible for participation in a popular front. The New Left, whose behavior is often charged to the communists for opportunistic reasons, is a liability to the party; the communists would like nothing more than to see the movement disappear.

The future of the New Left is an open question. One possibility is that the movement is now in a stage comparable to that of utopian socialism in pre-Marxist days, in which case it may develop a popular program and become an importance force. However, this means that it would have to resolve its internal contradictions: it cannot, for example, advocate economic collectivism and political anarchy at the same time. The other possibility is that the New Left will simply die out—not, however, without having made important contributions by exposing many skeletons in the closet.

Herbert Marcuse: Philosopher of the New Left

If the New Left has a philosopher, he is Herbert Marcuse (1898–), whose philosophical thought draws on a variety of sources. His utopia is derived from a reformulation of various Freudian ideas; his critique of contemporary Western society is partly Marxist and partly post-Marxist; and his critique of the Soviet Union is somewhat Trotskyist.

Marcuse accepts the Freudian position that libidinal repression is a source of human unhappiness; but while Freud believed that repression is the price man has to pay for culture, Marcuse takes the position that repression is the result of a society in which man has to toil. If changes are made in institutional arrangements, man, by virtue of his natural endowments, could then enjoy all the pleasures of which he is capable.

If Prometheus is the culture-hero of toil, productivity, and progress through repression, then the symbols of another reality principle must be sought at the opposite pole. Orpheus and Narcissus [*i.e.*, *love in general*] . . . *stand for a very different reality. They have not become the culture-heroes of the Western world: theirs is the image of joy and fulfillment; the voice which does not command but sings; the gesture which offers and receives; the deed which is peace and ends the labor of conquest.* . . . [13]

In that hoped-for future, the individual will be fully autonomous and his society will be "polymorphous"; that is, it will lend itself to the great variety of institutional arrangements autonomous individuals require. But the character of modern industrial civilization, which, though it has created the potentiality for the abundance that is a prerequisite for human liberation, denies the realization of this potential because of the socioeconomic structures both in the West and in the Soviet Union.

In the West, capitalism is based on the constant manufacture of wants that are meaningless for human growth. At the same time, in order to satisfy these artificially created wants, people are forced to work instead of enjoying life. Not only is this work unnecessary in any real sense; it maintains a relationship of domination and subservience, which a progressive reduction of labor would gradually eliminate.

The capitalist system, with its unique traits of domination, also depends on the maintenance of a state of warfare, which is the basis for "prosperity." Economists may point out that the money now spent on defense establishments could be used for other prosperity-maintaining purposes, but, given the fractured character of society and its many interests, which are not only uncoordinated but are generally short term, the necessary political will cannot be marshaled to make the required substitutions.

Even so, the creation of artificial wants and the maintenance of the warfare state are not, in themselves, enough to support the capitalist economy, which also requires the exploitation of underdeveloped countries. If the Third World countries want to emancipate themselves from Western dominance, they must combine national liberation with social revolution. Success in this dual endeavor would not only be a psychological blow to the self-confidence of the ruling elites of the Western countries (which is based on the assumption of the universal applicability of their values), it would also have revolutionary repercussions within the Western countries themselves.

Despite all the shortcomings of the capitalist system, on the conscious level the majority of people are satisfied with it. They may occasionally sense that something is wrong but they do not know what it is, and their general satisfaction with the system makes radical change very difficult, if not impossible. Moreover, the establishment's tolerance of the most diverse points of view becomes, in effect, oppressive. It is impossible for the antiestablishment point of view to get an unencumbered hearing, because the apparent tolerance of the establishment of different opinions deepens the belief of the vast majority of people in the fairness of their political system and thus enhances their loyalty to it. Furthermore, though the mass media permit the expression of a great range of opinions, they treat all opinions equally and accord misinformed people the same attention as informed people. Marcuse argues that one cannot be equally tolerant of truth and falsehood: to be tolerant of falsehood is to be intolerant.

Marcuse feels that because of the conditions in which man finds himself in the West, freedom must assume a new meaning.

New modes of realization [*of freedom*] *are needed, corresponding to the new capabilities of society.*

Such new modes can be indicated only in negative terms because they would amount to the negation of the prevailing modes. Thus economic freedom would mean freedom from *the economy—from being controlled by economic forces and relationships. . . . Political freedom would mean liberation of the individuals* from *politics over which they have no effective control. Similarly, intellectual freedom would mean the restoration of individual thought now absorbed by mass communication and indoctrination, abolition of "public opinion" together with its makers.*[14]

Marcuse believes that the system can transform itself only through revolution. But he hedges his commitment to revolution with so many reservations (including those of an ethical nature) that they constitute a practical denial of his commitment.

Marcuse's attitude toward the Soviet Union is similar to Trotsky's: "the Revolution was betrayed." He believes that an unimaginative bureaucratic apparatus has taken hold of the country, repressing people, distorting truth, and inhibiting all creative efforts. The regime sacrifices the present generation for the alleged welfare of future generations. At the same time, the type of millennial society it envisages is primarily one of technicians and engineers.

Marcuse not only criticizes the perverted form of socialism exhibited by Soviet communism; he challenges some basic tenets of classical socialism itself. He maintains that the objective identity between humanism and socialism has been dissolved. Shifting the means of production from private control to public control is only a quantitative change, not a qualitative one. What is needed is a total reconstruction of society along lines that are different from the tenets of both capitalism and traditional socialism. According to Marcuse, four forces will bring about the desired revolutionary changes: (1) the alienated intelligentsia in the West; (2) the disadvantaged peoples, particularly the blacks, in the United States; (3) the reawakened revolutionary left in Europe, particularly in France; and (4) the revolutionary forces in the Third World.

In the end, Marcuse pins his hopes on the Third World, for he thinks that the West and the Soviet Union have little chance of escaping from the quagmire of "economism." The Third World, not yet having entered this stage, may be in a position to bypass it (a thought Marcuse shares with Mao Tse-tung).

The historical advantage of the late-comer, of technical backwardness, may be that of skipping the stage of the affluent society. Backward peoples by their poverty and weakness may be forced to forego the aggressive and wasteful use of science and technology, to keep the productive apparatus à la mesure de l'homme, *under his control, for the satisfaction and development of vital individual and collective needs.*[15]

NOTES

1. Karl Marx, "Economic and Philosophical Manuscripts," *Early Writings,* tr. and ed. T. B. Bottomore (New York: McGraw-Hill, 1964), pp. 122–25.
2. *Ibid.,* p. 130.
3. *Ibid.,* p. 131.
4. Quoted in David McLellan, "Marx's View of the Unalienated Society," *Review of Politics,* Vol. XXXI (October 1969), pp. 464–65.
5. Predrag Vranicki, "Socialism and the Problem of Alienation," in *Socialist Humanism: An International Symposium,* ed. Erich Fromm (Garden City, N.Y.: Doubleday, 1965), pp. 275–76.
6. *Ibid.,* p. 278.
7. Quoted in Walter Odajnyk, *Marxism and Existentialism* (Garden City, N.Y.: Doubleday, 1965), pp. 105–06.
8. Adam Schaff, "Marxism and the Philosophy of Man," in Fromm, *op cit.,* pp. 134–35.
9. Quoted in Charles Andras, "The Christian-Marxist Dialogue," *East Europe,* Vol. XVII (March 1968), p. 12.
10. *Ibid.*
11. *Ibid.*
12. Edmund Taylor, "Revolution and Reaction in France," *Foreign Affairs,* Vol. XLVII, No. 1 (October 1968), p. 103.
13. Herbert Marcuse, *Eros and Civilization: A Philosophical Inquiry into Freud* (Boston: Beacon Press, 1966), pp. 161–62.
14. Herbert Marcuse, *One-Dimensional Man: Studies in the Ideology of Advanced Industrial Society* (Boston: Beacon Press, 1964), p. 4.
15. Herbert Marcuse, *Eros and Civilization: A Philosophical Inquiry into Freud,* p. xviii.

CHAPTER FOURTEEN

THE REVOLUTION AGAINST DISCRIMINATION

BLACK NATIONALISM

Black Nationalism has been one response to the failure of the American "melting pot" idea—an idea that has never been totally descriptive of the American experience. Earlier European ethnic groups had established community institutions out of sentimental as well as economic reasons. While these groups were not fully integrated into society, they were part of the body politic; there was no discrimination against them in the exercise of their franchise. In some cases, these groups experienced social discrimination, but members of most minority groups were not denied entrance to restaurants, places of amusement, or other quasi-public places. If these European newcomers did not integrate themselves into American society, their children were generally free to do so. If, for whatever reason, they retained bonds with their ethnic communities, it was usually a matter of choice and not necessity.

In the case of the black, the situation has been quite different. Whatever else may have been involved, the mere difference in color has had special consequences. Awareness of the more important differences in the situation of blacks as compared with other ethnic groups has been long in coming. Nor was it fully understood that legal rights and statutory prescriptions do not have the power of social transformation. Thus the rise of Black Nationalism has resulted from a number of disappointments and misapprehensions.

Black Liberation Movements

The early emancipation attempts of the blacks were based on self-improvement and were characterized by deference to white prejudice. Th "father" of this form of accommodation, Booker T. Washington (1856–1915), took the position that blacks would have to "earn" both the respect of whites and the right to equality. Espousing vocational training for blacks, he reassured whites that if they supported his program a docile labor force would result. The following passages from Washington's address at the Cotton States and International Exposition in Atlanta (in September, 1895) illustrate the humble self-abnegation that characterized this early movement.

As we have proved our loyalty to you in the past, in nursing your children, watching by the sick-bed of your mothers and fathers, and often following them with tear-dimmed eyes to their graves, so in the future, in our humble way, we shall stand by you with a devotion that no foreigner can approach, ready to lay down our lives, if need be, in defence of yours, interlacing our industrial, commercial, civil, and religious life with yours in a way that shall make the interests of both races one. In all things that are purely social we can be as separate as the fingers, yet one as the hand in all things essential to mutual progress. . . .

The wisest among my race understand that the agitation of questions of social equality is extremest folly, and that progress in the enjoyment of all the privileges that will come to us must be the result of severe and constant struggle rather than of artificial forcing. No race that has anything to contribute to the markets of the world is long in any degree ostracized. It is important and right that all privileges of the law be ours, but it is vastly more important that we be prepared for the exercises of these privileges. The opportunity to earn a dollar in a factory just now is worth infinitely more than the opportunity to spend a dollar in an opera-house.[1]

Self-help through vocational training found expression in the establishment of Tuskegee Institute in 1881, of which Washington was the head. The National Urban League, founded in 1910 and composed of blacks and whites, became an instrument on the national level for helping blacks adjust to urban life by training them for jobs in factories. Washington's philosophy discouraged blacks from fighting for civil rights and seeking political power. Its underlying assumption was that the underdog's honest striving would eventually be rewarded. This approach overlooked the fact that striving requires an incentive, which was denied the blacks, and that accommodation to prejudice reinforces rather than eradicates it.

Washington's position was challenged by W. E. B. Du Bois (1868–1964), who urged the self-assertion of the black. Washington had advocated vocational training; Du Bois took the position that the black needed his own intelligentsia, the "talented tenth." Washington had shifted the burden for emancipation to the black; Du Bois shifted it to the nation:

While it is a great truth to say that the Negro must strive and strive mightily to help himself, it is equally true that unless his striving be not simply seconded, but rather aroused and encouraged, by the initiative of the richer and wiser environing group, he cannot hope for great success.

In his failure to realize and impress this last point, Mr. Washington is especially to be criticized. His doctrine had tended to make the whites, North and South, shift the burden of the Negro problem to the Negro's shoulders and stand aside as critical and rather pessimistic spectators; when in fact the burden belongs to the nation, and the hands of none of us are clean if we bend not our energies to righting these great wrongs.[2]

Can the masses of the Negro people be in any possible way more quickly raised than by the effort and example of this aristocracy of talent and character? Was there ever a nation on God's fair earth civilized from the bottom upward? Never; it is, ever was and ever will be from the top downward that culture filters. The Talented Tenth rises and pulls all that are worth the saving up to their vantage ground. This is the history of human progress; . . .

How then shall the leaders of a struggling people be trained and the hands of the risen few strengthened? There can be but one answer: The best and most capable of their youth must be schooled in the colleges and universities of the land.[3]

In 1905, to implement his ideas, Du Bois founded the Niagara Movement, from which the National Association for the Advancement of Colored People (NAACP) emerged in 1910. The NAACP proposed to fight against discrimination in the courts and to organize a political lobby, which would rely to a large extent on the support of white liberals. The NAACP was, and is, an elitest biracial organization that has not been interested in creating a mass movement among blacks. It has also been legalistic, fighting bad laws and unfair interpretations. Its solution for the black has been assimilation—that is, integration into the lifestream of America. From 1910 to 1960, the black emancipation movement was dominated by the NAACP approach.

But during this period there were other stirrings among the black masses. The Movement for African Unity, founded by Marcus Garvey (1887–1940) in 1917, appealed to the black as "a new Negro who stands erect, conscious of his manhood rights and fully determined to preserve them at all costs." [4] Garvey spoke of Negroes as a mighty race that can accomplish anything it sets its mind to, but he appealed mostly to the uneducated masses. The educated black thought of him as a combination demagogue and buffoon; nevertheless, his movement had lasting significance: "The inner shame over blackness was by no means exorcised, but after Garvey it was never again quite the same as it had been." [5]

The first important instance of mass action occurred in 1941 when A. Philip Randolph (president of the Brotherhood of Sleeping Car Porters) threatened to march on Washington, D.C., unless blacks were given jobs in defense industries. President Franklin D. Roosevelt issued Executive Order 8802 in response, which prohibited discrimination in defense-job hiring and established the Fair Employment Practices Committee. But Garvey's movement and Randolph's threat were but straws in the wind.

The high point in the NAACP approach to the "Negro problem" was the school desegregation decision of the Supreme Court in 1954 (Brown *vs.* The Board of Education of Topeka). However, this decision did not accomplish what many had hoped it would. Though legal segregation was abolished, *de facto* segregation was not. Whites who could afford to do so moved to the suburbs and the schools in the city became increasingly black; the scholastic progress of black children was, therefore, not better or faster than before. Middle-class blacks benefited by the desegregation decision, but for the masses in the ghettos it was irrelevant. Inner-city black children might sit for a few hours next to white children, but their socio-economic backgrounds were too dissimilar for this association to modify the barriers between the white and the black communities.

The worsening situation in the ghettos exposed the limitations of the NAACP approach, with its emphasis on integration through legal means and the cooperative efforts of a black elite and white liberals. The elitist approach of the NAACP was challenged by the Congress of Racial Equality (CORE), which was founded in 1942 and in the 1950's assumed a heightened militancy. Representing the new temper of the black community, CORE emphasized mass action and greater awareness of the economic issues in the emancipation struggle. The Montgomery, Alabama, bus boycott of 1955–57 and the student sit-ins in 1960 and 1961 were peaceful direct-action tactics. (Such demonstrations were the modern descendants of the black boycotts of segregated trolley cars at the turn of the century and the boycotts of stores during the First World War under the slogan "Don't buy where you can't work.") The direct action of the 1950's and early 1960's was conceived as a combination of economic pressure and moral appeal to the consciences of the white community. This was the particular philosophy of the Southern Christian Leadership Conference (SCLC), established in 1957 under the leadership of Dr. Martin Luther King, Jr. (1929–68). Still, all of these efforts were directed toward integration. Then, in the middle 1960's, Black Nationalism arose.

The Rise of Black Nationalism

In contrast to the earlier position that black emancipation would follow from the removal of barriers to the advancement of individual blacks, it was now generally held that emancipation was a collective enterprise. For where discrimination and oppression are severe the individual cannot rise above the status of the group. It is only through the emancipation of the group that the individual can be emancipated. Even if an exceptional individual succeeds in "making it" on his own, his existence is "unauthentic" if he is thereby divorced from his original background. Moreover, the individual successes of members of a minority are only too often misused by the majority to obscure existing discrimination.

One favorite technique is for a majority to appropriate the achievements of a minority but dissociate itself from the latter's shortcomings: a gold medal won by an American black at the Olympics is credited to the United States, but crimes committed by American blacks are popularly classified as "Negro crimes." When the achievements of a member of a minority are recognized as such, there tends to be a certain patronizing attitude. This recognition, moreover, is frequently used by members of the majority to relieve guilt feelings without having to change basic attitudes.

Finally, the full emancipation of a few individuals may deprive the minority of its leadership. Those who are accepted by the majority may only too easily persuade themselves that their advantages and prestige will automatically accrue to the others, which is not necessarily true. Only if the prestigious members of the group constantly identify with it by fighting for the common cause will their success be of significant use to the group.

Black Nationalism must be understood in the context of these contemporary attitudes. Indeed, to take the position that Black Nationalism is racism in reverse is to miss an important point: the nationalism of the strong is aggressive whereas the nationalism of the weak is defensive. The purpose of the former is domination; the purpose of the latter is liberation. One should not be deceived by the fact that the nationalism of the strong is often casual while the nationalism of the weak is strident. Casualness comes with security of position while stridency reflects the need to compel attention within and outside the minority group.

In examining the specific forms of Black Nationalism, we must first distinguish between those groups that want complete separation from the white community and those who see cohesion of the masses and mass action as the means for achieving equality—although the line between the two is not very distinct. Very often the insistence on separatism stems from an abandonment of hope that a fulfilling life is possible for blacks within the white community. When this situation exists a positive response by the white community to the needs of the black community would shift the latter's emphasis from complete separatism to nationalism of a more limited scope. Extreme nationalists call for the ceding of certain territories to blacks so that they can establish their own, separate state—as advocated by the New Africa Movement. This movement was launched in 1967 when the National Conference on Black Power met in Newark, N.J., and passed a resolution calling for a national dialog on the desirability of partitioning the United States into two separate and independent nations, one black and the other white. They also demanded substantial "reparations" from whites, and expressed the possibility of also relying on assistance from other countries.

Another form of nationalism is the proposed takeover of cities in which blacks comprise a substantial portion of the population. These cities would be run as special enclaves in which blacks would provide all the services and have their own police force. In contrast to the separate state proposal, the black-enclave theory does not deal with economic implications, only with the issue of political communal autonomy.

Finally, there is the nonterritorial form of nationalism which simply involves the self-definition of blacks as a people with a common historical experience and a common culture. Black intellectuals have a particular significance in this type of nationalism. Their role is similar to the roles played by the intellectuals of many earlier nationalist movements, in which historians created the "history" of their peoples, writers captured their mood in tales and drama, and composers transformed ancient folk tunes into symphonies—all of which asserted a collective genius that called for a collective destiny. This collective consciousness was particularly significant in the case of the "historyless" peoples of Eastern Europe (who for centuries had lived under the domination of others). In many respects the establishment of the group consciousness was synthetic, but it was nevertheless wholly effective.

One very pronounced form of Black Nationalism has been that represented by the Black Muslims. To consciously choose to separate oneself from the religion of the dominant group is one of the strongest expressions of separatism. It tells the majority—in no uncertain terms—that the minority does not care for it, and it provides a firm basis on which the minority can develop its group consciousness without fear of being subverted. (Obviously, religious differences of long historic standing have different implications than those that derive from a conscious break during the recent past.)

The person who did most to dramatize the meaning of the Black Muslim movement was Malcolm X (1925–65), who in the end broke with the official leader, Elijah Muhammed, because (though continuing to advocate the idea of black separatism) he had come to see the stultifying consequences of viewing the white man as a "devil." Malcolm X appealed both to the black masses and the intellectuals, but he was bitterly opposed by members of the black middle class. He was particularly incensed by the hypocrisy of the Northern liberal because it confused the black community.

The white Southerner, you can say one thing—he is honest. He bares his teeth to the black man; he tells the black man, to his face, that Southern whites never will accept phony "integration." . . .

The word "integration" was invented by a Northern liberal. The word has no real meaning. . . .

Human rights! Respect as human beings! *That's what America's black masses want. That's the true problem. The black masses want not to be shrunk from as though they are plague-ridden. They want not to be walled up in slums, in the ghettoes, like animals. . . .*

The American black man should be focusing his every effort toward building his own business, and decent homes for himself.[6]

Social Ideology and Tactics

None of the groups of Black Nationalists that have appeared thus far is clear about the social content of the movement. The question of the social content of Black Nationalism is of significance vis-à-vis the changes that have occurred in capitalism. Until recently, ethnic minorities in America could advance economically through independent individual efforts such as family farms or small businesses. Although there are still limited opportunities for small business, particularly in the service field, with the era of large-scale enterprise, most employment opportunities are provided by corporations. But corporations as a rule are motivated more by efficiency and profit considerations than by social concerns; they tend not to make the sustained effort necessary for the economic integration of submerged groups. Thus many blacks are caught between the limitations of black capitalism and the uncertainties of corporate paternalism.

This situation has led some groups to espouse socialist solutions. The Student Nonviolent Coordinating Committee (SNCC), founded in 1960, articulated its mission as a struggle against racism, capitalism, and imperialism, uniting white and black radicals in a biracial effort. For white radicals such cooperation with blacks was ideologically related to their belief in the role of blacks as a vehicle for social transformation. (As has been pointed out, many white radicals assign to the blacks the same role the earlier radicals assigned to the proletariat.)

More recently, however, SNCC has receded in importance, and its program has been somewhat taken over by the Black Panthers, a militant group which at one time espoused urban guerrilla tactics. For a time the Black Panthers caught the imagination of many blacks; but internal division and public hostility have reduced their activity and influence.

The banner under which the black struggles of the sixties took place was that of *black power*. Yet the interpretation of black power has varied with different groups. For Urban League and NAACP integrationists—if they use the term at all—it means employing the political, and particularly the electoral, process for the betterment of blacks. For others it may mean "political" action in the form of demonstrations, boycotts, and marches—activities that are not very different from those used by the labor movement in its earlier quest for better pay and working conditions.

One particular form of this "political" action is civil disobedience, for which Martin Luther King, Jr., provided the philosophical basis. King did not see the tactic as limited to his own group; he felt that it lent itself to universal application. King's model was Gandhi's campaign for gaining India's independence from Great Britain. King took the position that passive resistance is a sign of strength, not weakness. "While the nonviolent resister is passive in the sense that he is not physically aggressive toward his opponent, his mind and emotions are always active, constantly seeking to persuade his opponent that he is wrong. The method is passive physically, but strongly active spiritually." [7]

Nonviolence does not seek to humiliate the opponent but to win his friendship; it is not directed against the people but against injustice. (By making the issues abstract, nonviolence attempts to make them psychologically manageable.) Another characteristic is that nonviolence does not seek to retaliate; it accepts suffering without inflicting it. Accordingly, King quotes Gandhi on this subject: "Rivers of blood may have to flow before we gain our freedom, but it must be our blood." [8] King justified this attitude by pointing out that suffering has "tremendous educational and transforming possibilities" and that nonviolence avoids not only physical violence but violence of the spirit, or hate. It tries to put love in the center of social existence.

But black power is also sometimes associated with the use of violence. Black Nationalist proponents of violence argue that violence against an oppressor is violence only in a technical sense, for the oppressor has already utilized terror and force in an attempt to keep the victim in check. They point out that violent revolution has always been an acceptable way of changing social conditions; the United States was born in revolution, and later engaged in a civil war. Perhaps it is helpful first of all to differentiate between criminal violence, with its isolated attacks on life and property for the benefit of the perpetrators, and revolutionary violence, which is organized and is directed toward social transformation. (In times of revolution, incidentally, criminal violence always declines.) The moral issues in revolutionary violence center on two questions: whether the desired goals can or cannot be achieved peacefully, and whether the evil to be corrected is grave enough to warrant the social price to be paid in the use of violence.

On a more practical level, the use of violence by a small minority whose grievances are, at best, only vicariously shared by the majority will have limited success. Initially, violent outbursts may dramatize discontent and may move the majority to action, but repetition of such outbursts is bound to lead to repression. Revolutionary rhetoric has an even more ironic consequence: opponents of such minority groups, by identifying words with actions, can make mere rhetoric the basis for the advocacy of repressive measures.

NOTES

1. Booker T. Washington, "The Atlanta Exposition Address, 1895," in *Negro Protest Thought in the Twentieth Century,* eds. Francis L. Broderick and August Meier (Indianapolis: Bobbs-Merrill, 1965), pp. 6–7.
2. W. E. B. Du Bois, "The Souls of Black Folk, 1903," in *ibid.,* p. 39.
3. W. E. B. Du Bois, "The Talented Tenth, 1903," in *ibid.,* p. 42.
4. Harold Isaacs, quoted in Charles E. Silberman, *Crisis in Black and White* (New York: Random House, 1964), p. 137.
5. *Ibid.*
6. Malcolm X, *The Autobiography of Malcolm X* (New York: Grove Press, 1964), pp. 274–75, 278–79.
7. Martin Luther King, Jr., "Nonviolent Resistance to Evil," in Broderick and Meier, *op. cit.,* p. 264.
8. *Ibid.,* p. 265.

EPILOGUE

THE FUTURE OF IDEOLOGY

The future of ideology was first debated in the late 1950's by the advocates of the "end of ideology" school and its opponents. The end of ideology school maintains that ideologies have exhausted themselves in the West. Daniel Bell, the school's foremost representative in the United States, wrote: "The events behind this important sociological change are complex and varied. Such calamities as the Moscow Trials, the Nazi-Soviet pact, the concentration camps, the suppression of the Hungarian workers, form one chain; such social changes as the modification of capitalism, the rise of the Welfare State, another." [1] Another reason for the demise, as Bell and others see it, is the fact that ideologies are too simplistic to be relevant in complex Western societies. In fact, ideologies are not only irrelevant, they are harmful.

For obvious reasons, proponents of the end of ideology school do not deny the role of ideology in underdeveloped countries, nor do they deny the need for utopias even in the West. Where both need and frustration are great, only a powerful faith can release the single-minded energy that is necessary if backward countries are to move ahead. Pragmatism, with its trial-and-error method, may be sufficient for the routine process of advanced countries, but it is of little help to struggling nations. A man who is trying to save himself from drowning should not be confused by conflicting advice from myriad onlookers. He needs a voice of authority and confidence to shout unambiguous commands. Only such a voice can help the drowning man marshal the energy and determination that might save him. Faith can still move mountains.

Paul Hoffman, the former administrator of the Economic Cooperation Administration, told of having dinner with a prominent Asian statesman whose country had received technical aid from the United States. After thanking Mr. Hoffman for the aid, the statesman commented, "Occasionally we wish you would send us one-armed economists." Mr. Hoffman looked puzzled and his companion continued, "The economists you send us would usually write reports which would state 'on the one hand we think you should do this but on the other you should do that,' and there would follow if not the very opposite of the first recommendation something which was quite different from it." A poor and struggling country, he said, like a drowning man, needs unequivocal advice that is given with assurance.

In the West, according to Bell, utopias have to be empirical.

There is now, more than ever, some need for utopia, in the sense that men need—as they have always needed—some vision of their potential, some manner of fusing passion with intelligence. Yet the ladder to the City of Heaven can no longer be a "faith ladder," but an empirical one: a utopia has to specify where *one wants to go,* how *to get there, the costs of the enterprise, and some realization of, and justification for the determination of* who *is to pay.*[2]

The critics of the end of ideology school have argued that the "end of ideology" is itself ideological and that the argument about the complexity of society and the simplification of ideology is spurious. C. Wright Mills, for one, has dealt with the first issue:

It is a kindergarten fact that any political reflection that is of possible public significance is ideological: *in its terms, policies, institutions, men of power are criticized or approved. In this respect, the end-of-ideology stands, negatively, for the attempt to withdraw oneself and one's work from political relevance; positively, it is an ideology of political complacency which seems the only way now open for many writers to acquiesce in or to justify the* status quo.[3]

Henry David Aiken took up the issue of simplification as follows:

It . . . seems necessary to remind the anti-ideologist that simplification, so far from being a fault peculiar to ideology, is . . . a large part of the saving virtue of rationality itself. To oppose simplism on principle, in politics as in every other sphere of activity, is not to make a legitimate demand for recognition of the complexities and diversities of political life, but, in effect, to ask for an abandonment of policy and a fatal acquiescence in the drift of events. For simplification is an essential feature of any rational initiation of action. To refuse to simplify when one confronts a problem is in effect to reject the obligation to reach a solution; it is to make a game of possibilities and hence to move automatically outside the context of agency and choice. Every procedure that helps us to make decisions does so precisely by reducing the range of possibilities which we may reasonably be expected to consider. And every method, in setting a limit to the con-

siderations that ought to be taken into account, thereby secures our deliberations against an endless spread of doubts.[4]

In a sense, Bell conceded an important point to his opponents by advocating the need for utopias, but he refused to carry this idea to its logical conclusion. Is not his empirical utopia, aside from its conservative implications, a psychological impossibility? Is it not something closer to the bureaucratic process involved in budget planning than to the fusion of passion and intelligence that, according to Bell, is the hallmark of Utopia? Moreover, the emphasis on the empirical in the end of ideology school seems to imply that the empirical represents truth while the ideological means distortion of the truth. Since this is a rather widespread assumption, a few explanations are in order.

Those who take the position that an ideological commitment is somehow incompatible with truth argue that in contrast the empirical approach permits one to look at the facts as they are and, in general, to view social life objectively. However, the problem with this position is that facts, as well as the perception of social life, are enveloped in values. When we deal with facts, we not only select those that are meaningful, we also interpret them—both of which processes involve evaluation. Furthermore we must realize that facts themselves are a result of evaluation.

Only by an evaluation do we call the Eroica "music," not noise, and so assimilate the "fact" of its composition to the history of music rather than to acoustics. . . .

. . . all statements of fact, however free of evaluation they may seem, are possible only *when some fundamental act of appraisal has already legislated for the manner of their entertainment, formulation and assertion.*[5]

Take another example of greater social relevancy: a particular person may be referred to as a Negro, a black, or an Afro-American. All three statements are factual. Nevertheless, each of these "factual" descriptions involves an act of appraisal across the spectrum from integration to separatism. As to "objectivity," on closer inspection, it reveals itself as a frame of mind inclined to the acceptance of existing values.

There is a tendency to assume that empirical studies in a pragmatic society are scientific per se. The reasoning goes as follows: A prag-

matic society is non-ideological, hence it permits the study of social phenomena as to their true nature. If this opportunity meets with the mind of one who does not have preconceived notions of his own, true social science scholarship emerges. The fallacy of this argument becomes clear if we recognize that being a pragmatic society only means that such a society does not have long-range goals; it does not mean that such a society does not have values and values which are strongly held. The empiricist who approaches the study of such a society "without preconceived notions" approaches it in the spirit of the assumptions which underlie it. To say the least he will accept reality to be as it is seen through the eyes of the particular society. This makes him in effect an ideologue of the status quo.[6]

The extent to which pragmatism is dissociated from objectivity becomes clear when one notes that today's pragmatic society was in most cases yesterday's ideological society. American society, for example, is considered one of the most pragmatic in the world, but its roots are thoroughly ideological. One of the fundamental ideas underlying American society is the ringing assertion in the Declaration of Independence that all men are created equal—an ideological statement if ever there was one!

Citizens of the older nation-states accept national loyalty with complete naturalness; for them, the nation-state is a pragmatic framework and therefore nationalism is pragmatic. But during the late eighteenth and the early nineteenth centuries, at the time of the dynastic state, nationalism was still an ideology for many. Similarly, since the nationalism of the newly emerging nations represents a break with the past, their people—as well as outside observers—experience it as an ideology.

The difference between a pragmatic and an ideological society is not that the pragmatic society is more objective than the ideological society; the difference is that the pragmatic society is more tolerant. A pragmatic society, with its basic values firmly established and its ideological roots all but forgotten, will be tolerant of many different points of view provided they do not challenge the fundamentals of the existing order. In contrast, an ideological society, because it is in the process of establishing new values, will be suspicious of even trivial deviations.

In evaluating the end of ideology school, we must consider the historic circumstances at the time of its rise. The Stalinist era had just ended and Khrushchev had just revealed Stalin's "crimes," so that there was a tendency to identify the consequences of ideology per se with the consequences of this particular ideology. Fanaticism and totalitarianism were added to the definition of ideology rather arbitrarily. At the same time, the West, particularly the United States, experienced unprecedented prosperity; since the end of ideology school, in line with classical Marxism, viewed the matrix of ideology as economic conflict, this prosperity seemed to suggest that ideology was withering away. It did not occur to the end of ideology school that social problems would persist in spite of general prosperity or that new problems would arise irrespective of prosperity—much less that they would be productive of ideologies.

Stalinist communism gave rise to Western self-righteousness, and the assumption by the West that it had the solution for all social problems in turn gave rise to smugness. Indeed, in the early 1960's, as communism began to change, smugness was becoming the new nemesis of the West. Raymond Aron, who had fathered the end-of-ideology school with his *Opium of the Intellectuals* (published in 1955 but based on earlier essays) avowed in the foreword to the 1962 English edition of his book: "Ten years ago, I thought it necessary to fight ideological fanaticism. Tomorrow it will perhaps be indifference which seems to me to be feared. The fanatic, animated by hate, seems to me terrifying. A self-satisfied mankind fills me with horror." [7]

As developments in the latter part of the 1960's showed, Aron need not have worried about a self-satisfied mankind. In the United States, for example, the black revolution, the New Left, and the reassessment of military intervention and power politics as a result of the Indochina war indicated the dissatisfaction of at least some of the people with the status quo. And these movements involve, of course, ideological commitments.

There will always be issues that trouble mankind. Moreover, there is the perennial problem of human purpose, which requires an image of a world better than the one into which one was born. This better world cannot merely be "more of the same," as an empirical utopia would suggest. It must involve qualitative improvements, including hoped-for changes in human nature itself.

NOTES

1. Daniel Bell, "The End of Ideology in the West," in *The End of Ideology,* rev. ed. (New York: Collier Books, 1962), p. 300.

2. *Ibid.,* p. 301.

3. C. Wright Mills, *Power, Politics and People,* ed. Irving Louis Horowitz (New York: Ballantine Books, 1963), p. 251.

4. Henry David Aiken, "The Revolt Against Ideology," *Commentary* (April, 1964), p. 38.

5. Marjorie Greene, *The Knower and the Known* (New York: Basic Books, 1966), p. 160.

6. Max Mark, "Reality and Theory," *Ethics,* Vol. LXXIII (October 1962), p. 58.

7. Raymond Aron, *The Opium of the Intellectuals,* tr. Terence Kilmartin (New York: Norton, 1962), p. xvi.

BIBLIOGRAPHY

CHAPTER ONE: MAN, THE MEASURE

* Arendt, Hannah. *The Origins of Totalitarianism.* New York: Harcourt Brace Jovanovich, 1960.
* Beloff, Max. *The Age of Absolutism 1660–1850.* London: Hutchinson's University Library, 1954.
* Fromm, Erich. *Escape from Freedom.* New York; Farrar Straus & Giroux, 1941.

Hallowell, John H. *The Moral Foundation of Democracy.* Chicago: University of Chicago Press, 1954.

Kirscht, John, and Ronald C. Dillehay. *Dimensions of Authoritarianism: A Review of Research and Theory.* Lexington: University of Kentucky Press, 1967.

Kornhauser, William. *The Politics of Mass Society.* Glencoe, Ill.: Free Press, 1959.

* Loewith, Karl. *From Hegel to Nietzsche: The Revolution in Nineteenth Century Thought.* Tr. David E. Green. New York: Holt, Rinehart and Winston, 1964.
* Manuel, Frank E. *Age of Reason.* Ithaca, N.Y.: Cornell University Press, 1959.

Randall, John Herman, Jr. *The Making of Modern Mind.* Boston: Houghton-Mifflin, 1940.

* Schumpeter, Joseph A. *Capitalism, Socialism and Democracy,* 3rd ed. New York: Harper & Row, 1950.
* Talmon, Jacob L. *The Origins of Totalitarian Democracy.* New York: Praeger, 1961.

CHAPTER TWO: LIBERALISM

Bullock, Alan Louis C., and Maurice Shick, eds. *The Liberal Tradition from Fox to Keynes.* New York: New York University Press, 1957.

Dewey, John. *Human Nature and Conduct.* New York: Holt, Rinehart and Winston, 1944.

Edman, Irwin. *John Dewey: His Contribution to the American Tradition.* Indianapolis: Bobbs-Merrill, 1955.

Galbraith, John Kenneth. *The New Industrial State.* Boston: Houghton-Mifflin, 1967.

Lekachman, Robert. *Age of Keynes.* New York: Random House, 1966.

* Paperbound edition also available.

Loewi, Theodor. *The End of Liberalism: Ideology, Policy and the Crisis of Public Authority*. New York: Norton, 1969.

Russell, Bertrand. *Freedom Versus Organization*. New York: Norton, 1939.

Shonfield, Andrew. *Modern Capitalism: The Changing Balance of Public and Private Power*. New York: Oxford University Press, 1966.

CHAPTER THREE: MARXISM

* Avineri, Shlomo. *The Social and Political Thought of Karl Marx*. Cambridge, Eng.: Cambridge University Press, 1968.

* Bober, Mandell M. *Karl Marx's Interpretation of History*, 2nd rev. ed. Cambridge, Mass.: Harvard University Press, 1948.

* Feuer, Lewis S., ed. *Marx and Engels: Basic Writings on Politics and Philosophy*. Garden City, N.Y.: Doubleday, 1959.

* Freedman, Robert. *Marx on Economics*. New York: Harcourt Brace Jovanovich, 1961.

* Hook, Sidney. *From Hegel to Marx*. New York: Humanities Press, 1950.

* Lichtheim, George. *Marxism: An Historical and Critical Study*. New York: Praeger, 1965.

* ———. *The Origins of Socialism*. New York: Praeger, 1969.

* Meyer, Alfred. *Marxism: The Unity of Theory and Practice—A Critical Essay*. Cambridge, Mass.: Harvard University Press, 1959.

CHAPTER FOUR: CONSERVATISM

* Bell, Daniel, ed. *The Radical Right*. Garden City, N.Y.: Doubleday, 1963.

* Kirk, Russel. *The Conservative Mind: From Burke to Santayana*. Chicago: Regnery, 1953.

Viereck, Peter. *Conservatism: From John Adams to Churchill*. Princeton, N.J.: Van Nostrand-Reinhold, 1956.

CHAPTER FIVE: RACISM

* Benedict, Ruth. *Race: Science and Politics*. New York: Viking Press, 1959.

Davis, David B. *The Problem of Slavery in Western Culture*. Ithaca, N.Y.: Cornell University Press, 1966.

Dvorin, Eugene. *Racial Separation in South Africa: An Analysis of Apartheid Theory*. Chicago: University of Chicago Press, 1952.

Handlin, Oscar. *Race and Nationality in American Life*. Boston: Little, Brown, 1957.
Jenkins, William Sumner. *Pro-Slavery Thought in the Old South*. Chapel Hill, N.C.: University of North Carolina Press, 1935.
Montagu, Ashley. *Man's Most Dangerous Myth: The Fallacy of Race*. Cleveland: World, 1964.
Rose, E. J. B. *Color and Citizenship: A Report on British Race Relations*. New York: Oxford University Press, 1970.

CHAPTER SIX: EUROPE, GREAT BRITAIN, FRANCE, AND GERMANY

Beer, Max. *A History of British Socialism*. New York: Norton, 1942.
* Brinton, Crane. *English Political Thought in the 19th Century*. London: Benn, 1949.
* Bullock, Alan Louis C. *Hitler: A Study in Tyranny*, rev. ed. New York: Harper & Row, 1962.
* Butz, Otto. *Modern German Political Thought*. Garden City, N.Y.: Doubleday, 1955.
Hearnshaw, F. J. L. *Conservatism in England: An Analytical, Historical and Political Survey*. New York: Macmillan, 1935.
Kohn, Hans. *Making of the Modern French Mind*. Princeton, N.J.: Van Nostrand-Reinhold, 1955.
McBriar, A. M. *Fabian Socialism and English Politics 1884–1918*. Cambridge, Eng.: Cambridge University Press, 1962.
Soltan, Roger. *French Political Thought in the Nineteenth Century*. New Haven, Conn.: Yale University Press, 1931.
* Stern, Fritz. *The Politics of Cultural Despair: A Study in the Rise of the German Ideology*. Berkeley, Cal.: University of California Press, 1961.

CHAPTER SEVEN: THE UNITED STATES

Banfield, Edward C. *The Unheavenly City: The Nature and Future of Our Urban Crisis*. Boston: Little, Brown, 1970.
* Commager, Henry S. *The American Mind: An Interpretation of American Thought and Character Since the 1880's*. New Haven, Conn.: Yale University Press, 1950.
* Free, Lloyd, and Hadley Cantril. *The Political Beliefs of Americans*. New Brunswick, N.J.: Rutgers University Press, 1967.
* Galbraith, John Kenneth. *The Great Crash, 1929*. Boston: Houghton-Mifflin, 1955.
* Harrington, Michael. *The Other America: Poverty in the United States*. New York: Macmillan, 1962.

* Hartz, Louis. *The Liberal Tradition in America: An Interpretation of American Political Thought Since the Revolution.* New York: Harcourt Brace Jovanovich, 1955.
* Hofstadter, Richard. *The American Political Tradition.* New York: Knopf, 1948.
———. *Social Darwinism in American Thought,* rev. ed. New York: Braziller, 1959.
Howe, Irving, and Lewis Coser. *The American Communist Party: A Critical History.* New York: Praeger, 1957.
* Jacobs, Jane. *Death and Life of Great American Cities.* New York: Random House, 1961.
* Kolko, Gabriel. *Wealth and Power of Social Class and Income Distribution.* New York: Praeger, 1962.
* Lens, Sidney. *Radicalism in America.* New York: Crowell, 1969.
Seidler, Murray B. *Norman Thomas, Respectable Rebel.* Syracuse, N.Y.: Syracuse University Press, 1961.
* Theobald, Robert, ed. *Guaranteed Income: Next Step in Economic Evolution.* Garden City, N.Y.: Doubleday, 1966.

CHAPTERS EIGHT AND NINE: THE SOVIET UNION

Berdyaev, Nicolas. *The Russian Idea.* New York: Macmillan, 1948.
Feifer, George. *Justice in Moscow.* New York: Simon and Schuster, 1964.
Madison, Bernie G. *Social Welfare in the Soviet Union.* Stanford, Cal.: Stanford University Press, 1968.
* Maynard, John. *Russia in Flux.* New York: Macmillan, 1948.
* Meyer, Alfred G. *Leninism.* New York: Praeger, 1962.
* Nove, Alec. *The Soviet Economy: An Introduction.* New York: Praeger, 1966.
* Schapiro, Leonard. *Government and Politics of the Soviet Union.* New York: Random House, 1965.
Wallace, Donald M. *Russia on the Eve of War and Revolution.* New York: Random House, 1961.
Wolfe, Bertram. *Three Who Made a Revolution (Lenin, Trotsky, Stalin).* New York: Dial Press, 1948.

CHAPTER TEN: COMMUNIST CHINA

* Fairbanks, John King. *The United States and China,* rev. ed. Cambridge, Mass.: Harvard University Press, 1958.
Fitzgerald Charles P. *China: A Short Cultural History,* 3rd ed. New York, Praeger, 1967.

Hsiung, James Chieh. *Ideology and Practice: Evolution of Chinese Communism.* New York: Praeger, 1970.
Hsu, C. Y. *The Rise of Modern China.* New York: Oxford University Press, 1970.
* North, Robert C. *Moscow and Chinese Communism,* 2nd ed. Stanford, Cal.: Stanford University Press, 1963.
* Schram, Stuart R., ed. *The Political Thought of Mao Tse-tung.* New York: Praeger, 1963.
* Schurman, Franz. *Ideology and Organization in Communist China.* Berkeley, Cal:. University of California Press, 1968.

CHAPTER ELEVEN: THE REVOLUTION AGAINST POVERTY

* Adam, Thomas R. *Government and Politics in Africa South of the Sahara,* 3rd rev. ed. New York: Random House, 1965.
* Alexander, Robert J. *Today's Latin America,* 2nd ed. New York: Praeger, 1968.
DeBray, Regis. *Revolution in the Revolution: Armed Struggle or Political Struggle in Latin America.* New York: Grove Press, 1967.
* Fanon, Frantz. *The Wretched of the Earth.* New York: Grove Press, 1965.
Guevara, Ernesto ("Che"). *Selected Works.* Tr. Rolando E. Bonaches and Nelson P. Valdez. Cambridge, Mass.: MIT Press, 1969.
Kenner, Martin, and James Petras, eds. *Fidel Castro Speaks.* New York: Grove Press, 1969.
Scheer, Robert, and Maurice Zeitlin. *Cuba: Tragedy in Our Hemisphere.* New York: Grove Press, 1963.
Sigmund, Paul E., Jr., ed. *The Ideologies of Developing Nations.* New York: Praeger, 1963.
Wilkie, James W., and Albert L. Michaels, eds. *Revolution in Mexico: Years of Upheaval 1910–1940.* New York: Knopf, 1969.

CHAPTER TWELVE: THE REVOLUTION AGAINST AUTHORITARIANISM

* Burks, Richard V. *The Dynamics of Communism in Eastern Europe.* Princeton, N.J.: Princeton University Press, 1961.
DeGeorge, Richard T. *New Marxism: Soviet and East European Marxism Since 1956.* New York: Pegasus, 1968.
Gabarnikow, Michael. *Economic Reforms in Eastern Europe.* Detroit: Wayne State University Press, 1968.
Hoffman, George W., and Fred W. Neal. *Yugoslavia and the New Communism.* New York: Twentieth Century Fund, 1962.

* Lichtheim, George. *Marxism in Modern France.* New York: Columbia University Press, 1966.
Russian Institute, Columbia University, ed. *The Anti-Stalin Campaign and International Communism.* New York: Columbia University Press, 1956.

CHAPTER THIRTEEN: THE REVOLUTION AGAINST ALIENATION

Barrett, William. *What Is Existentialism?* New York: Grove Press, 1964.
* Fromm, Erich, ed. *Socialist Humanism: An International Symposium.* Garden City, N.Y.: Doubleday, 1965.
Fyvel, T. R. *Troublemakers: Rebellious Youth in an Affluent Society.* New York: Schocken Books, 1962.
Garaudy, Roger. *Marxism in the Twentieth Century.* Tr. René Hague. New York: Scribner's, 1970.
* Josephson, Eric and Mary, eds. *Man Alone: Alienation in Modern Society.* New York: Dell, 1962.
* Lipset, Seymour M., and Sheldon S. Wolin, *The Berkeley Student Revolt: Facts and Interpretations.* Garden City, N.Y.: Doubleday, 1965.
MacIntyre, Alastair. *Herbert Marcuse: An Exposition and a Polemic.* New York: Viking Press, 1970.
* Marx, Karl. *Early Writings.* Ed. T. B. Bottomore. New York: McGraw-Hill, 1964.
* Odajnyk, Walter. *Marxism and Existentialism.* Garden City, N.Y.: Doubleday, 1965.
* Oglesby, Carl. ed. *The New Left Reader.* New York: Grove Press, 1969.
* Pappenheim, Fritz. *The Alienation of Modern Man: An Interpretation Based on Marx and Tönnies.* New York: Monthly Review Press, 1959.
* Venable, Vernon. *Human Nature: The Marxian View.* New York: Knopf, 1965.

CHAPTER FOURTEEN: THE REVOLUTION AGAINST DISCRIMINATION

Broderick, Francis L., and August Meier, eds. *Negro Protest Thought in the Twentieth Century.* Indianapolis: Bobbs-Merrill, 1965.
* Carmichael, Stokeley, and Charles V. Hamilton. *Black Power: The Politics of Liberation in America.* New York: Random House, 1967.

Cronon, E. D. *Black Moses: The Story of Marcus Garvey and the Universal Negro Improvement Association.* Madison, Wisc.: University of Wisconsin Press, 1969.

De Graft-Johnson, J. C. *African Glory: The Story of Vanished Negro Civilization.* New York: Walker, 1966.

Du Bois, W. E. B. *An ABC of Color.* New York: International Publishers, 1969.

Malcolm X. *Autobiography.* New York: Grove Press, 1964.

Myrdal, Gunnar. *An American Dilemma: The Negro Problem and Modern Democracy.* New York: Harper & Row, 1969.

* Silberman, Charles E. *Crisis in Black and White.* New York: Random House, 1964.

EPILOGUE: THE FUTURE OF IDEOLOGY

Bell, Daniel. *The End of Ideology,* rev. ed. New York: Collier Books, 1962.

Greene, Marjorie. *The Knower and the Known.* New York: Basic Books, 1966.

Lichtheim, George. *The Concept of Ideology and Other Essays.* New York: Random House, 1967.

Shklar, Judith N., ed. *Political Theory and Ideology.* New York: Macmillan, 1966.

GLOSSARY

Alienation: *Originally:* A metaphysical concept; man's "being in the world."
In Hegel: The process by which the products of man's mind, such as language, law, techniques, slip from his control and become "alien" to him in the sense that they develop laws of their own to which he becomes subjected.
In Marx: Alienation is basically identified with alienated labor.

Analytic statement: A statement that must be true because of the meaning of its terms. For example, "Fire burns." The opposite of a synthetic statement.

A posteriori statement: An empirical statement, that is, a statement that can be confirmed or disproved by reference to evidence based on experience. The opposite of an a priori statement.

A priori statement: A statement that is necessarily true independent of any factual state of affairs. The opposite of an a posteriori statement.

Capitalism: An economic order under which the bulk of the means of production is privately owned.

Communism and socialism: Because of the different meanings attributed to the terms *socialism, communism, socialist, and communist,* their use gives rise to a considerable amount of confusion. Their meaning depends on the context in which they are used and on who uses them. For communists *socialism* and *communism* refer to two stages of development. In the stage of socialism people receive compensation for their efforts in line with the quantity and quality of their work. In the higher stage of communism they receive their income on the basis of their needs. Officially the Soviet Union is still in the stage of socialism (though it is in the process of building communism). Hence the official name, Union of Soviet *Socialist* Republics. But in referring to themselves, communists employ *socialist* and *communist* interchangeably.

Communism and *socialism* are used by noncommunists in a radically different sense. *Communism* refers to a system whose characteristics are a *planned society* (including economy) and *authoritarian* rule, while *socialism* is understood to involve a *moderately planned economy* (with *some* nationalization of industry) under a *democratic* government. According to this distinction the British Labour Party, the Euoropean socialist parties, and the Norman Thomas socialists in the United States are socialist—that is, they ascribe to social democracy—and the Soviet Union and Communist China are communist. A socialist, then, is a believer in socialism (social democracy) and a communist is a believer in communism (a society managed by a self-appointed elite).

Unfortunately, the adjective *socialist* has a less precise meaning in noncommunist terminology. When it refers to a government or a political system, it means social-democratic. However, if it refers to an economy, it is (regrettably) often used as the equivalent of *planned,* irrespective of whether planning goes hand in hand with the complete or only partial public ownership of the means of production, and irrespective of whether planning is done democratically or not. While the *government* of the Soviet Union can hardly be referred to as socialist, its economy is often referred to in the West as socialist.

In the eyes of communists, social-democrats are not viewed as fellow-socialists. In the past all kinds of epithets have been used by communists for social-democrats; at one time they went so far as to call them "social fascists." In recent years the custom has been to refer to them simply as social-democrats. If social-democrats are hostile to the Soviet Union, they are referred to as right-wing social-democrats. If they show some degree of sympathy for the Soviet

Union, they are identified as left-wing social-democrats.

Additional difficulties in terminology have recently arisen. Before the emergence of the formerly colonial countries, the movement for strict social planning under elitist rule went hand in hand with guidance by an international center. Now we see a number of countries emerging that have such planning without being run by the Soviet Union or China. To apply the term *communist* to these countries would be misleading. To refer to them simply as *socialist* would also be misleading, since in the West the term in connection with political regimes means social-democratic. Hence, the best way of defining these regimes is to call them authoritarian-socialist.

Finally, attention should be called to the cases in which the character of a communist regime or party undergoes a drastic change without its name being changed. Revisionism has, for instance, greatly affected the Italian Communist Party. Not only does it insist on independence from Moscow, its party program is definitely not revolutionary but reformist. These changes have led many sophisticated observers to suggest that the Italian Communist Party be henceforth considered a left-wing social-democratic party.

Dialectic: *In Plato:* The method by which one can arrive at ultimate truth through rational argument without help from the senses.
In Aristotle: A method of disputation through question and answer.
In Hegel and Marx: The movement of reality from lower to higher stages through the process of thesis to antithesis to synthesis. The opposite of metaphysical.

Empiricism: The theory that all knowledge is derived from experience and that no knowledge is given a priori. The opposite of rationalism.

Epistemology: The theory of knowledge that deals with the question of how man gains knowledge.

Essence: The distinctive nature of a thing; its inner substance.

Existentialism: As a philosophy, existentialism makes a distinction between essence and existence. Existentialism denies that man has an immutable essence that is a basic human nature. Rather his essence is a result of his self-definition, which, in turn, follows from his living, thinking, and acting. Accordingly, existence comes before essence.

Fascism: *In a technical sense:* A reactionary movement in an *advanced* country based on a mass party and a charismatic leader espousing an extreme form of nationalism. Fascism rises on the support of a lower middle class that is beset by status anxiety and on the support of an upper bourgeoisie that is afraid of social radicalism.
In a general sense: Any reactionary nationalist movement in an advanced country.

Idealism: *In ontology:* The view that only mind or ideas are real. The opposite of (ontological) materialism.
In ethics: The orientation toward ideals. The opposite of (ethical) materialism.
In politics: The view that political decisions should be governed by ideals either because ethics demand this or because ideals do motivate people in practice. The opposite of (political) realism.

Ideology: The term was coined at the end of the eighteenth century by the French philosopher Destutt de Tracy. De Tracy was one of a group of Enlightenment philosophers who wanted to get at truth through the elimination of all those mystifications that had been the result of faith and authority. As a step in this direction, De Tracy considered it necessary to purify ideas by accepting as true only those that corresponded to sense perceptions. To his efforts he gave the name *ideology*—that is, the science of purification of ideas.

Later the term acquired a negatvie connotation. Napoleon attacked the "ideologues" as subversive of his rule. For Marx, too, the term had a pejorative meaning, but for different reasons. He called all those ideas that were the result of a false consciousness ideologies. Today the term is neutral. Ideology is any organized set of ideas about the good life and the institutional framework for their realization. However, usage has increasingly become less strict so that any combination of sociopolitical values having a connecting rationale is referred to as ideology. For example, people speak about the ideology of the American businessman.

Legal positivism: The philosophy of law that holds that law is man-made and that law is any command that emanates from a sovereign authority either directly or through its delegation. The opposite of natural law.

Logical empiricism or logical positivism: The philosophy that accepts as meaningful only those statements that are either analytical or verifiable by experience. It relies on logic and experience.

Materialism: *In ontology:* The notion that only matter is real. The opposite of (ontological) idealism.
In Marx: The "matter" of society is its economy (hence economic materialism).
In ethics: The doctrine that a person's actions should be governed by consideration of self-interest defined in material comfort. The opposite of (ethical) idealism.
(Note: A person may be a materialist ontologically and an idealist ethically.)

Metaphysical: Nonverifiable; beyond experience.
In Marx: The opposite of dialectical.

Metaphysics: An approach to those philosophical matters that are not subject to empirical investigation and hence invite speculative inquiry. Ontology and epistemology have traditionally been part of metaphysics. (The term *metaphysics* was first used in the first century B.C. by Andronicus of Rhodes to describe that part of Aristotle's philosophical work that came after his "Physics.")

Natural law: *In a religious sense:* The view that there is a higher law than that of man which is God-given. Human law, in order to be law, must conform to this higher law.
In a secular sense: The view that above the law of individual sovereignties there is the law of civilized mankind to which the former must conform in order to be considered law. The opposite of legal positivism.

Ontology: The branch of philosophy that deals with what existence itself is; philosophical efforts at determining the fundamental categories of being.

Pragmatism: A theory of truth that holds that an idea is true if it works satisfactorily; that is, if it leads to an anticipated experience.

Rationalism: 1. The belief in reason. The opposite of irrationalism.
2. The theory of knowledge that holds that knowledge is possible through the use of reason without involvement of sense perceptions. The opposite of empiricism.

Realism: *In philosophy:* The theory according to which physical objects exist independently of our perception.
In politics: The view that the central phenomenon in politics is power and hence an understanding of politics must be derived from the mapping of power relations in society. The opposite of (political) idealism.

Revisionism: *Earlier:* The reformist school of Marxism at the turn of the century that minimized the class struggle and believed that incremental social reforms would lead to socialism.
Modern:
1. At one time, the derogatory description by the Soviet Union of the policies of Yugoslavia.
2. At present, description by the Chinese Communists and their allies of the ideological "deviations" of the Soviet Union and of the communist parties supporting the general line of the Soviet Union.

Socialism: *See* Communism and socialism.

Synthetic statement: A statement in which the subject does not imply the predicate. A statement whose truth cannot be established through logical analysis. The opposite of an analytic statement.

Teleology: Any theory that concerns itself with ends. The study of events from the standpoint of assumed purposes.

Voluntarism: The view that the essence of social reality is will. The notion that it is will that determines human events.

INDEX

1 2 3 4 5 6 7 8 9 10 11 12 13 14 15 88 87 86 85 84 83 82 81 80 79 78 77 76 75 74 73